Baedeker
Majorca/Minorca

Baedeker's
MAJORCA

Imprint

146 colour photographs
6 special plans, 4 town plans, 2 ground-plans, 4 drawings, 1 map of islands

Text (partly on basis of "Baedeker's Compact Guide to Majorca and the Balearics"):
Peter M. Nahm, Ostfildern-Kemnat

Editorial work: Baedeker Stuttgart

English Language Edition: Alec Court

Design and layout:
Creativ GmbH, Ulrich Kolb, Stuttgart

General direction:
Dr Peter Baumgarten, Baedeker Stuttgart

Cartography:
Gert Oberländer, Munich; Mairs Geographischer Verlag GmbH & Co., Ostfildern-Kemnat
(large map of Majorca and Minorca)

English translation: James Hogarth
David Cocking (revision and amendment)

Source of illustrations:
Baden Provincial Library, Karlsruhe (1); Baedeker-Archiv (1); Fotoperator (1); Historia-Photo
(2); Ludwig (6); Nahm (43); Perlas Majorca (1); Pfaffinger (78); Schweiger (1); Subirats
Casanovas (2); Süddeutscher Verlag (1).

To make it easier to locate the various sights listed in the "A to Z" section of the Guide, their
co-ordinates on the large map of Majorca and Minorca are shown in red at the head of each
entry.

Following the tradition established by Karl Baedeker in 1844, sights of particular interest and
hotels of particular quality are distinguished by either one or two asterisks.

Only a selection of hotels can be given: no reflection is implied, therefore, on establishments
not included.

The symbol ⓘ on a town plan indicates the local tourist office from which further
information can be obtained. The post-horn symbol indicates a post office.

In a time of rapid change it is difficult to ensure that all the information given is entirely
accurate and up to date, and the possibility of error can never be completely eliminated.
Although the publishers can accept no responsibility for inaccuracies and omissions, they
are always grateful for corrections and suggestions for improvement.

4th English edition
© Baedeker Stuttgart
Original German edition

© 1994 The Automobile Association
United Kingdom and Ireland

© 1994 Jarrold and Sons Ltd
English language edition worldwide

Distributed in the United Kingdom by the Publishing Division of the Automobile Association,
Fanum House, Basingstoke, Hampshire, RG1 2EA.

Licensed user:
Mairs Geographischer Verlag GmbH & Co., Ostfildern-Kemnat bei Stuttgart

The name *Baedeker* is a registered trademark

Printed in Italy by G. Canale & C. S.p.A – Borgaro T.se – Turin

ISBN 0 7495 0858-2

Contents

General · Geography · Climate · Flora and Fauna · Population · Language and Literature · Customs · Economy and Transport

Alaró · Alayor · Alcudia · Alfabia · Algaida · Andraitx · Artá · Bañalbufar · Binisalem · Buñola · Cabo Formentor · Cabo Salinas · Cabrera · Cala d'Or · Cala Figuera · Cala Millor · Cala Pí · Cala San Vicente · Calas de Mallorca · La Calobra · Calviá · Campanet · Campos del Puerto · Ca'n Picafort · Capdepera · Ciudadela de Menorca · Colonia de San Pedro · Colonia de Sant Jordi · Costa de los Pinos · Ermita de Nuestra Señora de Bonany · Ermita de San Salvador · Esporlas · Estellencs · Felanitx · Fornalutx · Gorch Blau · Inca · Isla Dragonera · Lloseta · Llubí · Lluch Monastery · Lluchmayor · Mahón · Manacor · Mercadal · Minorca · Miramar · Montuiri · Muro · Orient · Paguera · Palma de Mallorca · Petrá · Pollensa · Porreras · Porto Colóm · Porto Cristo · La Puebla · Puigpuñent · Sancellas · San Juan · San Lorenzo del Cardessar · Santa Margarita · Santa María del Camí · Santañy · Santa Ponsa · San Telmo · Selva · S'Estanyol · Sineu · Sóller · Son Servera · Valldemosa · Villafranca de Bonany

Accommodation · Airlines · Airport · Banks · Bicycle and Motorcycle rental · Boat Trips · Camping and Caravanning · Car Rental · Currency · Customs regulations · Diplomatic and Consular offices · Electricity · Emergencies · Events · Excursions · Food and Drink · Getting to Majorca/Minorca · Golf courses · Hotels · Information · Inter-island transport · Maps and Plans · Motoring · Museums · Opening times · Postal services · Public holidays · Rail travel · Restaurants · Roads · Shopping and souvenirs · Telephone · Time · Tipping · Travel documents · Vacation apartments · Walking · Water sports · When to go · Youth hostels

The Principal Sights at a Glance

Preface

This pocket guide to Majorca and Minorca is one of the new generation of Baedeker guides.

Baedeker pocket guides, illustrated throughout in colour, are designed to meet the needs of the modern traveller. They are quick and easy to consult, with the principal places of interest described in alphabetical order, and the information is presented in a format that is both attractive and easy to follow.

The present guide is devoted to the north-eastern Balearic islands – Majorca, the largest and most important island in the group; Minorca, lying to the north-east of Majorca; and the small island of Cabrera, off the south coast of Majorca. The guide is in three parts. The first part gives a general account of the islands, their geography, climate, flora and fauna, population, language and literature, customs, economy, notable personalities, history, culture and art. A number of suggested itineraries introduce the second part, in which the towns, villages, monasteries, etc., of tourist interest are described. The third part contains a variety of practical information. Both the sights and the practical information are listed in alphabetical order.

The Baedeker pocket guides are noted for their concentration on essentials and their convenience of use. They contain numerous specially drawn plans and colour illustrations, and at the end of the book is a large map making it easy to locate the various places described in the "A to Z" section of the guide with the help of the co-ordinates given at the head of each entry.

Facts and Figures

General

This guide is concerned with the islands of Majorca (in Spanish Mallorca), Minorca (Spanish Menorca) and Cabrera, which form the north-eastern part of the group of Spanish islands in the western Mediterranean known as the Balearics.
A separate Baedeker pocket guide is devoted to the islands of Ibiza and Formentera, in the south-western part of the group (Islas Pityusas).

The Balearic Islands, lying in the western Mediterranean between latitude 38° and 40° N and between longitude 1° and 4° E, off the south-east coast of the Spanish mainland, consist of the Balearics proper (Islas Baleares), with the two principal islands of Majorca (3640 sq. km (1405 sq. miles)) and Minorca (700 sq. km (270 sq. miles)), the Islas Pityusas, with Ibiza (in Ibizan Eivissa; 572 sq. km (221 sq. miles)) and Formentera (100 sq. km (40 sq. miles)), together with some 150 smaller islands, including Cabrera (17 sq. km (6½ sq. miles)), and numbers of rocky islets, some of them serving military or nautical purposes, others completely unused.
The islands constitute the Spanish Province and Autonomous Region of the Balearics (Comunidad Autónoma de las Islas Baleares/Comunitat Autonoma de les Illes Balears), with a total area of 5014 sq. km (1936 sq. miles), the capital of which is Palma de Mallorca.

The Balearics were granted autonomy on 22 February 1983 under the Spanish policy of decentralisation. The organ of government is the Interinsular Council-General of the Balearic Islands (Consell General Interinsular de les Illes Balears).
Autonomy has also had an effect on language. While formerly Spanish (Castilian, *lengua castellana*) was officially favoured as the written and generally accepted language, the local idioms, Majorcan and Minorcan, which are forms of Catalan, are increasingly gaining ground. Many place-names have two forms, and where road signs do not give both forms they are frequently amended with the aid of aerosol paint. Recently, however, there have been counter-moves aimed at giving more emphasis to Castilian once again. Nevertheless, overall there is still a far greater degree of ambivalence in the Balearics than there is in the Catalan region of mainland Spain, where Catalan is spoken almost exclusively.
For further information on language see p. 14.

The origin of the name Balearics is not known with certainty. There may be a connection with the Greek word *ballein*, "throw", possibly referring to the islanders' reputation in ancient times for their skill with the sling (see History on p. 26).

Palma de Mallorca is 132 nautical miles from Barcelona, 140 from Valencia, 172 from Algiers, 287 from Marseilles and 439 from Genoa.

The Balearic group

Autonomous status

Origin of name

Distances from mainland

◄ *An old windmill on Majorca*

9

Spain

Geography

The Balearics are the continuation of the folded Andalusian mountains which extend from Gibraltar by way of the Sierra Nevada to Cabo de la Nau, separated from the Iberian peninsula in the Late Tertiary era by tectonic movements which led to massive subsidences and submersions. The archipelago is now separated from the Spanish mainland by a submarine trench up to 1500 m (5000 ft) deep. Both the Balearics proper and the Islas Pityusas have their own continental shelf.

Majorca

Sierra del Norte

Majorca is made up of three markedly different zones of relief. Running parallel to the north-west coast is the Sierra del Norte (Majorcan "Serra de Tramuntana"), a 90 km (55 mile) long range of wooded hills with clusters of bizarrely shaped rocks, reaching a height of 1443 m (4734 ft) in Puig Mayor and falling steeply down to the sea in much-indented cliffs which form picturesque little coves and creeks (*calas*).

Serranía de Levante

In the south-east of the island are the ridges of hills which form the Serranía de Levante, rising to 509 m (1670 ft) at San Salvador, with a number of stalactitic caves. Here, too, the coast is broken up into innumerable *calas*.

Llanura del Centro

Between these two upland regions, in which Mesozoic limestones predominate, the large bays of Alcudia and Pollensa to the north-east and Palma to the south-west cut deep into the Llanura del Centro, a fertile plain given up to intensive agriculture (arable, fruit-growing, vines), with isolated hills of some size such as the Puig de Randa (542 m (1778 ft)) and the Puig de Santa Magdalena (304 m (997 ft)).

Minorca

The north-west of Minorca consists of a gently rolling upland region, reaching a height of 357 m (1171 ft) in Monte Toro, with fjord-like inlets reaching in from the north-west coast. In the south-west is an extensive area of low-lying land, fringed by cliffs enclosing small rocky coves.

Climate

Thanks to their maritime situation the Balearics enjoy a very temperate Mediterranean climate with mild, rainy and almost always frost-free winters and dry and not unduly hot summers. There are, however, quite marked differences from island to island.

Cold dry winds blowing in from the north (the *tramontana*) give Minorca a relatively rough climate, reflected in the typical wind-blown aspect of the vegetation. On Majorca the winds come up against the barrier of the Sierra del Norte, and in summer fresh winds blowing down from the hills (the *maestral* or *mestral*) bring coolness to the central plain.

Winds

Annual average rainfall decreases steadily from Minorca southward (Mahón 580 mm (23 in), Palma de Mallorca 480 mm (19 in)). On Majorca the Sierra del Norte acts as a weather barrier: while in the hills at Lluch Monastery annual precipi-

Rainfall

Catalan wind rose

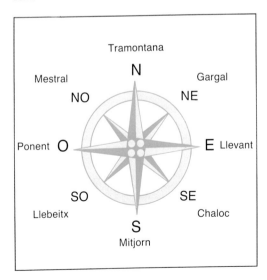

11

tation (in winter not infrequently in the form of snow) is over 1460 mm (57 in) but only 400–500 mm (16–20 in) in the plain.

Water-supply

Given the intermittent character of their watercourses Majorca and Minorca had in the past to depend mainly on ground-water or rainwater, raised by windmills or by *norias* (the water-wheels operated by draught animals which were introduced by the Moors). These archaic but efficient and economical methods are now giving place to modern irrigation systems with water circulating under pressure. Majorca has abundant reserves of fresh water, Minorca only very limited resources; having said that, however, even Majorca can experience short-ages during the high season.

Flora and Fauna

Flora

The typical form of vegetation up to heights of about 700 m (2300 ft) is the *garigue*, an open scrub woodland of Aleppo pines mingled with holm-oaks, wild olives, arbutus, carob trees and the endemic dwarf palms. Between 700 m and 950 m (3100 ft) this gradually gives place to a macchia consisting of *Erica multiflora*, rosemary, myrtle, laurel and broom, inter-spersed with areas of bracken. In the *alta montaña* only a sparse vegetation of wiry grasses, stonecrops and cushions of low-growing rosemary finds a foothold among the bare rocks. Minorca has practically no woodland, which suffers badly from the perpetually blowing sharp north winds, and here, too, the cork-oak is almost completely absent. On the little island of Cabrera the original tree cover has been destroyed by the goats which roam wild there.

In private gardens and well-maintained public parks, however, the whole flora of the Mediterranean can be seen in all its splendour and variety – bougainvilleas (also used in hedges), oleanders, many species of geranium, hibiscus, palms (includ-ing the date palm, recognisable by the clusters of fruit hanging like bunches of grapes), agaves and even bananas (though these do not ripen here). A distinctive feature of the landscape is the prickly pear (*Opuntia*), sometimes growing wild; clumps of these are often planted behind peasants' houses, still some-times serving in place of the "smallest room", since their sharp smell keeps off insects. The fruit, which ripens in summer, is used as pig food or made into jam. When the plants spread too much they are chopped up and ploughed in to lighten and fertilise the soil.

Fauna

The islands' original fauna, which never comprised a great variety of species, has been decimated by the expansion of cultivation, and there are now practically no deer, mountain goats or wild sheep.

The relatively limited fish stocks in the waters immediately surrounding the islands offer sufficient food for any consider-able numbers of sea and wading birds only during the rainy season. In the hills there are birds of prey (eagles, falcons), partridges and in many areas hoopoes. Visitors will be struck by the large numbers of songbirds and ornamental birds in cages on the fronts of houses. The abundance of insects and the heat provide favourable conditions for reptiles such as lizards, geckos and several species of snake, including the poisonous horned viper and Levantine viper.

Bougainvillea

Prickly pear

Olive tree

Carob tree

Lonely rocky coves round the coasts of the islands provide a home for large numbers of crayfish – a much-esteemed but not particularly cheap speciality of the regional cuisine.

Population

The Autonomous Region of the Balearics has a total population (almost exclusively Roman Catholic) of some 660,000, 530,000 of whom live on Majorca and 56,000 on Minorca. The highest density is found in the Palma de Mallorca conurbation.

In physical type and in character the people of the Balearics are markedly different from mainland Spaniards. They are a rather stolid but friendly and honest race, whose characteristics and qualities will be more evident to the visitor during the winter months, when the large numbers of seasonal workers from the mainland have left the islands.

The eventful history of the islands, situated as they are at the crossroads of Mediterranean seafaring traffic, has created out of the mingling of ethnic groups of Moorish, Jewish and Catalan origin, roughly equal in strength, together with smaller numbers of Italians, Basques, French, Greeks and British (particularly on Minorca), a dark-haired type of stocky build. The most recent influx of settlers has brought in influences from Central Europe, Scandinavia and North America.

Language and Literature

Language

On the Balearics as in the rest of Spain the official language and the language of business is Spanish (Castellano, Castilian); but the everyday languages of the islanders are Majorcan (Mallorquí) and Minorcan (Menorquí) – two closely related dialects of Catalan (Catalá), an independent Romance language spoken in north-eastern Spain (Catalonia) and in the extreme south-west of Mediterranean France which differs from Castilian in significant respects and shows considerable Provençal influence in its vocabulary.

Although English is widely understood, particularly in hotels, restaurants, shops, etc., in the main tourist centres, it is an advantage for visitors to have some Spanish, and if they can manage a few words of Catalan it will give great pleasure to the people they are speaking to, some of whom, if their schooling has been limited, may have difficulty with the pronunciation of Spanish.

The Majorcan dialect of Catalan – which, it is said, is not spoken but shouted – shows marked differences from Castilian Spanish both in pronunciation and in vocabulary. Thus it lacks the Spanish diphthongisation of Latin vowels (Latin *portus* gives Castilian *puerto* but Catalan *porto*; *bonus* gives Castilian *bueno* but Catalan *bo*), and final vowels disappear altogether (Castilian *dulce*, Catalan *dulc*; Castilian *muerte*, Catalan *mort*). In addition to the verb types in -ar, -er and -ir of standard Spanish, Catalan has a fourth type ending in -re (e.g. *prendre*, "take"). The definite article, in Catalan *el* or *la* (plural *els*, *las*), is replaced in the "*parlar salat*" ("salty language") of the Balearics and the Costa Brava by *es* (*s'*) and *sa* (*s'*), and the plural forms *es* (*ets*) and *ses*, derived from the Latin demonstrative pronoun *iste*. As examples of Provençal influence on vocabulary the words for "table" (Castilian *mesa*, Catalan *taula*), "corn" (Castilian *trigo*, Catalan *blat*) and "window" (Castilian *ventana*, Catalan *finestra*) may be cited.

As in Portuguese, unaccented *a* and *e* almost disappear in pronunciation, and unaccented *o* is pronounced like a short *u*. The Castilian *j*, and *g* before *e* or *i*, pronounced like *ch* in "loch", is pronounced in Catalan *zh*, like the *j* in French "journal". *Ll*, pronounced in Castilian like *l* followed by consonantal *y* (as in "William"), is normally pronounced in Catalan like a consonantal *y* (as in "yes"); where, exceptionally, *ll* is to be pronounced like a double *l* this is indicated by a point, or less commonly by a hyphen, between the two letters (e.g. *sil-laba*, "syllable"). The Spanish letter *ñ* is replaced in Catalan by *ny* (the only situation in which the letter *y* is used). *Ch* is always pronounced like *k*; the modern practice is to use *c* by itself. The letter *x* is almost always pronounced *sh*. The Castilian *ch* (pronounced as in English) is replaced by *tx* and at the end of a word frequently by *-ig*, giving rise to such curious endings as *-aitx* (pronounced *atch*), *-oig* (pronounced *otch*) and *-uig* (pronounced *ootch*). *Z* and *c* before *e* or *i* are not lisped as in Castilian but, like *s*, are frequently voiced. Catalan, unlike Castilian, has a double *s*.

The rules for the use of accents are the same as in Spanish, except that where the letter *i* is stressed in the ending *-ia* the *i* bears no accent (Castilian María, Catalan Maria). The use of the grave or acute accent varies according to the pronunciation of the vowel: *a* always takes a grave accent, *i* and *u* an acute, while open *e* and *o* take a grave (*cafè*, *arròs*), closed *e* and *o* an acute (*consomé*, *fórmula*).

Pronunciation

With the conquest of the Balearics by Jaime I in 1229 and the subsequent Christianisation of the islands Catalan became the official language in place of Arabic, which has left its mark only in a few expressions in the Majorcan dialect and in numbers of place-names (Alcudia, Binisalem, Bañalbufar, Algaida, etc.). Catalan enjoyed an early flowering as a literary language on Majorca, to an extent never subsequently equalled, through the work of the philosopher and missionary Ramón Llull (Latinised as Raimundus Lullus; 1233–1314). Llull, perhaps Majorca's greatest son, wrote most of his treatises, novels and poems – works of great influence on the thinking of the West – in his native tongue as well as in Latin and Arabic. Among writers active between the 14th and 16th c. particular mention may be made of Anselm Turmeda, Guillem de Torroella and Jaume d'Olesa, whose vivid descriptions of the life of their time afford valuable glimpses of the past of the Balearic island world.

After the unification of Spain the Castilian spoken at the Court gained in importance during the 16th and 17th c., and in 1715 it was declared the official language of the whole kingdom, including the Balearics. Majorcan was downgraded to become the colloquial language of the peasants and the lower orders of the population, and only occasionally achieved written form in folk-songs and popular tales. It was not until the early 19th c., with the revival (Renaxensa) of Catalan during the Romantic movement, that it again gained access to intellectual and literary circles. Societies were formed to promote its use, and it became the subject of detailed linguistic study. The philologist Maria Aguiló (1825–97) produced a pioneering "Lexicon of Classical Catalan" and Tomás Forteza (1838–89) published a

Literature

"Catalan Grammar". Most poetry and prose remained popular in tone and of purely local interest. The literature of the islands gained a wider appeal only with the work of Miguel Costa i Llobera (1854–1922) and Joan Alcover (1854–1926).

During the political controversies of the late 1970s, with their emphasis on separatist tendencies, an additional boost was given to Catalan, now again recognised as an official language, and with it to Majorcan and Minorcan, and this trend was still further reinforced by the granting of autonomy to the Balearics.

Customs

Little in the way of traditional customs has survived on the Balearics. The old regional costumes are worn only on special occasions or in folk performances, though some women still occasionally wear the *rebozillo*, a white tulle headscarf, often embroidered, which is tied under the chin.

On the Balearics, as in the rest of Spain, fiestas feature prominently in the annual round, and these naturally reflect old folk traditions. All over the islands there are sumptuous processions during Holy Week and at Corpus Christi; every community celebrates the festival of its patron saint (*fiesta*) with pilgrimages (*romerías*), parades and popular celebrations (*ferias*); and on the days of high festival and at the great summer fairs there are equestrian pageants (in particular the historical play "Moros y Cristianos") and bullfights.

The bullfights

Bullfights (*corridas*) were held in Spain until the 16th c. as a form of weapon training as well as on the occasion of fiestas, mounted *caballeros* with their lances being pitted against the bulls. At the beginning of the 17th c. bullfighting began to take a less hazardous form, and the present rules are attributed to Francisco Romero, who was born in Ronda about 1700. With the building of the first large bullring (*plaza de toros*) in Madrid in 1749 it finally became a public spectacle, in which only professional *toreros* now take part.

The bullring is exactly circular, with the dearer seats on the shady side (*sombra*) and the cheaper ones in the sun (*sol*).

The bullfight (*lidia*) has three main parts (*suertes*). After a brief prologue during which the *capeadores* tease the bull by playing it with their brightly coloured cloaks (*capas*) there follows the *suerte de picar* or *suerte de varas*, in which the mounted *picadores* provoke the bull to attack them, plunge their lances (*garrochas*) into its neck and withstand the charges of the infuriated beast as best they can. When the bull has been sufficiently weakened (*castigado*) by his wounds (*varas*) the second stage, the *suerte de banderillas*, begins. The *banderilleros* run towards the bull carrying several *banderillas* and, skilfully eluding its charge at the last moment, stick them into its neck. The normal banderillas are sticks 75 cm (30 in) long with barbed points and paper streamers; the *banderillas a cuarta* are only 15 cm (6 in) long. Bulls which are too fierce or vicious are distracted by plays with a cloak (*floreos*). When three pairs of banderillas have been planted in the bull's neck the *suerte suprema* or *suerte de matar* begins. The *espada* or *matador*, armed with a red cloth (*muleta*) and a sword (*estoque*), begins by teasing the bull with the cloth and then seeks to manœuvre it into a position in which he can deliver the death stroke (*estocada*), after which the *coup de grâce* is administered by a *punterillo* with a dagger. If the bull has shown itself courageous and aggressive it will be loudly applauded; unskilful bullfighters will be loudly criticised and booed. The show is repeated six or eight times until the onset of darkness. Following protests by visitors to the islands from central Europe, bullfighting on the Balearics is less common.

During the main holiday season visitors will have the opportunity of seeing performances by local folk-dance groups. In addition to group dances (*bailes de figura* or *bailes moriscos*, Moorish dances) such as the "Cossiers" or "Ball de Cossis" danced in the Alaró area, the "Cavallets" round Felanitx or the "Aguiles" and "Dimonis de Sant Antoni", there are pair dances (*bailes populares*), which are of two kinds: in the hill regions the dances are mostly hopping dances, to a fairly stately rhythm, accompanied by shawms and tambourines, while the dances of the lowland areas, particularly the *jotas*, are livelier. The most characteristic Majorcan dances are the "Copeo" of the hill regions and the "Mateixes". Towards the end of the 19th c. *boleros* and *boleras* from Castile came to the island, where their melodies blended with native tunes, giving rise to the "Parado" (Valldemosa, Selva). The celebrated flamenco was also taken over from mainland Spain.

Popular musical instruments include the guitar, the fiddle, the flute, the shawm and the bagpipe. An instrument of unusual type, probably of Arab origin, is the *zambomba*, a drum shaped like a flowerpot and spanned with rabbit-skin, with a round stick protruding from it; the stick is moistened with water and moved up and down, producing a very curious sound.

Folk-dances

Economy and Transport

The Balearics have little in the way of minerals, and until the coming of the tourists agriculture was almost their only source of income. From the beginning of the 14th c. the land was worked under the *aparcería* system introduced by Jaime II – a form of share-cropping in which the crops were shared equally between the landowner and the tenant farmer. Since nowadays, in line with the expectations of workers on the land, no account is taken of variations in yield in good and bad years and losses are borne almost entirely by the lessor rather than the tenant, many landowners have sold their land for building. As a result the Balearics, which formerly exported much of their agricultural produce, now cannot produce enough to meet their own needs.

In the fertile, artificially irrigated central plain, the Llanura del Centro, and in the uplands of south-eastern Majorca large areas are used for fruit-growing. In January and February the pink and white splendour of the almond-blossom attracts large numbers of visitors and displays in the most spectacular way the great extent of the orchards. Apricots and figs are also grown in these areas. The land between the rows of trees is frequently used for grazing, and around Lluchmayor, Llubí and Campos del Puerto for the growing of capers. Here, too, several crops of grain, pulses, citrus fruits, artichokes, vegetables (in particular early vegetables for export to Central Europe) and alfalfa are taken every year; in recent years flower-growing has become increasingly important. Around Binisalem, Santa Margarita and Felanitx excellent wine is produced, but in view of

Agriculture

the superabundance of wine in mainland Spain this finds only a local market. At the foot of the relatively well-watered north-western slopes of the Sierra del Norte a great system of terraced fields with drystone retaining walls, mainly devoted to the growing of oranges and lemons, has been laboriously built up over the centuries. Oranges and lemons are also grown in the *huertas* (gardens), the fertile valleys of Sóller, Palma and La Puebla (where some rice is also grown). The once-famous vineyards of Bañalbufar were largely destroyed by phylloxera and have been replaced by vegetable-growing (principally tomatoes). The higher and dried levels are occupied by olive groves, often centuries old.

There is also a limited amount of stock-farming on Majorca (horses, donkeys, mules, black Majorcan pigs, sheep, goats, poultry). In the area of Campos del Puerto there is some dairy-farming (milk, cheese).

On Minorca dry agriculture predominates, producing grain, pulses, vegetables, root vegetables for forage and wine; exceptions are the better watered areas around Mahón and Ciudadela. The small fields are often sheltered from the wind by high drystone walls (*tancas*). The almost perpetual wind makes the growing of fruit trees practically impossible, apart from figs, peaches and carobs in some sheltered spots. Stock-farming is of considerable importance, and dairy-farming is developing (cheese, particularly around Mahón).

Fishing

Local catches of fish can meet the needs of the islands only outside the tourist season; during the summer supplies have to be brought in from mainland ports. This is because the Mediterranean is only moderately well stocked with fish, and stocks are particularly poor near the islands with their considerable depth of water; moreover there is generally more pollution in the Mediterranean than, for example, in the Atlantic.

Salt production

Although most of the islands' production of sea salt comes from Ibiza, salt is also produced on Majorca (Los Estanques, Ses Salinas, Colonia de Sant Jordí, around La Puebla) by methods which were already practised by the Phoenicians. Sea-water contained in large shallow salt-pans is left to evaporate for several months, producing great sheets of crystallised salt (sodium chloride, with small admixtures of other salts), which is exported as table salt, mainly to Scandinavia and Asia. Its impurities make it unsuitable for use as industrial salt.

Craft products

Leatherworking is of great economic importance on Majorca (shoes, handbags, etc., at Palma, Inca, Binisalem, Lloseta and Lluchmayor) and Minorca, as is the production of textiles (embroidery, cloth, carpets, blankets).

Pottery and ceramics are old-established traditional crafts. Painted tiles (*azulejos*, the predominant colour being blue, *azul*) are produced particularly at Felanitx, faience at Inca (both on Majorca). Faience, originally introduced to Spain by the Moors, is made from natural-coloured clay with a water-resistant tin glaze. During the Middle Ages it was exported from Spain by way of the Balearics to Italy, where it became famous under the name of majolica (from Majorca). It has been made on the Balearics since the 16th c.

Glassware is produced mainly at Algaida and Inca, silver and other jewellery around Palma.

Terraced fields: a man-made landscape ▶

Rural idyll: sheep grazing near Palma

Manacor is famous for its artificial pearls (also made at Felanitx and Sóller), which are claimed to be superior in durability and brilliance to other artificial pearls and to be almost indistinguishable from natural pearls.

The manufacture of spirits (Palma, Binisalem, Santa María, Algaida) has considerably expanded in recent years, largely owing to demand from tourists. Beer is becoming increasingly popular, and much of it comes from local breweries.

Industry and craft production is almost exclusively in the hands of small and medium-sized firms. Domestic craft production is an important subsidiary source of income for the rural population.

Minerals
Power production

Lignite is worked in the Lloseta and Alaró areas, providing part of the fuel requirements of a power-station at Puerto de Alcudia. There is another power-station at Palma de Mallorca, which also has an oil refinery. Marble and other building stones are worked on Minorca, where fertilisers (superphosphates) are also produced.

Transport

Majorca has two railway lines, from Palma to Sóller (with a tram service from there to Puerto de Sóller) and from Palma to Inca. Practically all places of any size are served by buses. Minorca has no railway but a number of bus services. On all the islands there are ample facilities for the rental of cars, motorcycles, scooters and bicycles.

Shipping

From the earliest times the Balearics had a substantial fleet of vessels for overseas trade. The most important harbour and commercial port is Palma de Mallorca, which links the islands with Europe, Africa and America. From the ports of Alcudia, Pollensa and Sóller on Majorca and Mahón (naval base) and Ciudadela on Minorca there are regular services between the islands and to the Spanish mainland.

To meet the needs of the heavy tourist traffic Majorca and Minorca have excellent airports catering for international services, connections with mainland Spain and local services between the principal islands in the group.

Air services

Since the end of the Second World War tourism has developed into the islanders' principal source of income. Majorca now depends primarily on the tourist and holiday trade, and Minorca is also attracting increasing numbers of visitors. More than half the total tax revenue of the Balearics region comes from tourism. Most of the tourist facilities are on the coasts. Income is generated not only by the hotels, restaurants, etc., catering directly for visitors but also by transport services, shops, the manufacture of souvenirs and by the building industry which provides the new hotels, restaurants and holiday and recreational facilities required.

Tourism

The tourist boom has severely damaged, and sometimes destroyed, the established economic structures of the Balearics, and it is now being questioned whether the development of the last three decades has brought only benefits to the islanders. It

Traditional-style pottery from La Granja

is increasingly being suggested that a brake should be put on any further expansion of the tourist trade. This tendency was also reflected in the general conditions for building rights and protected areas which were adopted in 1988.

Notable Personalities

Frédéric (Fryderyk) Chopin
(1.3.1810–17.10.1849)

Frédéric Chopin, the son of a French father and a Polish mother, was born in the little town of Zelazowa-Wola near Warsaw. In 1830 he went to Paris, where he quickly made a name as a piano virtuoso. His own compositions, blending elements of Polish folk-music with new and personal harmonics, also attracted much attention. Chopin, suffering from tuberculosis, spent the winter of 1838–39 on Majorca with the celebrated and unconventional French authoress George Sand (see p. 24), hoping that the island's climate would provide a cure. Among the music he composed during his stay was the "Raindrop Prelude" (op. 28, no. 15).

Miguel Costa i Llobera
(4.2.1854–16.10.1922)

Miguel Costa i Llobera, born in Pollensa, studied law at Barcelona and Madrid before turning to theology. After being ordained as a priest and taking his doctorate he returned to his native island, where he served as a priest in Pollensa and later in Palma.

Costa i Llobera is now celebrated as one of the pioneers of modern Catalan literature. The dominant themes of his work, written in Spanish and Catalan and modelled on classical forms, are the serene contemplation of nature and religious mysticism.

Gaspar Melchor de
Jovellanos
(15.1.1744–27.11.1811)

Gaspar Melchor de Jovellanos was born in Asturias, in northwestern Spain, and his connection with the Balearics came about by chance. A lawyer, he became a judge in Madrid and in 1797 Minister of Justice. In this capacity he opposed Charles IV's pro-French and conservative favourite Manuel de Godoy (Duke of Alcudia), and was imprisoned for his liberal views, first in Valldemosa Monastery and then in Bellver Castle in Palma. When Godoy was overthrown in 1808 and the French moved into Spain he became a member of the Junta Central, the anti-French popular government which led the fight against the occupying forces and fostered a new national consciousness in Spain.

Jovellanos was a highly cultivated man, perhaps the principal representative of the Spanish Enlightenment. His works bear the strong imprint of his political objectives and of what he saw as the basic problems of his country and his period. He wrote

Frédéric Chopin

Ramón Llull

Ludwig Salvator

not only on economic and didactic subjects but also on purely literary themes, and his prose provided a model for later generations of writers.

Ramón Llull was born in Palma de Mallorca. The son of a noble family, he went to the Court of the King of Aragon at the early age of fourteen. He was at first entirely given up to the pleasures of the world, but at the age of thirty he had visions of Christ which brought about a complete change in his personality. Thereafter he devoted his life to missionary activity in distant lands, travelling extensively in North Africa, the Near East, Italy and France, where he also became a university lecturer. He is said to have been stoned to death in the Algerian town of Bejaia (Bougie). His tomb is in the Church of San Francisco in Palma.

Raimundus Lullus – so Latinised in accordance with humanist practice – wrote novels and poems as well as numerous religious, philosophical and scientific works. Much of his work was written in Catalan, which he made a fully valid means of poetic expression, and he is also regarded as the founder of Catalan prose literature. He also wrote in Latin and Arabic.

Ramón Llull
(Raimundus Lullus)
(1235–29.6.1316)

Ludwig Salvator, second son of Grand Duke Leopold of Tuscany, was born in Florence. A great amateur of the natural sciences, he pursued his researches during his travels in the Near East and the Mediterranean area. The works in which he published the results of his researches, illustrated by himself, at first appeared anonymously. Between 1869 and 1891 he published a seven-volume work on the Balearics which is still of value. From 1860 to 1913 he lived mostly on Majorca, in his country houses of Miramar and Son Morroig.

Ludwig Salvator,
Archduke of Austria
(4.8.1847–12.10.1915)

Joan Miró, born at Montroig, near the Catalan capital Barcelona, received his first artistic impulses from the French Realists and above all from the new Cubist school, with which he became acquainted in Paris, where he went for the first time in 1919. Soon afterwards he became one of the signatories of the Surrealist Manifesto; then in 1923 he turned completely away from traditional painting – and from Cubism – to develop his own characteristic style. In his pictures vigorous lines, often suggesting calligraphic forms, combine with intense colours to

Joan Miró
(20.4.1893–25.12.1983)

23

Notable Personalities

Joan Miró

George Sand

Catalina Thomás

create compositions devoid of all abstraction and stimulating a wide range of representational associations. Miró also devoted much attention to graphic techniques, ceramics and sculpture. Until 1940 Miró lived mostly in Paris, but when German troops advanced on the French capital he sought refuge in Spain. When Paris was liberated by the Allies in 1944 he returned to France. After the war he moved to Majorca, where he died on Christmas Day 1983.

George Sand
(Amandine-Lucie-Aurore
Dupin, Baronne Dudevant)
(1.7.1804–8.6.1876)

George Sand, born Aurore Dupin at Nohant in central France, is less known today as a writer than for her association with Frédéric Chopin. At the age of eighteen she married Baron Dudevant, but separated from him in 1831 and entered into a liaison with the writer Julien Sandeau (1811–83), who used the pseudonym J. Sand. Along with him she wrote a number of novels, at first sharing his pseudonym; then, after separating from him, she began to call herself George Sand. There followed a series of friendships and acquaintances with leading writers and artists of the day, including Alfred de Musset, Franz Liszt, Hector Berlioz, Eugène Delacroix and Honoré de Balzac. She and Chopin (see p. 22) spent the winter of 1838–39 in the Monastery of Valldemosa, and in 1842 she published "Un Hiver à Majorque" ("A Winter on Majorca"), which was severely critical of the Majorcans and reflected the difficulties of life in the country for this spoiled woman of letters (who did not endear herself to the local people by her habit of wearing male dress and smoking cigars). The book does, however, contain descriptions of nature and scenery which are still valid.

After the 1848 Revolution, which she had supported ideologically and in her writings but which could claim no significant success, George Sand withdrew from public literary life and thereafter lived in the Château of Nohant, which became the meeting-place of the leading literary and artistic figures of the day.

Fra Junípero Serra
(24.11.1713–28.8.1784)

Miguel Jose Serra Ferrer was born in the little Majorcan town of Petrá, where he attended the school run by the Franciscan Friary of San Bernardino. At the age of fifteen he went to Palma to begin his theological studies, and in 1731 he took his vows in the Franciscan Friary of Jesús there, adopting the name in religion of Junípero. After taking his doctorate at Palma

University he gave lectures in philosophy at the university, without neglecting his duties as a preacher.

Fra Junípero found his real vocation, however, in missionary activity, and at Easter 1749, along with some thirty companions, he sailed for the Spanish possessions in America. It was not until the beginning of December that the party arrived at the port of Veracruz in the Gulf of Mexico. Then, starting from Ciudad de Méjico (Mexico City), he set out to convert the natives. This missionary activity took him to the Mexican peninsula of Baja California (Lower California) and the territories which are now the American States of Texas and California. Here the Jesuits had already established mission stations, and after the dissolution of the Jesuit Order the Franciscans, under the leadership of Junípero, took over their pastoral inheritance. An arduous journey, partly by water and partly on land, took them farther north, and Fra Junípero established the first mission station of his own at San Diego. Further foundations followed, including San Carlos Borromeo del Río Carmelo at Monterey (1770), San Antonio de Padua (1771), San Luís Obispo (1772), San Juan de Capistrano (1776) and – the culmination of Fra Junípero's activity – San Francisco de Asís (1776), which was to develop into a great American city. Fra Junípero died on 28 August 1784 in the Mission of San Carlos in Monterey and is buried there, on 25th September 1988 he was beatified by Pope Paul II.

All over Majorca can be seen evidence of the veneration accorded to Santa Catalina Thomás. Born in Valldemosa in 1531, she spent most of her life as a nun in the Convent of Santa Magdalena in Palma, where her body is now preserved in a glass coffin. She was canonised by Pope Urban VIII in 1627. She now features prominently in popular piety as the "island saint", and many churches have statues and polychrome representations of the Saint on tiles.

Catalina Thomás
(1.5.1531–1.9.1574)

History

There are abundant remains of the prehistoric and early historical periods, some of them excellently preserved, on Majorca
and Minorca. They belong predominantly to the Talayot culture
(from Arabic *atalaya*, "lookout"), a megalithic culture which
flourished between 1500 B.C. and the Roman occupation (123
B.C.), erecting the characteristic Balearic *talayots* – towers built
of massive stone blocks – which have given their name to the
period. The total absence of any written or pictorial evidence
leaves great gaps in our knowledge of this early period, but it
seems to be established that by the 4th millennium B.C. Majorca
was inhabited by pastoral peoples of Iberian stock. The oldest
traces of human settlement which have so far been identified
come from a cave at Son Muleta (near Sóller), where human
remains were found which have been dated by radiocarbon
determinations to 3984 ±85 B.C.

At the same site were found thousands of skeletons of an
extinct dwarf antelope (*Myotragus balearicus*) which was pre-
sumably the staple food of the men of that period. Pottery
fragments found on the site date from a later period (probably
about 2000 B.C.). Other finds from Son Matge (Valldemosa) are
dated to 3800 ± 150 B.C.

Remains of dwellings have been found dating from the Neo-
lithic period, which has left traces only on Majorca, and from
the Early Bronze Age, the so-called Pre-Talayot period
(c. 2000–1400 B.C.). These were either cave dwellings or huts
with stone walls and roofs borne on timber rafters (Ca Na
Cotxera; 1800 ±100 B.C.). Some idea of the archaic method of
construction of these houses can be gained from the small field
huts on Minorca, still used as sheds or stables. At Son Matge
(Valldemosa) remains of massive stone houses (1870 ±100
B.C.) were found, and also pottery with impressed or scratched
decoration. During the Pre-Talayot period the dead were buried
in either natural or man-made burial caves (Sa Tanca, Alcudia;
Son Mullet, Sóller; Son Oms, Sant Jordí and Es Rafal, Palma;
Son Sunyer Vell, El Arenal), which show a striking resemblance
to burial caves on Sardinia and Sicily and in Asia Minor.

The men of this period possessed astonishing skill in working
clay, making a great variety of pottery in colours ranging from
grey to reddish brown, either plain or with scratched decoration. They also had various small bronze objects (dagger
blades, arrowheads, coins). They were skilled in the use of the
sling, and numbers of sling-stones have been found. Later,
during the Punic Wars, the Carthaginians were to make use of
this skill, deploying against the Romans the much-feared
Balearic slingers (Latin *balearii*, perhaps from Greek *ballein*,
"throw", or from Semitic *baál yarah*, "skilled in throwing").
They seem already to have used lead balls, compelling the
Romans to armour their ships with plates of leather.

About 1400 B.C. the megalithic method of construction with
cyclopean walls (made with large irregular blocks) which is
characteristic of the Talayot Bronze Age culture (Balearic culture; 1400–100 B.C.) began to come into use. Some 100 talayots

have been located on Majorca, some 300 on Minorca. These
towers, usually round but sometimes square, served as dwellings and apparently also as burial places and cult centres. They
had a diameter of some 14·50 m (48 ft) at the base and originally
stood up to 8 m (26 ft) high. The form of the top cannot be
determined. The talayots often stood in the middle of surprisingly large settlements, as at Capicorp Vey in southern
Majorca, Ses Paises near Artá, Son Real at Ca'n Picafort and
Son Danús at Santañy. The settlements were surrounded by
defensive walls some 2 m (6 ft) high. Excavation has yielded
quantities of pottery, bronze weapons (swords, daggers, etc.),
jewellery and coins.
From the same period date the *taulas* (Catalan *taula*, from Latin
tabula, "table"), which are found only on Minorca. As the name
indicates, these are table-like structures with a large stone slab
resting horizontally on a vertical monolith. Like the talayots,
they were surrounded by a wall and seem to have served
purely cult purposes. They stand up to 4.20 m (14 ft) high
(Trepucó, south of Mahón), and occasionally have a second,
smaller taula beside them (Talatí de d'Alt; Torralba d'En Sort).
In addition to a small number of dolmens and dolmen-like
megalithic tombs (Torre d'en Gaumés, south-west of Alayor;
Montplé, west of Mahón; Son Bauló, Santa Margarita) the
other most notable monuments of this period are the *navetas*,
which have the form of an upturned boat and were the tombs of
clan chieftains, probably later used as dwellings. On Majorca
fifteen navetas are known, on Minorca sixty-four. The best
preserved is the Naveta d'es Tudóns (restored) near Ciudadela,
which is 14 m (46 ft) long by 6·5 m (21 ft) wide and consists of a
narrow vestibule leading into the main chamber, 9 m (30 ft)
long and 2–3 m (6–10 ft) high.

About 1000 B.C. a new phase known as the Post-Talayot period | Post-Talayot period
begins, with a geometric style of building influenced by
Greece. From the 6th c. B.C. – the time when Carthage was
preparing to conquer the neighbouring island of Ibiza – dressed
blocks of stone are used, producing right angles and smooth-
faced masonry. The Necropolis of Son Real (south-east of Ca'n
Picafort) yielded important material dating from this period.
The sculpture and pottery show clear Greek and Carthaginian
influences, the metal objects (bronze necklaces) influences
from Central Europe. During this phase, when Majorca and
Minorca were still politically independent, a degree of Romanisation, the result of trade and seafaring traffic, can be ob-
served.
The Greek historian Diodorus, in the 1st c. B.C., tells us that
Majorca and Minorca then had over 30,000 inhabitants.
According to the accounts brought back by Greek seafarers
they lived in caves and went practically naked.

The islands are settled by pastoral peoples of Iberian stock. | Stone Age and Bronze Age
Trading-posts are established by Phoenicians and Greeks; salt
is bartered for other goods.

During the Punic Wars the Balearics provide the Carthaginians | 3rd–2nd c. B.C.
with strategic bases. According to local legend their leader
Hannibal Barca was born in 247/246, on Ibiza or a small neighbouring island; in fact he was probably born in Carthage. In the
struggle against Rome he deploys Balearic slingers (cf. Trajan's
Column). His brother Mago is on Minorca about 205 B.C. From

Ramón Llull

Balearic slinger

about 200 B.C., as a result of the weakening of Carthage, a process of Romanisation develops through increased trading contacts.

123 B.C.	Roman forces led by Quintus Caecilius Metellus ("Balearicus") conquer the Balearics. Foundation of Pollentia (the island capital; at Alcudia), Palmaria (Palma), Cunici (Manacor), Sinium (Sineu) and Bocchoris (Puerto Pollensa).
from A.D. 200	The Balearics are Christianised. In 417 Severus, Bishop of Minorca, mentions the Carthaginian foundations of Iamnona (Ciudadela) and Magona (Mahón).
5th c.	Devastation and conquest of the islands by the Vandals under Gunderic (426); Vandal rule under Gaiseric (455–465).
6th c.	The Balearics are taken by Justinian's general Belisarius (533–534), and thereafter are under Byzantine rule.
798	Conquest by the Moors, whose rule lasts for some five centuries – an eventful period, but one that brings the islands prosperity and a flowering of culture,
11th c.	After the death of Al-Mansur (1002) and the disintegration of the Caliphate of Córdoba the Balearics are incorporated in the Arab Kingdom of Denia (1015). In 1076 the royal governor in Madina Mayûrqa (Palma) makes himself independent ruler of the islands. Piracy, particularly on the coasts of Catalonia, Provence and Italy, becomes the principal source of revenue.

With the support of the Pope and the Italian city republics of Pisa and Genoa, Count Berenguer III of Barcelona tries to put an end to piracy. Palma is unsuccessfully besieged but Ibiza is taken and destroyed.	1114
The Balearics under Almoravid rule.	1118–1203
The islands are incorporated in the Moorish (Almohad) kingdom of Granada.	1203
Increased activity by pirates. The raids by Abu Yahya in Catalonia are particularly infamous.	1226–27
Jaime (Jaume) I, King of Aragon and Count of Barcelona, known as El Conquistador, leads a successful punitive expedition against the Majorcan pirates, and after a victorious battle at Santa Ponsa enters Palma on New Year's Eve.	1229
Foundation of a Majorcan State with democratic institutions.	1230
After Jaime I's death his son Jaime II establishes the Christian kingdom of Majorca, in which Minorca is incorporated in 1287. The town of Ciutat (Palma) flourishes: thriving trade and shipping traffic, minting of coinage, much building activity, foundation of towns and monasteries, introduction of *aparcería* (share-cropping; 1301). The poet, philosopher and missionary Ramón Llull is active on Majorca, and from 1281 in North Africa and elsewhere.	1276
Majorca plays an important part in Mediterranean trade and produces a number of major cartographers. Jaime II's son Sancho is king from 1311 to 1324. His nephew and successor Jaime III is killed in a battle with his cousin Pedro IV of Aragon, who gains possession of the island. Majorca is incorporated in the Kingdom of Aragon.	14th c.
Peasant risings on Majorca (1450–52). As a result of the marriage of Ferdinand of Aragon and Isabella of Castile (1469) the Balearics become part of the Kingdom of Spain together with the rest of Aragon.	15th c.
After Columbus's discovery of America and the consequent opening up of the Atlantic, trade in the Mediterranean declines. 1521–22: rising by craftsmen ("Germania") on Majorca. Continual raids and attempted invasions by Moorish and Turkish corsairs operating from North Africa, particularly under the leadership of Khaireddin Barbarossa, devastate the Balearics and decimate the population. Building of fortifications (Palma), fortified churches and watch-towers.	16th c.
Brigandage, famine, plague.	17th c.
In the War of the Spanish Succession Majorca and Ibiza side with the Habsburgs against the Bourbons. In 1715 Palma is taken by Philip V's forces. In 1708 Minorca is occupied by Britain, anxious to gain possession of Mahón's fine harbour. Under the Treaty of Utrecht (1713) it is ceded to Britain together with Gibraltar. During the Seven Years' War France occupies Mahón (1756), but under the Peace of Paris (1763) is obliged to hand it back to Britain.	18th c.

Thereafter the island alternates between British and Spanish rule, until in 1808, with French help, it finally becomes part of Spain.

After the French Revolution refugees come to Majorca. Monasteries and Church possessions are secularised.

19th c.

The Polish composer Frédéric (Fryderyk) Chopin and the French writer George Sand spend the winter of 1838–39 together in Valldemosa Monastery on Majorca.

Archduke Ludwig Salvator of Austria lives on Majorca from 1860 to 1913, with brief interruptions, and writes his comprehensive study of the Balearics.

Majorca's first railway line is opened in 1875.

20th c.

During the 1920s there is a first modest development of the tourist trade on Majorca.

After 1933 there is an influx of refugees from Nazi Germany. During the Spanish Civil War (1936–39) Majorca and Ibiza are controlled by the Nationalists, Minorca by the Socialist People's Front.

After years of deprivation during and after the Second World War a rapid development of mass tourism begins in the 1950s. It soon becomes necessary to establish airports for jet aircraft on Majorca, Minorca and Ibiza; there is an uncontrolled building boom, and not only the landscape but the whole economic and social structure undergo far-reaching changes.

1983

On 22 February the Balearics become an autonomous region, the Comunidad Autónoma de las Islas Baleares. The organ of government is the Consell General Interinsular de les Illes Balears.

The regionalisation of administration is accompanied by a further upsurge of regional language and culture.

1988

In June the Insular Council adopts a series of regulations for improving the infrastructure of the Balearics. These include stricter control on hotel building, improvements in the provision of sewerage and the placing under legal protection of many undeveloped areas.

1990

Severe summer storms lead to widespread flooding and cause considerable damage to the countryside.

Culture and Art

Art and architecture bear eloquent witness to the progress and the different phases of historical development. The Talayot culture (see p. 26) was probably represented on Ibiza as on the other Balearic islands, but in the 6th c. B.C. it was Punicised by the Carthaginians. The new masters of the island no doubt pulled down the cyclopean masonry of the talayots and used the stones to build their own structures, as is evidenced by the megalithic blocks in the surviving remains of Punic walls. In contrast to Ibiza the Talayot peoples of Majorca and Minorca were largely able to escape subjection to Carthage. While Ibiza was important to the Carthaginians not only for its strategic situation but also for its salt-pans and lead-mines, they were content to establish only a few small military posts on the two larger islands without seeking to bring the native inhabitants under their control.

Talayot culture

The Roman conquest led to the rapid decline of the Balearic culture. The Roman governors set out at once to equip the islands, which were important for the maintenance of their new ascendancy in the western Mediterranean, with a well-organised administrative structure centred on Pollentia (present-day Alcudia; with theatre) as capital, convenient economic centres (Manacor and Palma) and a network of roads, which can still be traced.

Roman period

From the brief period of Byzantine rule there survive mosaics (now in the museum in Manacor) from an Early Christian church and the remains of a basilica at Son Bou on the south coast of Minorca.

Byzantine period

The Byzantine period was followed by some five centuries of Moorish rule which brought a great cultural and economic flowering to the Balearics. The castles of Capdepera and Felanitx, the strongholds of Santueri and Castell del Rey and the Arab Baths in Palma still bear witness to this time of prosperity, which had an enduring influence not only on art and architecture but also on the islands' customs and way of life.

Moorish period

The Romanesque period has left few traces on the islands. The only surviving example of Romanesque architecture is a church doorway at the Almudaina Palace in Palma.

Romanesque

When Jaime I conquered Majorca in 1229 the Gothic style was already in full flower. It is represented on the island by such magnificent buildings as the Cathedral and the Lonja in Palma and by Bellver Castle, one of the finest examples of Gothic military architecture.
Majorcan art and architecture were now within the sphere of influence of the Iberian mainland. The Late Gothic and Early Renaissance period gave birth to the Plateresque style of architecture, so called because its intricately patterned decoration recalled the art of the silversmith (*platero*). This style is finely represented by the doorway of the Church of San Jerónimo in Palma and by numerous patrician houses.

Gothic

Plateresque

Culture and Art

Baroque

About 1700 the variety of Baroque known as Churrigueresque (after a family of Spanish sculptors named Churriguera), with its overcharged ornament, came into fashion. This period produced not only churches but also numerous patrician town houses and country houses with finely decorated windows, oriels, spacious patios, grand staircases and beautiful coffered ceilings (*artesonados*).

Popular architecture

Popular architecture, largely unaffected by changing artistic trends, is exemplified by the houses of ordinary people in the smaller towns and by the farmhouses and cottages of country people. Generally these houses are gabled or pent-roofed and are built of dressed limestone with painted door-frames and shutters. On Minorca the terraced houses in towns show British influence, with sash-windows and painted doors with brass fittings. Notable features on Minorca, too, are the whitewashed copings of enclosure walls and the roof ridges of houses. Farms often have a circular threshing-floor.

The architecture of tourism

The growth of mass tourism has radically changed the traditional aspect of towns and coastal regions in the Balearics. Almost all beaches and bays of any size are now fringed by massive hotel complexes, often showing a regrettable lack of architectural imagination, and mushrooming holiday developments with great areas of chalet-type houses. Only the inland regions and cliff-edged stretches of coast have been largely spared by this blight. It must be said, however, that some of the more recent developments have been imaginatively conceived to fit better into the landscape.

A table for Titans: the Talatí de d'Alt ▶

Quotations

Gaspar Melchor de
Jovellanos
Spanish writer
"Memoria del Castillo de
Bellver" (1813)

Roughly half a mile from Palma, west-south-west of the city,
stands Bellver Castle, to which our unhappy history has given a
melancholy celebrity. Half a cannon-shot north of the sea and
some hundreds of feet above sea-level, it adorns and domi-
nates the surrounding countryside. The outer curtain-wall follows exactly the circular ground-plan of the castle, interrupted
only by three truncated round towers which rise from the foot
of the walls, looking east, south and west, ready to defend the
castle. Between them are four round oriels opening off the
upper wall-walk. Three of them are open to the sky; the fourth,
which is roofed, rises above the parapet. Of the same height
and diameter, they taper towards the foot, forming inverted
cones which are supported on the capitals of massive semi-
columns. The columns, projecting from the wall, follow the
wide, steep curve of the walls downwards to their base, which
then falls down to the bottom of the castle moat at an angle of
forty-five degrees. The moat, encircling the whole castle, is
wide and very deep; and it, too, follows the circular ground-
plan of the castle, diverging from it only at the towers and
oriels. On the high ground outside the moat is the esplanade
with its dilapidated redoubts. It is wide and spacious, following
the course of the moat which determines its extent.
On the west side, about the middle of the esplanade, an old and
ruinous keep projects from it. Between this and the drawbridge
the wall is defended by a strong battery of nine cannon, rebuilt
in the 18th century to return the fire of any enemy occupying
the neighbouring hills. Round the outside of the wall runs a
narrow wall-walk of irregular form and depth, and the whole
structure is surrounded by palisades with a covered access
passage and the glacis. These structures, too, are of recent
date.
From the outer walls a gate on the north side leads into the
castle. The moat is crossed on the drawbridge, beyond which is
another gate leading north-north-east. This gate also affords
access, by way of a bridge which was originally movable but is
now permanent, to the esplanade. With its two gates this is
now the only entrance to the interior of the castle; for the bridge
formerly on the south side is no longer there.

George Sand
French writer
"A Winter on Majorca"
(1842)

The monastery, situated at the top of this mountain pass, over-
looks a wide valley to the north which opens out and rises in a
gentle slope to the coastal cliffs, lashed and eroded by the sea.
One of the arms of the range heads in the direction of Spain, the
other runs east. And so from this picturesque Charterhouse we
look down on the sea on both sides. We can hear it rumbling to
the north, while to the south it can be seen as a thin brilliant line
beyond the hills which slope down to the vast plain beyond. It is
a sublime spectacle, framed in the foreground by black rocks
covered with firs, beyond this by the jagged outlines of mountains fringed by magnificent trees, and beyond this again by
rounded summits which are gilded in warm tones by the setting sun and on the flanks of which the eye can just distinguish,
a league away, the microscopic silhouettes of trees, delicate as
the antennae of a butterfly, sharp and black as a line drawn in

Indian ink on a background of sparkling gold. This background is the plain; and at this distance, when the mountain mists begin to rise and cast a transparent veil over the abyss, it could be taken for the sea. But the sea is still farther away, and when the sun returns and the plain is like a blue lake the Mediterranean traces a bright silver ribbon along the far margin of this dazzling prospect. . . .

The rain had at last stopped, and spring had suddenly come. It was February; all the almond trees were in flower, and the meadows were covered with sweet-smelling daffodils. Apart from the colour of the sky and the lively colours of the landscape this was the only difference the eye could perceive between the two seasons; for the trees in this area are mostly evergreen. Those which come into leaf are not subject to the danger of frost; the grass retains all its frankness, and the flowers need only a morning's sun to poke their noses out into the wind. . . .

But suddenly Perica opened a small gate out of the meadow, and we saw a path running round a large rock in the form of a sugar-loaf. We followed the path, and as if by enchantment found ourselves above the sea, above its immensity, with another shore a league away below our feet. The first effect of this unexpected spectacle was a fit of dizziness, and I sat down. Gradually I gained reassurance and was emboldened to walk down the path, although it had been made not by human feet but by goats. The sight before me was so beautiful that I felt myself equipped not with seven-league boots but with the wings of a swallow; and I set off, winding my way round the great hundred-foot-high limestone pinnacles which stood like giants along the coastal cliffs, seeking always to see the bottom of an inlet which cut deep inland to my right, with fishermen's boats appearing no bigger than flies. . . .

I might perhaps have seen Amphitrite in person under an arch of mother-of-pearl, crowned with a garland of rustling seaweed; but instead I saw only pinnacles of limestone rock, some climbing from ravine to ravine like columns, others hanging like stalactites from cave to cave, and all affecting bizarre forms and fantastic attitudes. Trees of prodigious vigour, but all misshapen and half uprooted by the wind, hung over the abyss; and from the bottom of this abyss another mountain rose up sheer to the sky – a mountain of crystal, of diamond and of sapphire. As is well known, the sea, when seen from a considerable height, produces the illusion of being a vertical surface.

(Cakes and how to make them)

Ensaimadas are a kind of soft round cake made from a dough consisting of the finest wheat flour (*Jéxa*), eggs, sugar and water. The dough is left for one or two days, according to whether it is the warm or the cold season, and is then rolled out on a wooden board, covered with a thin layer of lard (*saim*), turned over and shaped into cakes. These are then put into the oven, and after baking are sprinkled with powdered sugar. . . .
Cuartos, which are generally eaten with ice cream . . . are a Majorcan speciality, which for delicacy and digestibility rank among the finest cakes I have ever tasted. They are made in the following fashion. Egg yolk is whipped up in a basin (*ribella*) with sugar of the finest sort, and white of egg is whipped up in a separate basin. The two substances are then mixed together

Archduke Ludwig Salvator
of Austria
"The Balearics" (1869–91)

and thoroughly shaken, after which cornflour is added to the mixture through a small sieve so as to produce a fairly thick dough. The dough is then filled into small square tin or paper moulds and baked in the oven. When ready they are sprinkled with pounded sugar of the finest quality and taken out of the moulds. . . .

Congrets are small thin round cakes, rather concave in shape, with an almost chocolate-coloured outside and a white interior. The method of baking them is said to be a secret of the nuns, but according to a well-informed person it is as follows. The dough is made from 12 carefully whipped eggs, 1½ *libras* (pounds) of sugar and 5 spoonfuls of cornflour. The cakes formed from this dough are laid on a sheet of paper and baked in a hot oven. . . .

The *tordada reyal* is a large cake which is much esteemed on Majorca. It is made in the following way. A thin dough containing ground almonds, sugar, lemons and orange-peel is spread out in a cake-tin and covered with a dry layer of *pasta reyal*. Over this is spread a layer of apricot jam, and over this again another layer of *pasta reyal*. The whole thing is covered with icing made from white of egg and sugar, and the cake is then baked in the oven and finally decorated with sweets, flowers, etc.

Albert Vigoleis Thelen
German writer
"The Island of Second
Sight" (1953)

Deya is – to continue in Baedeker's language, since I cannot express it so well in my own – absolutely fantastic, extraordinary, delightful, extremely rewarding: I can quote no more, for I have just discovered that my 1929 Baedeker devotes only three-quarters of a line to the village. Later works, however, have compared the artistic activity of Deya with Worpswede and Ascona. I do not know Worpswede, but Ascona offers more naked flesh, more scandalous goings-on and less art than the Deya of those days, where world-famous painters had taken up their abode. To add variety there were a few writers, a few philosophers and one or two vegetarians; a Romanian fortune-teller; an Italian coloratura singer who had lost all her ornaments, so that she made use of her divine gift only on bright moonlight nights on a solitary rock; a dozen sculptors and a much-sought-after portrait photographer, a Russian.

One day I was strolling with Pedro on the Borne. It was around the time when the Majorcan takes his constitutional or hires an iron chair from the tourist office and makes passers-by run the gauntlet. We had no money to hire a chair, so we walked up and down in the jostling parade. Suddenly there was a commotion; the promenaders came to a halt and all eyes were turned upwards. A bird of prey – some kind of falcon – had swooped down out of the sky, its target evidently a tame pigeon. The bird pulled out of its dive just above our heads and shot up into the air again. The pigeon lay in the street with its wings spread wide. The air battle was over so quickly that the Spaniards had no time to shout their "olés" in support. Everyone looked at the pigeon, still paralysed with fright. Then there was a further movement in the street. An elderly man in a white linen suit with a bundle of books under his arm was running down the middle of the Borne. The crowd opened up to let him through, and he was within an ace of trampling on the pigeon. Some people laughed, others were angry. Then a boy caught up the pigeon and carried it off to safety from further murderous attacks.

(Minorca, an archaeologist's paradise)
Minorca can claim with justice to be a paradise for archaeologists. A professional archaeologist, or an amateur, would find a lifetime's occupation and interest here, even if he confined himself to the stone memorials of prehistoric times – the monuments of the megalithic culture (from Greek *mega-*, "big", and *lithos*, "stone"). These massive remains, which show that man lived here in prehistoric times and which on Majorca are found only occasionally and are confined to certain forms, are present on Minorca in great abundance and variety; some of them are of types peculiar to the island. Even the ordinary visitor notices them without even looking for them, and the question is inevitably asked: what do these monuments mean and what purpose did they serve?

The questions raised by the prehistoric inhabitants of Minorca are numerous and complex. Why were the talayots built, what was the purpose of the taulas – those huge stone tables standing in the fields which may perhaps once have borne the meals of some imaginary giants? Or the boat-like structures which stand by themselves, far from any known settlement, and from their shape have been given the name of *navetas* ("little boats")?

The archaeological richness of Minorca is impressive, and all visitors to the island – even those who have little interest in these problems – should make a point of seeing some of its prehistoric monuments.

Luis Ripoll
Spanish writer
"Minorca" (1961)

If you take the road which runs south-east from Petrá and makes its way into the southern half of the island you will soon observe an extraordinary change in the landscape. You are leaving the un-irrigated land and encountering increasing numbers of windmills which draw water up from the earth, and you will also notice innumerable drystone walls bordering the road and dividing the fields up into squares. They are very reminiscent of Minorca, the neighbouring island; and this feeling becomes stronger as you go towards the south coast of Majorca, developing into a striking similarity which extends even to the towns and villages in this area. Felanitx is more like a Minorcan village than any other town on Majorca. Felanitx has, too, like almost every town on Majorca, its *puig*, a hill with a monastery containing a much-revered image of the Virgin. In this case it is an almost solitary hill 500 m (1640 ft) high from which the view extends over the whole of Majorca's south coast, only a few kilometres away, from Cala Millor, near Son Servera, to Porta Petro and Cala d'Or, near Santañy, and over the sea to the island of Cabrera. The *puig* at Felanitx is one of the finest viewpoints on Majorca.

José Moll Marqués
Spanish writer
"In Quest of my Majorca"

Suggested Itineraries

Visitors who are planning a stay of some length on Majorca or Minorca should make sure that they see something of the interior of the islands. The best way of doing this is to hire a car; and a small car like the Ford Fiesta, the Opal Corsa, the Fiat Panda or Seat Marbella is particularly suitable for this purpose: these little cars are very manœuvrable and are quite adequately powered for the narrow island roads.

In this section we suggest a number of itineraries for Majorca, starting and finishing at Palma, from which all the island's main roads radiate and which is surrounded by a unified motorway and expressway system linking all the main roads.

Similar suggestions for Minorca will be found in the entries on Alayor, Ciudadela, Mahón and Mercadal in the "A to Z" section of this guide.

Places which are the subject of an entry in the "A to Z" section are indicated by bold type.

The distances given are the total mileage from and to Palma.

Through the western and central Sierra del Norte (c. 150 km (95 miles))

Leave **Palma** on the wide street (Paseo Marítimo/Passeig Maritim, then Avenida Gabriel Roca) which runs west and then south-west from the harbour, and continue on the main road which passes through numerous coastal resorts (with the motorway running parallel as far as Palma Nova). Beyond Palma Nova the road turns away from the coast and comes to **Santa Ponsa**, on the bay of the same name.

From Santa Ponsa the route is direct (or with a detour to the inland town of **Calviá) via Paguera** and **Andraitx** (on road C 719 to here) to **San Telmo**, with the **Isla Dragonera** lying off the coast.

Then return to Andraitx and continue north on the C 710. After the Coll de Sa Cremola (343 m (1125 ft)) the road descends to the rugged and very picturesque north coast and continues through beautiful scenery, with some superb views, to **Estellencs** and **Bañalbufar**.

The road again leaves the coast and follows a winding course to the country house of La Granja (road junction, with a rewarding detour to **Puigpuñent**), near **Esporlas**. From here it is possible to return to Palma on the same road; alternatively, continue for another 3 km (2 miles) in the direction of the coast and at a road junction turn right into the C 710 for **Valldemosa** (off the road to the right), with the monastery where Chopin and George Sand spent the winter of 1838–39, and the beautifully situated country house of Son Marroig near **Deija**.

The next place of any size on the road is **Sóller**, with the picturesque little port of Puerto de Sóller (rewarding detour to the hill village of **Fornalutx**). From Sóller the C 711 runs through beautiful hill scenery, over the Col de Sóller (496 m (1627 ft); road-tunnel being built) and past the country house of **Alfabia** and the little market town of **Buñola** to return to Palma.

Through the central and northern Sierra del Norte (c. 130 km (80 miles))

Leave **Palma** on the road to Sóller (the C 711: see preceding route). At **Buñola** a narrow road goes off on the right and traverses very beautiful scenery to **Orient**. This road then continues through the hills, which are much eroded by karstic action, to **Alaró** (excursion to the Castillo de Alaró) and Consell, where it joins the road (C 713) running along the north edge of the central plain from Palma to Inca and Alcudia. Along this road to the right (5 km (3 miles)) is **Santa María del Camí**. Turning left along the C 713, we come to the leather-working town of **Inca** (detour to **Lloseta**), and from there take a road which turns north and after passing through **Selva** climbs into the hills. Just beyond a major road junction on the northern flank of the hills a minor road diverges to the left to the famous Monastery of **Lluch**. The main road (C 710) continues west, passing through a wild karstic landscape, to the junction with the narrow and winding road which runs down to **La Calobra**. Just beyond this lie the artificial lakes of **Gorch Blau** and Embalse de Cúber, at the foot of the Puig Mayor, Majorca's highest hill. The road then continues via **Fornalutx** to **Sóller**, from which the C 711 leads back to Palma.

Along the north of the central plain to Cabo Formentor

(c. 150 km (95 miles))

From **Palma** take the C 713 (with the motorway running parallel to it as far as Marratxi), which leads north-east through **Santa María del Camí** and **Binisalem** to **Inca** (see previous route) and then passes between **Campanet** (stalactitic caves), to the left, and **La Puebla** (Sa Pobla), to the right. Just beyond La Puebla take the road to **Pollensa**, on the left. From here, after a side road to the attractive little resort of **Cala San Vicente**, the C 710 leads north-east to the Bahía de Pollensa and the picturesque road which continues along the peninsula to **Cabo Formentor**, through some of Majorca's finest scenery.

The return to Palma can be by the same route; but an attractive variation is to take the road along the Bahía de Pollensa to the old walled town of **Alcudia**, from which the C 713 leads back to Palma.

Over the central plain to the Bahía de Alcudia (c. 220 km (135 miles))

From **Palma** take the C 713, the road to Alcudia, which offers the possibility of detours to **Sancellas**, **Sineu**, **Llubí**, **Muro**, **Santa Margarita** and **La Puebla**, all in the Llanura del Centro. From Alcudia we take the C 712, which follows the wide sweep of the beautiful Bahía de Alcudia to **Ca'n Picafort** (12 km (7½ miles) beyond which is a side road to **Colonia de San Pedro**) and **Artá**. **From here the C 715 runs east to**

Evening in Palma Bay

Capdepera with its commandingly situated castle, near which is Cabo Capdepera, Majorca's most easterly point. From Capdepera a secondary road leads south-west at some distance from the coast (attractive detours to the resorts of **Costa de los Pinos** and **Cala Millor**) and just beyond **San Lorenzo del Cardessar** joins the C 715, coming from **Artá**. Just off the C 715 on the left is **Manacor**, from which a road runs east to the little port of **Porto Cristo**. The return to Palma is on the C 715, passing through **Villafranca de Bonany** (detours to visit **Petrá, San Juan** and the **Ermita de Nuestra Señora de Bonany**), **Montuiri** and **Algaida**.

From Palma to the south and south-east coast (c. 150 km (95 miles))

Leave **Palma** on the motorway (which for the most part leads away from the coast and has several junctions) to the airport and continue round the Bahía de Palma, passing through a series of seaside resorts. At El Arenal, where the motorway ends, take the road which turns inland and at **Lluchmayor** joins the C 717. From here there are possible detours to **Porreras** (to the north) and the coastal resorts of **Cala Pí** and **S'Estanyol** (to the south). The C 717 runs south-east to **Campos del Puerto** and **Santañy**, near Majorca's southern tip. From Santañy there are rewarding deviations to **Cabo Salinas**, the most southerly point on the island, and the resort of **Cala Figuera**.

From Santañy a secondary road leads north-east at some distance from the coast, with side roads to **Cala d'Or** and **Porto Colóm**. 15 km (9 miles) from Santañy a road branches off on the left to **Felanitx** and the **Ermita de San Salvador**.

Farther north we come to the beautifully laid out holiday village of **Calas de Mallorca** and beyond this **Porto Cristo**. A few kilometres west is **Manacor**, from which the C 715 returns to Palma.

Bad weather tour (*c.* 140 km (85 miles))

When the sky is overcast, or if the heat is too much for comfort, the following route is recommended. It follows the Palma–Manacor road (C 715).

Just before **Algaida**, to the south of the road, is the Prehistoric Park (large signpost), with numerous plastic reproductions of prehistoric animals.

Beyond this, on the left of the road, is a battlemented structure resembling a medieval castle – the Gordiola Glassworks, where visitors can watch the glass-blowers at work and visit a very interesting glass museum and a showroom displaying fine examples of modern glassware as well as items produced for the mass market. A few hundred metres farther on another pseudo-ancient building houses the showroom and shop of a leather-working factory.

Manacor is famous for its artificial pearls, and a tour of one of the factories is a must for all visitors.

From Manacor the road continues to **Porto Cristo**. Just before the town, on the right, is the entrance to the Cuevas del Hams, caves famous for their delicate stalactitic formations. On the south side of Porto Cristo are the Cuevas del Drach, also celebrated for their stalactites and stalagmites. Near by is a large aquarium.

The return to Palma is by the same route, on the C 715 via Manacor. An alternative for the return to Palma is to follow the southern route through the island from Porto Cristo through **Felanitx**, **Campo del Puerto** and **Lluchmayor**.

Sights from A to Z

Alaró

Island: Majorca
Altitude: 225 m (738 ft)
Population: 4000

Alaró lies 25 km (15 miles) north-east of Palma de Mallorca on the northern edge of the Llanura del Centro, at the foot of the Sierra del Norte.

Situation

In the centre of this friendly little country town stands the 14th c. Parish Church of San Bartolomé.

The town

**Castillo de Alaró

The main feature of interest in the area is the Castillo de Alaró, reached by taking a charming country road which runs north from Alaró, signposted to Sollerich, and in 2 km (1¼ miles) turning left (west) into an asphalt road. This road, which is not particularly wide to begin with, soon becomes even narrower and the asphalt surface comes to an end. The road winds steeply uphill through terraced olive groves, affording magnificent views but presenting problems for drivers not accustomed to mountain roads. In some 4 km (2¼ miles) it reaches an inn with a car park, from which there is a superb prospect southward of Alaró and the central plain. To the east is a steep-sided crag which rears up to a height of 822 m (2697 ft), crowned by the old castle, and is itself known as "Puig del Castell".

From the car park a footpath (not signposted) continues uphill past terraced fields, many of them in a state of picturesque neglect, and then through scrub woodland, passing a number of dilapidated Stations of the Cross. From the path, particularly at the higher levels, there are attractive views of the plain below. After about 45 minutes' walking (comfortable non-slip footwear advisable) the path passes through an old gateway on to the extensive summit plateau, covered with a dense growth of carob trees and enclosed for most of its extent by a wall. On the summit is the Pilgrimage Church of Nuestra Señora del Refugio (in Majorcan Mare de Déu del Refugi; founded 1622), which has a 17th c. figure of the Virgin; adjoining the church is a hospice. On the highest point of the hill rises a radio mast. From the plateau there are superb views in all directions. To the east, in limestone country much eroded by karstic action, lies the village of Sollerich. To the south the view extends over a spur of hill, covered with a dense growth of leathery leaved evergreens, to the Llanura del Centro.

The origins of the Castillo de Alaró, which guarded the approaches to the Orient and Sóller valleys, go back to Moorish and perhaps to Roman times. After Majorca was recovered from the Moors and became a Christian kingdom Jaime I, recognising the importance of the castle for the defence of the island kingdom, had it rebuilt.

◀ *The Lion of Sineu, emblem of a royal residence*

43

Castillo de Alaró

The Castillo de Alaró was the scene of a tragic episode during the conquest of Majorca by Alfonso III of Aragon in 1285, when his forces laid siege to the castle, the last Majorcan stronghold. The castle was defended by two loyal servants of Jaime II of Majorca, Guillermo Cabrit and Guillermo Bassa, who refused to surrender and put up a fierce resistance. When the castle eventually fell they were taken prisoner, condemned to death, impaled and burned alive. Cabrit and Bassa now rank among the great figures of Majorcan history, venerated almost as if they were saints.

Alayor (Alaiort) B12

Island: **Minorca**
Altitude: 130 m (427 ft). Population: 6000

Situation

Alayor (Minorcan Alaiort) lies on a hill on the western edge of the plain which extends westward from Mahón into the centre of Minorca.
The ancient sites in the surrounding area form part of Alayor's Museo Arqueológico al Aire Libre (Open-Air Archaeological Museum).

The town

The economy of this little town of whitewashed houses, the chief place in the district of the same name, is centred on wine production and shoe manufacture. It is dominated by its massive parish church (Santa Eulalia; 1674–80). Lower down, on

Torralba d'en Salort

Torre d'en Gaumés

the east side of the hill on which the town is built, stands the 17th c. Church of San Diego, with a cloister; it originally belonged to a Franciscan friary.

Torralba d'en Salort

B12/13

Situation
3 km (2 miles) SE

Near the centre of Alayor a minor road branches off the main road and runs south-east to the Taula de Torralba d'en Salort, a massive stone slab standing just beside the road, beyond a wall. Opposite this, in the middle of a field, can be seen a talayot with a hypostyle chamber (roofed with stone slabs). Nearby is a prehistoric spring 46 m (150 ft) deep.

The minor road continues south and joins a main road coming from Mahón; along this to the right is the seaside resort of Cala'n Porter (see Mahón).

**Torre d'en Gaumés

B12

Situation
5 km (3 miles) SW

From Alayor take the road to Son Bou, which leaves the west side of the town and runs south-west, passing occasional small windmills. In 2·5 km (1½ miles) a narrow country road goes off on the left, signposted to the Torre d'en Gaumés. This megalithic settlement, excavated in 1942, lies on a flat-topped hill and contains the remains of three massive round towers and the foundations of numerous other structures. A narrow asphalt road crosses the site. Beside the highest of the towers is a taula, from which there are fine views southward of the coastal area, eastward of Mahón and northward of Alayor. Close by is the stump of a second tower with a narrow opening

45

The hypostyle chamber of Torre d'en Gaumés

on one side. Lower down, near the road, are extensive remains of foundations and a small cave with drystone masonry enclosing the entrance. The ground in this area is extensively undermined, and in some of the foundations are cavities which give access to natural underground caves. To the south the road ends at a unique hypostyle chamber, constructed partly underground, with great monolithic slabs supporting the roof.

Son Bou   B12

Situation
8 km (5 miles) SW

The hotel and holiday colony of Son Bou is reached by continuing south-west on the road from Alayor beyond the turning for Torre d'en Gaumés. Shortly before Son Bou the road cuts through a ridge of white rock in a short tunnel to enter the resort's extensive area of modern development.

Above the resort to the east, in an expanse of fairly impenetrable macchia, are the foundations of an Early Christian basilica, possibly dating from the 5th c., near which are a number of graves.

San Jaime Mediterráneo

To the west of Son Bou is San Jaime Mediterráneo (Minorcan Sant Jaumé Mediterrani), a huge complex of villas set in beautiful gardens on the hillside and attractive little terrace houses along the edge of the coastal plain. The Club San Jaume has a double water-chute.

*Beach

The beautiful beach of clean light-coloured fine sand within easy reach of the new development is one of the longest continuous sandy beaches on Minorca. It slopes gently down to the sea and is very suitable for children. When the wind is in the

The long sandy beach of Son Bou

south, however, caution is required, since the beach faces directly on to the open sea and there may be a strong surf.
To the west is another modern development, Sant Tomás (below). To reach it by car it is necessary to make a long detour through the interior of the island. If, instead of returning to Mahón, you want to continue to Ferrerías and Ciudadela the best plan is to take the road which runs north-east from San Jaime to join the main road running from end to end of the island.

Sant Tomás

B12

The holiday settlement of Sant Tomás is reached by taking the main road from Alayor towards Mercadal and in 3 km (2 miles) turning off into a side road on the left which runs due west and then turns south.

Situation
16 km (10 miles) SW

Just beyond the junction with a road coming in on the right from Mercadal is San Cristóbal (in Minorcan Sant Cristofol), a little town of whitewashed houses. South of this, just off the road, are the Talayot of Sant Agusti Vell and the remains of other round towers.

San Cristóbal

The road to Sant Tomás and San Aldeolato (Sant Aldeolat) descends through a beautiful green valley to the coast (little room to park outside the holiday development). There is a beach of fine sand, which is very narrow but extends for a considerable distance, with a number of coves and limestone rocks eroded into bizarre shapes. From the beach a fringe of pine woods extends inland.

The beautiful Valley of Sant Tomás

The Sant Tomás development, on privately owned land, consists of several large hotels and numbers of holiday homes and apartments. It is a resort much favoured by British holiday-makers. Higher up, on the hillside, are handsome private villas.

Ferrerías

Situation
17 km (10½ miles) SW

B12

The attractive little town of Ferrerías (in Minorcan Ferreries; alt. 80 m (260 ft); pop. 3000) can be reached from the main road which traverses the centre of the island from Mahón via Mercadal to Ferrerías and Ciudadela, or direct from San Cristóbal (above). It lies in a sheltered situation at the foot of the 275 m (900 ft) high hill of Inclusa (in Minorcan S'Enclusa). The parish church is believed to have been founded by Jaime III in 1331. 2·5 km (1½ miles) south-east of the town is the Naveta de Son Mercer de Baix.

Santa Agueda

To the north of Ferrerías rises the island's second highest hill, Mount Santa Agueda (260 m (853 ft)), on which are the ruined Castle of Santa Agueda and a military radar station. The military road up the hill is closed to civilian traffic, but the main road to Ciudadela (in 2·5 km (1½ miles), below the road on the right, a Roman bridge) goes past the foot of the hill, from which it is a climb of 4·5 km (3 miles) to the ruined castle, the Moorish stronghold of Sen Agayz. This was the last refuge of the Moors before the Christian Reconquest.

The sheltered bay of Cala Santa Galdana

Cala Santa Galdana

*Situation

7 km (4¼ miles) south of Ferrerías, on a road which branches off the main road beyond the west end of the town, lies the holiday resort of Cala Santa Galdana. The road runs through gently rolling and rather barren country traversed by stone walls enclosing the fields, then, as it approaches the coast, through dense pine woods. Cala Santa Galdana lies in a beautiful wide bay surrounded by almost vertical rock walls. On the west side, where the slopes are less steep, the hillside is covered with pine woods and the houses reach up to the summit plateau, with roads and stepped lanes leading up to them.

The east end of the main beach, with the large hotel of Los Gavilanes, gets the sun only late in the morning. At the west end of the beach, which is of fine sand for the whole of its length, is a large crag of rock, from the top of which there is a fine view of the bay. Beyond this the mouth of a small river, spanned by a footbridge, serves as a haven for fishing-boats and other small craft. Farther upstream the rocky gorge of the river is very picturesque. Much the finest view of the bay is to be had from the precipitous rim of the plateau on its east side. From the hotel a steep stepped path climbs up the vertical rock face; at the top, to the right, is a viewpoint.

B6

Alcudia

Island: **Majorca**
Altitude: 0–16 m (0–50 ft). Population: 4000

Alcudia

Situation

The old-world little town of Alcudia lies on a narrow strip of land between the Bahía de Pollensa to the north and the wide Bahía de Alcudia to the south. From the town the peninsula extends north-east, reaching a height of 444 m (1457 ft) in the Atalaya de Alcudia and ending at the Cabo del Pinar (military area, closed to the public).

History

The advantages of the site were recognised in prehistoric times, and some of the earliest traces of human occupation on Majorca have been found here. The first organised settlement was established by Phoenicians. In the 1st c. A.D. the Romans founded the island's capital of Pollentia (Power) here – not to be confused with the present-day town of Pollensa (see entry) to the north-west. During the period of the Great Migrations (5th c. A.D.) the town was devastated by the Vandals, then pushing into the Iberian peninsula. It was rebuilt by the Moors, who had conquered the Balearics about A.D. 800, and it has preserved the Arabic name they gave it, Al Kudia (On the Hill). After the Christian Reconquest the town was surrounded by the imposing circuit of walls still to be seen today.

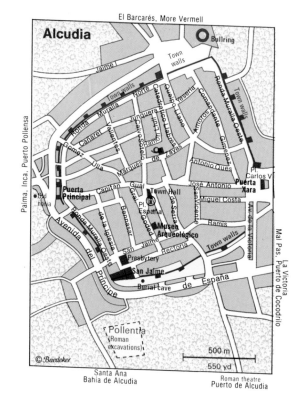

The walled town of Alcudia

Sights

The old part of the town is surrounded by an excellently pre-served and almost complete circuit of walls, interrupted by a major gap only on the south-east side. Originally dating from the 14th c., the walls were extensively rebuilt in the 17th c. The road from Palma enters the town through the massive Puerta Principal or Puerta de San Sebastián (large car park nearby), from which the main street runs east to the Puerta Xara (below). For motorists the best plan is to turn right into the road running outside the town, the Avenida del Príncipe de España; there is further room to park on the south side of the town, where the market is held. From here it is only a few paces to the Puerta Xara, the old harbour gate, standing by itself in the Plaza Carlos V.

*Town walls

At the south-west corner of the circuit of walls is the Parish Church of Sant Jaume, built on the corner bastion in the 13th–16th c. and largely rebuilt in neo-Gothic style in the 19th c. To the right of the gate leading into the old town, in the moat surrounding the walls, can be seen a prehistoric burial cave. To the south-west, beyond the road which encircles the town, are the excavations of the old Roman town (below).

Parish Church of St Jaume

A few yards to the north of the Parish Church, at Calle Sant Jaume No. 2, will be found the Museo Monográfico de Pollentia (open 10 a.m.–1.30 p.m. and 5 p.m.–7.30 p.m.; closed Sun. afternoons and Mon.). On display are excavation finds from the former Roman island capital of Pollentia (see below).

Museum

51

Remains of Roman Pollentia

The walls continue north to the Puerta Principal. They can be followed either outside or, on the inside, on the Ronda Muralla.

Old town

From the Puerta Principal it is possible either to continue round the walls or to turn right into the town, which has a number of handsome burghers' houses. In the centre stands the Casa Consistorial (Town Hall), a modern building in the style of the past. To the south of this is the Archaeological Museum (Museo Arqueológico), mainly displaying Roman material (pottery, mosaics).

Excavations

The excavations of Roman Pollentia (no connection with the present-day town of Pollensa), immediately south-west of the Church of Sant Jaume, are freely open to the public. After the Christian Reconquest stone from the Roman town was used in the construction of the town walls and other buildings, so that only scanty remains survive on the site (foundations of dwelling-houses, stumps of columns).

Oratorio de Santa Ana

A few hundred yards along the road to Puerto de Alcudia, which passes the excavation site, are (on the right) the cemetery and (on the left) the little Oratorio de Santa Ana (13th c.), which is believed to be Majorca's oldest church.

Roman theatre

Farther along the Puerto de Alcudia road, off to the right (poorly signposted), is the theatre of Roman Pollentia. As a stone on the outside of the auditorium records, it was excavated and conserved in 1953 at the expense of the American William L. Bryant Foundation. Of modest dimensions, the theatre was built in a hollow in the hillside in the 1st c. B.C. It is almost entirely unrestored, and is badly weathered. The remains include the tiers of seating in the auditorium, the orchestra and the foundations of the stage building; no structures survive above ground. Here and there are tomb chambers, hewn from the rock in the Late Roman or early medieval period.

Ermita de la Victoria

The road from the Puerta Xara goes east and then turns northeast along the north coast of the peninsula. 5 km (3 miles) from Alcudia on this very beautiful road is the Ermita de Nuestra Señora de la Victoria, situated at a height of 140 m (460 ft), with a fortress-like church.

From the Ermita there is a rewarding climb to the summit of the Atalaya de Alcudia (444 m (1457 ft)), from which there are fine panoramic views extending over the bays of Pollensa and Alcudia and Cabo Formentor (see entry) to the north. The road to Cap de Pinar is closed to civilian vehicles.

Atalaya de Alcudia

B6

Puerto de Alcudia

3 km (2 miles) south-east of Alcudia, at the north end of the wide Bahía de Alcudia, is Puerto de Alcudia, a fishing and commercial port and a small naval base. It now caters extensively for the tourist trade, with numerous restaurants, souvenir shops, etc., and there is additional building activity on the outskirts of the town.

With its large bars and discothèques the resort extends for a

Alcudia Bay – not always so deserted

long way south round the bay. The long beach with its fine white sand and turquoise-green water is fringed by dunes and pines. The new hotels and apartment blocks are notable for their unusual and richly varied architecture; there is an obvious attempt to avoid repeating the architectural sins of the past.

Hidropark

In the "Magic Center" tourist complex is the large fun-pool known as "Hidropark", with several swimming pools and flumes.

The road runs some distance inland from the beach and the hotels between the bay and the Lago Grande (or Lago Espe-ranza) to the west, with occasional glimpses of the sea and the lake. It then comes to the alluvial plain of La Albufera (The Lagoon: see La Puebla), where the new development contin-ues almost without a break into the resort of Playa de Muro.

Muro

See entry

Alfabia

C4

Island: Majorca
Altitude: 300 m (985 ft)

Situation

The estate of Alfabia, celebrated for its gardens, lies 20 km (12½ miles) north of Palma on the southern approach (C 711; tunnel being built under the pass) to the Coll de Sóller. Its lush growth of vegetation is fostered by its sheltered situation between the Sierra de Alfabia to the north and the Serreta de Alfabia to the south.

This was once the residence of the Moorish Viziers, who, with their skill in organising water-supplies, created here, on an island ill provided with surface water, a garden which even today makes it easy to forget this lack. It is said that the property once belonged to an Arab named Benabet, who during the Reconquest became a convert to Christianity together with his whole household, and was therefore allowed to retain posses-sion of his estates.

**The house and gardens

Opening times: Daily
In summer
9.30 a.m.–7 p.m.;
in winter
9.30 a.m.–5.30 p.m.

Admission charge

After passing through the great entrance gate (in front of which is a car park) we continue along an avenue of plane trees leading up to the massive Baroque doorway of the mansion. At the top we turn left at a small water-basin and walk up a flight of shallow steps flanked by date-palms with their characteristic bunches of fruit. Looking right at the top of the steps, we see, beyond a Baroque window, a massive vaulted cistern which supplies water to the gardens on either side of the steps. Be-yond this, on the right, is a charming shady pergola leading to other elaborately laid out gardens. Adjoining these are groves of oranges and lemons, continuing down the slope of the hill. The other part of the gardens, lying lower down at the foot of the double flight of steps, has an almost jungle-like aspect, with dense plantations of palms and a thicket of bamboos bordering a pool of crystal-clear water. Near here is a refreshment stall (open only during the main holiday season).

The house is in Late Baroque style. Approaching it from the lower gardens, we come first to the entrance hall, where the tour begins. In the library on either side of the entrance door are two Late Gothic reliefs portraying Christ's Passion; on the walls of the large drawing-room which follows is a large frieze with panels of island scenes (including Palma Cathedral, the Castillo de Bellver, coastal landscapes, etc.); above the frieze hang some large Baroque oil-paintings. In the next room are numerous engravings and etchings as well as a 14th c. bishop's chair. Finally we come to the bed-chamber (doors with rocaille carving); in the anteroom is another frieze with country scenes. In the courtyard is a huge plane tree, under which stands an octagonal fountain basin.

Passing through the great Baroque doorway on the far side of the courtyard, we return to the avenue of plane trees which leads back to the entrance gate.

Algaida

D5

Island: Majorca
Altitude: 195 m (640 ft). Population: 3500

The little market town of Algaida lies in the fertile Llanura del Centro, Majorca's central plain, at the foot of the Puig de Randa (see below). The main road from Palma (20 km (12½ miles) west) to Manacor (27 km (17 miles) east) runs just to the north of the town.

Situation

The town

Algaida, set in attractive surroundings, has a number of old windmills. The Gothic parish church (SS Pedro y Pablo) dates

Olive-grove near Alfabia

from the 14th and 15th c.; it has a Gothic Virgin and Child in the tympanum of the main doorway, and high up on the wall of the south aisle are fine gargoyles. Built on to the nave is a vaulted chapel. At each end of the town are wayside crosses; adjoining the one at the south can be seen a small fountain-house.

*Gordiola Glassworks

2 km (1¼ miles) north-west of Algaida, on the main road, are the Gordiola Glassworks, housed in a large building in the style of a medieval castle which was erected in 1969 on the occasion of the firm's 250th anniversary. On the ground floor are the actual glassworks, where visitors can watch the craftsmen at work, fashioning the red-hot molten glass with extraordinary sureness of touch into a variety of products (jugs, vases, animal figures, etc.). Adjoining is a large showroom where an immense range of glassware is displayed for sale, including items of real quality side by side with products of little artistic merit as well as well-designed domestic glassware.

On the upper floor is a small museum of great variety and interest (admission free; access by staircase in rear courtyard), with examples of glassware from many different countries, including Spain and Italy (Murano). Of particular interest is the glass from the Far East and from ancient Greece and Rome. There is also a small case displaying terracottas from the Sahara. A few hundred yards east is another building in medieval style, occupied by a leather factory. Here, too, in a large showroom the factory's products (handbags, leather clothing and accessories, shoes) are offered for sale.

*Prehistoric Park

Opening times
daily from 10 a.m.

Admission charge

Farther west, near the planned but as yet unbuilt new development of Son Gual (signpost at roadside), is the Prehistoric Park, recently established in an area of barren karstic terrain with a covering of scrub woodland. The park contains life-size and reasonably accurate plastic and glass-fibre models of a whole range of prehistoric animals. The animals are numbered, and information about the various species is given in a folder issued to visitors at the ticket office.

Near the exit from the car park is a self-service restaurant.

**Puig de Randa

D5

Situation
8 km (5 miles) SE

The most attractive excursion from Algaida, and one of the most rewarding excursions on the whole island, is the ascent of the Puig de Randa (542 m (1778 ft)), a hill rising out of the Llanura del Centro with three monasteries which are much-frequented places of pilgrimage. The road which runs south from Algaida to Lluchmayor comes in 3·5 km (2½ miles) to the beautifully situated village of Randa, with a fine parish church. From here a road branches off on the left and climbs the hill through scrub woodland, with numerous hairpin bends.

Nuestra Señora de Gracia

Half-way up the hill, on the right, is a gateway with the inscription "Santuario de Gracia", through which an avenue leads up to the car park at the entrance of the Santuario de Nuestra Señora de Gracia. The monastery, founded in the

Gordiola: a glass-worker . . .   *. . . and the showroom*

A plastic monster in the Prehistoric Park

15th c. is magnificently situated under vertical rock faces, with crevices and crannies which provide nesting-places for numerous birds. The footpath through the precincts of the monastery ends at a platform from which there are wide-ranging views of the southern part of the central plain. The left wall of the nave of the little church snuggles up against the rock face. Note the paintings on the majolica tiles in the first side-chapel on the left (Christ's geneaological tree, the Annunciation of the Virgin Mary, the Nativity, etc.); on the main wall is a painted wooden statue of St Anna. In the apse can be seen a figure of the Virgin, access to which is through a door on the left (light-switch on the wall) and up a small flight of steps.

Sant Honorat

The road continues to wind its way up the hill, with fine views of Randa below. In about three-quarters of a mile a side road (signposted by a not very visible majolica plaque on the wall) branches off sharply on the right to the Santuario Sant Honorat. In the forecourt of this 14th c. hermitage are a number of old pines and carob trees, and from here, too, there are fine panoramic views. To the south can be seen the island of Cabrera (see entry). At the left-hand end of the façade of the monastery (majolica plaque, "Iglesia") is a passage giving access to the church which stands on the far side of a small courtyard. On either side of the passage are majolica plaques giving (in Majorcan) a brief account of the history of the monastery. In the courtyard is a coloured majolica group of the Virgin and Child (Nuestra Señora del Desert – the "desert" being the Puig de Randa) flanked by Ramón Llull and Arnau Desbrull, the latter being founder of the monastery. At the right-hand end of the façade (plaque, "Portería") is the entrance to the conventual buildings. Between the two entrances can be seen a majolica figure of St Honoratus. Inside the church are the "Stations of the Cross" painted on majolica tiles and a modern reliquary.

Nuestra Señora de la Cura

Continuing uphill, the road reaches the summit of the Puig de Randa, on which are a radio mast and, beyond this, the entrance to the extensive precincts of the Hermitage of Nuestra Señora de la Cura, which is Majorca's most important place of pilgrimage after Lluch Monastery (see entry). It was founded in the 13th c. by the poet, theologian and mystic Ramón Llull (1235–1316), who made it a major centre of intellectual and spiritual life. Since 1913 the monastery has been run by the Third Order of Franciscans. The monastery is entered through a large gateway (1682) with a welcoming inscription. To the right stands the church, with a majolica figure of Nuestra Señora de la Cura over the doorway giving access to the left-hand aisle. It is entered by the doorway on the main front. In the loggia to the right are a series of large majolica panels depicting in chronological order (from left to right) the Annunciation, the Visitation, the Nativity, the Adoration of the Kings, Jesus in the Temple, the Resurrection and the Coronation of the Virgin. In the church, on right, is a "Bethlehem Grotto" of the type common on Majorca; the figures are of different origins.

Museum

The 16th c. grammar school now houses a museum in which are displayed oil-paintings, including some small votive pictures, chasubles and domestic porcelain; showcases contain books and letters (some referring to Ramón Llull). In the left side-room can be seen exhibits from the Peru missionary region (textiles and small items of religious art); in the right side-room are illustrated broadsheets and folklore items.

Near the church another loggia houses a modern fountain with a statue of St Francis of Assisi. As a tablet on the wall records, Ramón Llull founded a grammar school here, the Colegio de la Cura, in which the Latin language was taught for 200 years after his time. On the far side of the monastic precincts extends a large terrace with tables and benches where pilgrims can sit in the shade of the trees. From here there are extensive views to the south-west and north; straight ahead Palma, to the right the Llanura del Centro with the Sierra del Norte beyond it, in the distance on the left the island of Cabrera. There is a road around the Santuario with everchanging views to the west, north and south-east. The monastery has beautiful stained glass depicting scenes from the life of Ramón Llull and a fine library. In the modern conventual buildings a restaurant caters primarily for pilgrims and organised groups.

D2

Andraitx (Andratx)

Island: **Majorca**
Altitude: 52 m (171 ft). Population: 6000

The little country town of Andraitx (Majorcan Andratx) lies 30 km (19 miles) from Palma in the wide and fertile Valley of the Torrent de Saluet, which flows down to the sea at the west end of the Sierra del Norte.

Situation

The town

The country house of Son Mas and the old watch-towers on a hill above the town date from the time when Majorca was

Monasteries . . .

. . . on the Puig de Randa

The fertile Valley of Andraitx

exposed to plundering raids by Barbary pirates. The fortress-like Church of Santa María (13th c.) also stands on high ground, with a view of the Saluet Valley and Puerto de Andraitx.

Puerto de Andraitx (Port de Andratz)

D2

Situation
5 km (3 miles) SW

The little port of Puerto de Andraitx (Majorcan Port de Andratz) is beautifully situated at the mouth of the Torrent de Saluet, which here opens out into a narrow bay forming an excellent natural harbour. The part of the town on the south side of the harbour has best preserved its old-world character, and until now has been relatively unspoiled by the tourist trade. Things are very different on the north side of the bay, with modern apartment blocks built on the steep hillside above the harbour entrance. Many luxury yachts can be seen in the harbour, but very few fishing boats.

Bathing in the immediate vicinity of the town is mainly from rocky beaches. There is a sailing school and there are good diving-grounds. Boat trips can be made from the harbour, for example to the Isla Dragonera and to San Telmo (see entries).

*Cap de Sa Mola

3 km (2 miles) south-west is Cap de Sa Mola (lighthouse), from which there are fine views (to the north-west, the Isla Dragonera). In recent years new development has extended to within a short distance of the cape.

Costa de Andratx

Near the southern end of the town a mountain road, part of which is quite steep, winds its way over a small mountain pass to Costa de Andratx. The beautiful bay is flanked by steep mountain slopes.

Puerto de Andraitx, once a fishing port, now a yacht harbour

Camp de Mar

D2

The holiday settlement of Camp de Mar, 5 km (3 miles) south of Andraitx and the same distance east of Puerto de Andraitx, is attractively laid out on the Playa Camp de Mar, on a coast which is partly rocky. There is a beautiful scenic road to Puerto de Andraitx (with a branch to Cap de Sa Mola; total distance 11 km (7 miles)).

Situation
5 km (3 miles) S

Artá

C8

Island: **Majorca**
Altitude: 120 m (395 ft). Population: 6000

The little medieval town of Artá lies near Majorca's most easterly point, in the middle of the peninsula at the north end of the Serranía de Levante.

Situation

The town

In the centre of the town is the Plaza de España, in which, beside the Town Hall, stands the Artá Regional Museum (open Mon., Wed. and Fri. 10 a.m.–noon), with a variety of material of local interest, including prehistoric and Roman pottery, jewellery and bronze utensils.

From the Plaza de España a street runs up to the Parish Church (originally Gothic) of the Transfiguration (Transfiguración del Señor). In the paving outside the wall of the nave can be seen a crude pebble mosaic of the Lamb of God with Alpha and

61

Artá

The battlements of Artá

Gateway of Ses Paises, a megalithic settlement

Omega (A and Ω) and the Chi-Rho monogram (XP, the first two letters in the Greek name of Christ). The church has a fine altar-piece of the Transfiguration and a wooden pulpit.

From the parish church a Way of the Cross flanked by cypresses ascends to the top of the hill, which is surrounded by battlemented walls. On the outside of the walls, to the left of the steps, a memorial commemorates the dead of the Civil War. From here there are extensive views, particularly to the north and east. Within the walls is the domed Pilgrimage Chapel of San Salvador (originally Baroque; rebuilt in early 19th c.), which has a number of interesting pictures and, high up behind the High Altar, a 17th c. Virgin and Child, with staircase leading up to it from the two arms of the transept.

*Ses Paises

In a wooded area south of the town, beyond the main road from Alcudia to Capdepera, are the remains, known as Ses Paises, of a megalithic settlement (c. 1000–800 B.C.) surrounded by a double ring of walls. Particularly well preserved is the gateway, built of massive blocks of stone. Within the walls can be seen the foundations (unrestored) of a number of large buildings, surrounded by a dense growth of carob trees. The site is open and accessible at all times.

*Cuevas de Artá

D8

6·5 km (4 miles) south-east of Artá, beyond a crossroads, stands the Torre de Cañamel, a massive battlemented tower dating from the 13th c. which has recently been restored.

Situation
10 km (6 miles) SE
Torre de Cañamel

The Cuevas de Artá, close to the coast, are a complex of caves extending for some 450 m (500 yd), with a constant temperature of 18 °C (64 °F). From the entrance, 40 m (130 ft) above sea-level, there is a very beautiful view. The entrance chamber was long occupied as a dwelling or hiding-place, and still shows soot marks from domestic fires. The caves contain an impressive variety of stalactites and stalagmites, notable among them a 22 m (72 ft) high stalagmite in the Salón de la Reina de las Columnas (Hall of the Queen of Columns).

1 km (¾ mile) west is the Playa de Cañamel, with a beach of fine sand and facilities for sailing and diving.

The Ermita de Belén (Majorcan Betlém), in the hills north-west of Artá, is reached on a narrow and winding road (10 km (6 miles); 2 hours on foot). Founded in 1805 on the site of an old Moorish house, it has a plain little church decorated with frescoes and a pilgrim hospice. Superb view over Alcudia Bay.

Ermita de Belén

Bañalbufar (Banyalbufar)

C3

Island: **Majorca**
Altitude: 100 m (330 ft). Population: 500

The village of Bañalbufar (Majorcan Banyalbufar) lies 26 km (16 miles) north-west of Palma on the steep seaward slopes of the Sierra del Norte. It is very popular with the local people as a summer resort.

Situation

The village

On the hillsides falling steeply towards the sea are the laboriously constructed terraced fields which are characteristic of the hilly regions of Majorca. The handsome old manor house of Sa Baronia (originally 14th c.) is now a *hostal* (closed November to March). Near the village are numerous remains of windmills and cisterns.

*Torre Atalaya de Ses Animas

1 km (¾ mile) west, high above the coastal cliffs, is the Torre Atalaya de Ses Animas, the stump of an old watch-tower. From a small parking area on the coast road a footbridge leads on to the spur of rock on which the tower stands. From here there are magnificent views of the sea and the steep coastal hills with their terraced fields.

Binisalem   C5

Island: **Majorca**
Altitude: 137 m (449 ft)
Population: 5000

Situation

The little country town of Binisalem lies 22 km (14 miles) north-east of Palma, to the left of the road to Inca.

The town

Binisalem's main source of income is the production of wine and spirits. In the centre of the town, which originally grew up

A modern medieval castle: the Foro de Mallorca

64

round an Arab country house, is a spacious square in which stands the parish church, originally built in the 13th c. (fine Gothic doorway on east end) but in its present form dates mainly from the 18th c. To the left of the church is a distant view of the Castillo de Alaró, and on its south side is a monument to local wine-producers (1985). The church has a good retablo.

There are some notable old houses in the town centre. To the right of the church can be seen a corner house with a beautiful loggia on the first floor, and a little way north are a number of handsome houses with the typical round-arched vaulted doorway framed in plain stone slabs.

Foro de Mallorca

3 km (2 miles) north-east of Binisalem on the road to Inca we come to the leisure centre known as the Foro de Mallorca, centred on an elaborately battlemented and turreted pseudo-medieval castle. This contains a wax museum (Museo Histo-rial; daily 9 a.m.–9 p.m.; admission charge) presenting events in the history of Majorca and notable people who have played a part in that history – the Balearic mercenaries of antiquity who were celebrated for their skill with the sling; scenes from the Moorish period; the execution of Cabrit and Bassa, the heroic defenders of the Castillo de Alaró (see entry); George Sand and Chopin in Valldemosa Monastery; and much else besides.

In the basement of the "castle" is a discothèque, and round it are an attractive garden restaurant with swimming-pools (including "Aqualandia" with a large water-chute), children's playgrounds, etc.

Consell

5 km (3 miles) south-west of Binisalem is the watershed between the Bahía de Palma and the Bahía de Alcudia. In this area, which is noted for its wine, lies the little town of Consell.

C4

Buñola (Bunyola)

Island: **Majorca**
Altitude: 233 m (764 ft)
Population: 3000

The little market town of Buñola (Majorcan Bunyola) lies 16 km (10 miles) north of Palma in the wooded southern foot-hills of the Sierra del Norte.

Situation

The town

In the Parish Church of San Mateo (1756) is an alabaster Virgin of the Snows (probably 14th c.).
Mount Namarich (666 m (2185 ft)), to the east of the town, is worth climbing for the sake of the view from the top.
4 km (2¼ miles) north, on the road to the Coll de Sóller, are the gardens of Alfabia (see entry).

Raixa/Raxa

2 km (1¼ miles) south of Buñola, at the foot of a hill to the west of the main road, stands the country house of Raixa (Majorcan Raxa), originally a Moorish property. The house was rebuilt and furnished as a museum in 1797 by Cardinal Antonio Despuig (1745–1813), a great lover of Roman antiquity. The collection was dispersed in 1910. The beautiful Italian-style terraced gardens have fountains and viewpoints, but the estate is now privately owned and is not open to the public at the present time.

Cabo Formentor (Cap Formentor)   B6/7

Island: **Majorca**

Situation

Cabo Formentor (Majorcan Cap Formentor), the most northerly point on Majorca, lies at the end of the long Formentor Peninsula (highest point Mount Morral, 353 m (1158 ft)) which encloses the Bahía de Pollensa on the north. The drive to Cabo Formentor is one of the island's most impressive excursions.

**Drive to Cabo Formentor

Puerto Pollensa

The starting-point of the trip (40 km (25 miles) there and back) is the port of Puerto Pollensa, originally the Roman settlement of Bocchoris and until quite recently a modest fishing village. The town lies round its beautiful harbour, now mostly used by pleasure-craft. At the east end of the inner bay, which is bounded by the Punta de la Avanzada (lighthouse), is a naval air station (closed area), which is skirted by the road on its way to the cape. In and around Puerto Pollensa are flat beaches of both sand and shingle.

**Mirador de Mal Pas

From Puerto Pollensa the winding but very beautiful road to the cape – in excellent condition at least as far as the Formentor Hotel – climbs north-east through hills eroded by karstic action, affording delightful views of the Bahía de Pollensa, and comes in 6 km (4 miles) to a saddle in the hills where there is a large car park. Off the road to the left is the Mirador de Mal Pas, with a chain of outlook terraces on the fringe of the cliffs, which here plunge vertically down to the sea 232 m (760 ft) below. To the west can be seen the Punta de la Troneta, to the north-east the little offshore island of El Colomer. Near the car park is a monument to Antonio Paretti Coll, the engineer who built the road to the cape.

**Atalya de Albercutx

There is a particularly rewarding detour to be made along a narrow and winding road from Mirador de Mal Pas to Atalya de Albercutx, standing high up on the ridge. There is limited parking at the bottom of the watch-tower; the final few yards must be covered on foot. There is a superb panoramic view to be enjoyed from the top.

Cabo Formentor, the northern tip of Majorca

View from Atalaya da Albercutz, with the Bay of Pollensa

Beyond the saddle (to the right, a link road to the south side of the peninsula) the road descends through extensive but rather sparse pine woods, with many hairpin bends and beautiful views, particularly to the north. Soon the Formentor Hotel comes into view, lying in a beautiful bay on the south side of the peninsula and reached by a side road on the right.

*Formentor Hotel

The Formentor Hotel was opened in 1930 by an Argentinian named A. Diehl on the Playa de Formentor, a very popular beach fringed by pine woods; there are large parking areas. Offshore is the little Isla Formentor. This luxury hotel (see Practical Information – Hotels), with beautiful terraced gardens reaching down to the sea, has a wide range of facilities for water-sports and other sports and recreations and swimming-pools as well as a bathing beach. Boats ply between here and Puerto Pollensa.

The road to the cape continues through a beautiful sparsely wooded valley, then climbs again and becomes narrower, tunnels under the Mirador Fumat (fine panoramic views) and comes to the Punta Tomás (signpost; small car park), from which there is a view across the little bay of the lighthouse on Cabo Formentor.

**Cabo Formentor

After a further winding stretch the road ends immediately below the lighthouse which stands on the bare headland. From here there is a striking view of the rugged and much-indented north coast of the peninsula. The lighthouse and its platform are not open to the public.

Cabo Salinas   F6

Island: **Majorca**

Situation

Cabo Salinas, some 50 km (30 miles) south-east of Palma, is Majorca's most southerly point.

The cape

The cape is most easily reached from Santañy (see entry). Leaving the town on the road to Ses Salines, we turn left, 1·5 km (1 mile) beyond the hamlet of Llombarts, into a side road (unsignposted) which runs through very beautiful pine woods (mostly privately owned and closed to the public) and ends just before a lighthouse, the Faro de Cabo Salinas (not open to the public). Here the island of Cabrera comes into view. 2 km (1¼ miles) north-west (footpath) is the Playa d'es Caragol, with a sandy beach.

Ses Salines

Continuing west from the turning for the cape, the road from Santañy comes in another 2·5 km (1½ miles) to the modest little village of Ses Salines, which takes its name from the large salt-pans to the south of the village. In the surrounding area are numerous prehistoric remains.

On the road from Ses Salines to Santañy (see entry) lies the first botanical garden in the Balearics, called "Botanicactus". In the gardens, which cover 15 ha/37 acres, there are over 150,000 plants of more than a thousand indigenous and exotic species; about a third of the total area is devoted to plants of the wetlands and includes an artificial circular lake. There are extensive propagation houses where plants may be purchased.

*Botanicactus

Cabrera

Area of island: 17 sq. km (6¼ sq. miles)
Practically no permanent inhabitants

The little island of Cabrera lies some 17 km (10½ miles) south-west of Cabo Salinas, the most southerly point on Majorca, and 60 km (37 miles) south-east of Palma, between latitude 39°7' and 30°13' N and between longitude 6°36' and 6°40' E.

Situation

Cabrera (Goat Island) is the principal island in a small archipelago which also includes Conejera (Conillera, Rabbit Island), where there are also many lizards, and Foradada (lighthouse), lying to the north, together with a number of smaller rocky islets. Cabrera, with a greatest width of 5–7 km (3–4¼ miles), has a much-indented coastline, with several irregularly shaped bays and inlets. As a result of centuries of over-grazing by wild goats the surface of this hilly island has been largely eroded by karstic action and much of it is covered with cushions of low-growing rosemary. The climate is particularly healthy.

The island

Cabrera, southern outpost of Majorca

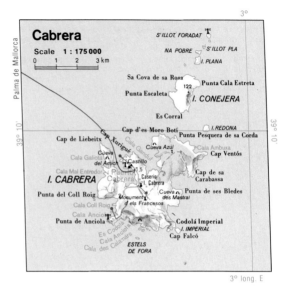

To the Romans the island was known as Capraria, and Pliny believed it to be the birthplace of Hannibal. In the Middle Ages it served as a corsairs' lair and a base for raids on Majorca. Towards the end of the 14th c. a castle was built above the harbour to prevent the corsairs from setting up a permanent establishment here.

After the French defeat at Bailén in July 1808 some 9000 French prisoners of war were confined on Cabrera, where they languished for almost three years, decimated by hunger and disease. Only 3600 of them survived to be repatriated to France in 1812.

Until the First World War Cabrera was owned by the Feliu family. To prevent the use of the harbour by the opposing navies the Spanish Government compulsorily acquired the island and established a small military garrison, which still remains.

Visiting the island

Cabrera has at present little to attract tourists, particularly since as a military area it is for the most part closed to visitors, and moreover can offer them no accommodation and little in the way of refreshment. If, however, you are sailing your own boat you will find in the island's harbour and in the coves (*calas*) around the coast quiet anchorages and clear water for swimming, diving and fishing. There are sandy beaches at Ganduf on the north-west coast, at Olla on the east coast and against the harbour breakwater.

The few non-military inhabitants of the island live in modest houses near the Puerto de Cabrera, an almost exactly circular natural harbour which ranks after Mahón (Minorca) as the best sheltered harbour in the Balearics; the entrance is only 330 m (360 yd) wide. By the harbour are a simple *cantina*, in which it is possible to get something to eat and drink, and the head-quarters of the military garrison.

During the hour or two that the regular boats spend in the harbour passengers have time to scramble up a steep and difficult path (care required because of crumbling rock and dangerous holes) to the ruined Castillo (14th–15th c.). Near by are a seamen's cemetery and a Guardia Civil post. From the castle and the adjoining crags there are magnificent views of the harbour, much of the rest of the island, a number of *calas* and, to the north, the main island of Majorca.

On the high cliffs of Punta Anciola, a small peninsula in the south-west of the island, stands an important lighthouse.

In the centre of the island (not at present accessible) is an obelisk set up in 1847–48 to commemorate the French prison-ers of war who died on Cabrera. It bears the following in-scription:

> A la Mémoire
> des Français morts
> à Cabrera
> L'Escadre d'évolutions
> de 1847
> commandé par
> S.A.R
> le Prince de Joinville

During the summer season it is possible to join a boat trip to the Cueva Azul (Majorcan Cova Blava; Blue Grotto), the most beau-tiful cave on Cabrera; the trip takes 20 minutes. The cave, which is accessible only from the sea, has a wide entrance and mea-sures approximately 50 by 160 m (55 by 175 yd). The high interior shimmers with a bluish light.

*Cueva Azul

Cala d'Or

E7

Island: **Majorca**
Altitude: sea-level

The summer holiday centre of Cala d'Or lies in the south-east of Majorca near the south end of the Serranía de Levante. Build-ing development is spreading further and further inland.

Situation

The resort

This huge holiday development extends round a series of coves – Cala Ferrera, Cala Esmeralda, Cala Gran, Cala d'Or and Cala Llonga. The villas and holiday homes, mainly of one or two storeys, are in a kind of pseudo-Mexican pueblo style and fit well into the landscape. There are almost always a number of luxury yachts anchored in the excellently equipped boating harbour. The resort has facilities for sailing and diving; glass-bottomed boats; tennis-courts and facilities for archery; dis-cothèques and night-clubs.

Porto Petro

Porto Petro, a little way south-west, is much quieter and more typically Majorcan than the ultra-modern Cala d'Oro. It has a

The harbour of Cala d'Or

small and well-sheltered harbour in an almost completely enclosed bay.

Above the south entrance to the harbour, on Punta de Sa Torre, is an old watch-tower. To the south-west lies the Cala Mondragó (sandy beach), with a new holiday development.

Cala Figuera

F6/7

Island: **Majorca**
Altitude: sea-level

Situation

The idyllic little fishing village of Cala Figuera lies near the southern tip of Majorca, 5 km (3 miles) south-east of Santañy.

The village

The houses of Cala Figuera are built along the fjord-like inlet which forms its harbour. The rocky shores, topped by dwarf pines, are much eroded and undermined by the sea. Above the north side of the harbour entrance are an old watch-tower and a lighthouse (fine views). This is a quiet and rather old-fashioned little resort which has a nostalgic charm; it has no big tourist hotels.

Cala Santañy

Some 5 km (3 miles) west of Cala Figuera is the holiday colony of Cala Santañy. A very steep road and some narrow steps lead down to the beach in the rocky bay.

Cala Llombarts

South-west of Cala Santañy lies the older and partially neglected holiday colony of Cala Llombarts (no large hotels). A

road leads down to the fairly large sandy beach; the rocky bay
is very well protected.

Cala Millor

Island: **Majorca**
Altitude: sea-level

The hotel colony of Cala Millor lies on the east coast of Majorca   Situation
in the Bahía de Artá, 15 km (9 miles) south of Artá.

The resort

Cala Millor, with the neighbouring little port of Cala Bona, is a
very popular holiday area with a sandy beach 1·5 km (1 mile)
long fringed by pine woods. The road to the resort and many
roads within it are also shaded by pines. In the last few years
Cala Millor has grown considerably to become a busy tourist
centre, with new developments springing up along the coast
and well inland, to join up with neighbouring towns. Most of
the hotels lie in the centre near the beach; further along the
coast becomes rocky.

South of Cala Millor, Punta Amer (with castle ruins) projects   Punta Amer
into the sea; on its south side lies the sandy Playa de Sa Coma,
a nature reserve.

African animals . . .   *. . . in relative liberty*

*Reserva Africana

Temporarily closed for
rearrangement

Admission charge

The Reserva Africana, to the south-west of Cala Millor, is an area of some 40 hectares (100 acres) in which African mammals and birds live in natural conditions. The best times to visit it are early in the day or in the late afternoon.

Within the reserve, which has no internal fences or divisions, ostriches, marabous, storks, elephants, Watusi cattle, antelopes, giraffes and many other species of animal roam freely. There are no dangerous beasts of prey.

Visitors can drive through the grounds in their own car or in one of the park's open jeeps; they are not allowed to go on foot. Even though there are no dangerous animals, visitors may not leave the vehicle in which they are travelling. The monkeys show no fear of man, and car windows should be closed when they are in the vicinity.

If your car breaks down help can be summoned by sounding the horn. Until it comes you must not leave your car.

It is useful to have binoculars. If you have a camera with interchangeable lenses, use the lens with the longest focal distance. There is also a separate "junior zoo", with enclosures containing a variety of species, including large felines (lions, leopards), and with a restaurant. Cars can be left in this area. Pedestrians can visit the "junior zoo" without going through the main reserve.

Cala Pí

E5

Island: **Majorca**
Altitude: sea-level

Situation

The Cala Pí development, now continuous with the built-up area of Vallgornera, lies half-way along the south coast of Majorca, almost due south of Lluchmayor.

**The resort

The road from Lluchmayor to the prehistoric settlement of Capicorp Vey (below) and Cala Pí cuts across a closed military area and ends in the extensive area of modern development. From here steps lead down to the fjord-like inlet, caught between high rock walls, the beauty of its crystal-clear water visible even from this height. The little cove forms an excellent sheltered natural harbour, with a small slipway for fishing-boats and a number of boat-sheds. There is also a good sandy beach; but outside the cove the coastal cliffs leave little scope for bathing.

On the spit of land to the left of the cove can be seen the stump of an old watch-tower. From here there is a good view of the island of Cabrera.

The development around the cove, which is still in progress, is in a style based on Moorish models, with low buildings which fit well into the landscape. Farther east, near the cliffs, are numbers of luxurious holiday villas.

**Capicorp Vey (Capocorp Vell)

E4

Capicorp Vey (Majorcan Capocorp Vell) is a site of the Pre-Talayot period (1000–800 B.C.), with remains which include five

Cala Pí: a rocky creek

talayots. The site is enclosed by a wall (admission charge; open Fri.–Wed. 10am–5pm, closed Thur.).
Near the entrance is the stump of a round tower, from the top of which there is a view of the island of Cabrera to the south.
Beyond the tower a monolithic slab of stone was set up in 1959 to commemorate the excavator of the site, A. J. Colominas Roca. The foundations of a number of rectangular buildings can also be seen, some of them with remains of the characteristic central pillar.

Cabo Blanco

E4

Beyond Capicorp Vey is a road junction, where the road to the left passes through a closed military area and in 5 km (3 miles) reaches Cabo Blanco, a rocky headland at the south-east end of the Bahía de Palma which is Majorca's most southerly point. From near the lighthouse, to the left of which is the stump of an old tower, there is a fine prospect of the sea and the island of Cabrera.
From Cabo Blanco a road follows the coast, usually at some distance from the cliffs, via the seaside resorts of Cala Blava, Bahía Azul and Bahía Grande to El Arenal (see Palma de Mallorca).

B6

Cala San Vicente (Sant Vincenç)

Island: **Majorca**
Altitude: sea-level

Calas de Mallorca

Cala San Vicente

Situation

The pleasant little holiday resort of Cala San Vicente (Majorcan Sant Vincenç), at the northern tip of Majorca, lies 6 km (4 miles) north-east of Pollensa and is most easily reached on a side road from there.

*The resort

From Pollensa (see entry) the road to San Vicente runs down the fertile Valle de San Vicente, between the Sierra de Cavall Bernat to the south-east and the Sierra de Sa Font to the north-west. The rocky bay has two small secluded sandy beaches, with the San Pedro Hotel on a promontory between them. On the left-hand side of the bay are two small slipways for fishing-boats. Close to the beaches are a number of other hotels, together with restaurants and bars. By the roadside can be seen a monument to the painter Llorenç Serda y Bisbal (1862–1955). The road continues along the bay to the right, rounds a promontory and ends in another small bay with some hotels and a number of privately owned houses. Inland from Cala San Vicente, scattered about in the pine woods, are other handsome holiday homes. Behind Cala Carbo a somewhat steep and winding road leads uphill to Sierra de Cavall Bernat and ends high above the sea, with a few platforms offering limited views. To the north, on the left-hand side of the bay, a footpath leads to the Punta de Covas Blancas (view).

Calas de Mallorca

E7

Island: **Majorca**. Altitude: sea-level

Situation

The resort area known as the Calas de Mallorca lies in the

southern half of Majorca's east coast in approximately the latitude of the little town of Felanitx.

The resort

The Calas de Mallorca (Coves of Majorca) are a large and carefully planned holiday settlement on the bare and much-indented coast between Cala Magraner and Cala Murada, with narrow inlets fringed by sandy beaches reaching deep into the rocky coast. The resort is dominated by a number of large hotel blocks, but much of the development is in single- and two-storey buildings.

La Calobra

B/C4

Island: **Majorca**. Length of road: 12 km (7½ miles)

The road known as La Calobra or the "Snake", so called because of its many sharp bends, runs steeply down from the Pollensa–Sóller road on the northern flank of the Sierra del Norte to the little Cala de la Calobra.

Situation

**To the Cala de la Calobra

The "Snake" leaves the main road just to the east of Gorch Blau (see entry) and winds its way down the barren karstic slopes to the sea; it is magnificently engineered but testing for the driver. Near the top, in what is known as the Nus de la Corbeta (Knot in the Tie), it turns through an angle of 270 degrees and passes under itself. Lower down it runs past labyrinthine rock formations and great monolithic pinnacles fluted and carved into bizarre shapes by erosion. One of the most striking points on the road is a narrow defile caught between high rock walls, the Cavall Bernat (alternating one-way traffic); just before this is a viewpoint looking down on the rocky cove below.

Nus de la Corbeta

Cavall Bernat

Near the lower end of the road the access road to the new development of Cala Tuent, in the cove of that name, branches off on the left.

Cala Tuent

The Cala de la Calobra is a little cove enclosed by sheer cliffs, with a restaurant and a number of small bars which are open only during the season. A road runs round the cove to the right or a short distance, ending at a car park, with a kiosk. From here it is 5 minutes' walk to the narrow gorge at the Torrent de Pareis, one of Majorca's most striking natural features.

Cala de la Calobra

The path follows two dark tunnels cut through the cliffs. After the first one, which has two window-like openings looking out to sea, a path on the left descends to the shore. Beyond this a second, longer, tunnel continues through the rock, using a natural cave (stalactitic and sinter formations) for part of the way, and emerges in the broad bed of the Torrent de Pareis, a circular basin framed in rock. To the south can be seen the gorge carved out by the stream; to the north, beyond a bank of shingle, the sea can be glimpsed between high rock walls (looking particularly beautiful on summer evenings towards sunset). Open-air concerts are occasionally given in this natural amphitheatre. It is also a popular picnic spot – as can, unfortunately, be seen from the traces left behind.

**Torrent de Pareis

La Calobra

Torrent de Pareis

The Torrent de Pareis Gorge is only some 30 m (100 ft) wide. Exploring it on foot is not without its hazards.
There are also boat trips from Puerto Sóller (see Sóller) to the Cala de la Calobra.

Calviá

D2/3

Island: **Majorca**. Altitude: 150 m (490 ft)
Population: 9000

Situation

The little town of Calviá lies inland below the south-west side of the Sierra del Norte, half-way between Palma and Andraitx.

The town

Calviá is the chief town of an extensive district which has prospered as a result of the busy tourist and holiday trade in the coastal region between Illetas and Fornells. The Parish Church of San Juan Bautista was originally built in 1245 in Early Gothic style but was altered in the 19th c. To the right of the church is the Balearic Library Centre. Passing between the two buildings, we come into a picturesque little inner courtyard with a draw-well.

A short way down from the main front of the church (car-park) stands the municipal music school; to the left of the main entrance there is a picture in the wall, measuring 4 by 7 m (13 by 23 ft), made of majolica tiles (1986) which shows a map of the district and episodes from the island's history.

4 km (2½ miles) north-west lies the modest little village of Capdella, with an 18th c. parish church (Virgen del Carmen) built at the expense of one Captain Barceló, celebrated as the "terror of the pirates".

Capdella

C5

Campanet

Island: **Majorca**
Altitude: 134 m (440 ft)
Population: 3000

Campanet lies in northern Majorca, to the left of the main road from Palma to Alcudia.

Situation

The town

The old-world township of Campanet lies on a low ridge of hills. The main sources of income of its inhabitants are farming, basketwork and the manufacture of glassware. The Parish Church of San Miguel (early 18th c.) contains the relics of the local saint, Victorianus. Campanet was the birthplace of the poet and humanist Lorenza Riber (1882–1958).

2 km (1¼ miles) north of Campanet is the Oratorio de San Miguel, originally built in the 13th c.
North-east of this, in a garden, is the entrance to the Campanet Caves.

Oratorio San Miguel

*Cuevas de Campanet

The Cuevas de Campanet, a complex of limestone caverns discovered only in 1945, are now open to visitors (conducted tours) for a total length of 1300 m (1425 yd); stout footwear is required. The caves maintain a constant temperature of 18–19 °C (64–66 °F). The sinter formations, in a range of colours from ochre to reddish brown, are very varied and of filigree delicacy: some are more than 3 m (10 ft) long but only 5 mm (0·2 in) thick. There is a restaurant at the entrance to the caves, and a pleasant view of the valley can be enjoyed from its terrace.

C5

Búger

The village of Búger lies on a hill on the opposite side of the Palma–Alcudia road from Campanet. On top of the hill stands the small 17th c. Parish Church of San Pere. There are several prehistoric burials in the surrounding area.

Situation
3 km (2 miles) SE

E6

Campos del Puerto

Island: **Majorca**
Altitude: 22 m (72 ft)
Population: 7000

The little town of Campos del Puerto lies in the southern part of

Situation

the Llanaura del Centro, 40 km (25 miles) south-east of Palma on the road to Santañy.

The town

The town has preserved something of its medieval aspect. On the main road through the town stands the Neo-classical Parish Church of Sant Julián, which has a fine painting by Murillo, "El Santo Cristo de la Paciencia" (17th c.). On the north side of the main street is the handsome and excellently restored 16th c. Town Hall, with a double-arched doorway; balustrades and coats of arms decorate the façade. There are a number of old defensive towers in the town.

The fertile plain to the south of Campos is intensively cultivated, with irrigation provided by numerous windmills. 5 km (3 miles) south-east is the prehistoric Necropolis of Son Toni Amer.

Ermita de San Blas

3 km (2 miles) south of Campos, to the east of the road to Colonia de Sant Jordi, can be found the Ermita de San Blas, one of the oldest hermitages on Majorca. In the dilapidated little church is a fine 15th c. retablo of Nuestra Señora de la Leche; the church is open on Sunday evenings only.

Baños San Juan

9 km (5½ miles) south of Campos on the road to Colonia de Sant Jordi lies the modest little rural spa of Baños San Juan de la Font Santa (Majorcan Banys de Sant Joan). To the west of the village are the evaporation basins of the Salinas de Levante.

Es Trenc

A narrow side road passes through the evaporating basins, ending in a large car park near the flat sandy beach. In the pinewoods are lagoons of brackish water and areas of marshland, where migrating birds rest on their journey.

Puerto de Campos

See Colonia de Sant Jordi

Ca'n Picafort

C6/7

Island: **Majorca**
Altitude: sea-level
Population: 4000

Situation

Ca'n Picafort, an old fishing village which has developed into a popular seaside resort, lies in north-eastern Majorca on the wide Bahía de Alcudia, here bordered by an alluvial plain.

The town

The life of Ca'n Picafort now centres on the tourist and holiday trade, with numerous hotels, restaurants, shops and bars. The beautiful beaches of light-coloured sand are fringed with pines for long stretches. From the town's seafront promenade there are views of the bay and the peninsula, with the Atalaya de Alcudia to the north.

Respectively south and south-east of the town are the prehistoric sites and cemeteries of Son Bauló and Son Real. They are not easy to find, so ask locally for directions.

Capdepera

Island: **Majorca**
Altitude: 70 m (230 ft)
Population: 5000

The little old-world town of Capdepera lies near the extreme eastern tip of Majorca at the northern end of the Serranía de Levante.
Capdepera is a centre of the Majorcan basketwork industry.

Situation

*Castle

To motorists approaching Capdepera from the west (the road from Artá) the imposing ruins of its 14th c. castle are seen on the slopes of the hill to the left. From the Plaza de Orient, the town's little main square, a stepped lane leads up to the ruins. A wall-walk, completely preserved in good condition, runs round the inner side of the battlemented walls. On the highest point in the circuit are the stump of a round tower and the small aisle-less Gothic Church of Nuestra Señora de la Esperanza (Our Lady of Good Hope; 1323), on an irregular ground-plan. Steps on the south side of the church lead up to the flat roof, designed for the collection of rainwater; there are fine panoramic views.

Opening Times:
Apr.–Sept. daily
10 a.m.–1 p.m.; 4–7 p.m.
Oct.–Mar. daily
10 a.m.–1 p.m.; 3–5 p.m.

Cala Ratjada

C8

Cala Ratjada, once a small fishing village, has developed in recent years into a seaside holiday resort which lives almost

Situation
3 km (2 miles) NE

Capdepera, huddled under its castle

Cabo Capdepera, Majorca's eastern tip

entirely from the tourist trade. There is only limited scope for bathing within the area of the town itself: much more attractive (and also very busy during the main holiday season) are the beaches in the surrounding area – Cala Guya (fine sand), Cala Mezquida, Playa Son Moll.

Casa March

A visit is recommended to the park known as Casa March, in which the well-known banking family of that name has built an open-air museum of contemporary art. It is best to make arrangements in advance by telephoning 56 30 33.

*Cabo Capdepera

Cabo Capdepera, the most easterly point on Majorca, is reached from Cala Ratjada in a short walk (2 km (1½ miles)) through beautiful pine woods or by road. On the cape are a lighthouse and the stump of an old watch-tower, the Torre Embucada. From here fine views of the sea and the inland hills can be enjoyed. There is a pleasant walk south over the plateau with its dense cover of stunted pines to a point where it falls sheer down to the sea below.

Ciudadela de Menorca (Ciutadella) — A/B10/11

Island: **Minorca**
Altitude: sea-level
Population: 20,000

Situation

Ciudadela de Menorca (Minorcan Ciutadella), Minorca's former capital, lies at the western end of the island, exactly on the 40th parallel of northern latitude.

Ciudadela de Menorca

Ciudadela was the capital of Minorca until 1722. In 1795 it became the seat of the re-established episcopal diocese of Minorca (a see originally founded in the 5th c.). In contrast to Mahón, Ciudadela is a town of Moorish and Spanish character. The town's thriving economy is centred on the leather and footwear industries for which it is famed and on the manufacture of jewellery. As a port Ciudadela is of merely local importance.

General

The town was founded by the Carthaginians as a military post, under the name of Yamma (The West), and is believed to be the oldest urban settlement on Minorca after Mahón. When the Romans occupied Minorca it became the island's administrative capital, under the name of Iamnona.
On 9 July 1558 the thriving little town was captured after a nine days' siege by a force of 15,000 Turkish corsairs. The town itself was almost completely destroyed, and the surviving inhabitants were carried off to slavery in Istanbul. Only a few structures survived this visitation and have been preserved. These include the Fuente and Borne bastions and the Muralla del Mar (a remnant of the town's circuit of walls with its five gates).
Ciudadela was the birthplace of J. A. Magín Farragut Mesquida, father of the American Civil War hero Admiral David Glasgow Farragut (b. 1801 in Campbell's Station, Tennessee; d. 1870 in Portsmouth, New Hampshire), who in 1862 forced a passage into the Mississippi with a fleet of forty-four Union vessels and thus made possible the taking of New Orleans. Admiral Farragut's mother, Elizabeth Shine, came from North Carolina.

History

Sights

Ciudadela is picturesquely situated above the long fjord-like harbour inlet (the Puerto), with many shoals allowing passage only to small vessels. At the tip of the promontory on the south-west side of the harbour entrance, outside the built-up area, stands a monument to Admiral Farragut, which occupies the site of the 17th c. Castillo de San Nicolás. Immediately adjoining is an old octagonal watch-tower.

A good starting-point for a tour of the old town centre of Ciudadela is the Plaza del Borne, above the south side of the inner harbour. In this square and in the broad Paseo del Puerto which runs west from here there is ample parking space. An obelisk in the centre of the square commemorates the destruction of the town in 1558. The Casa Consistorial or Town Hall (Ayuntamiento), on the west side of the square, stands on the site of the old Moorish Alcazar. From the balustrades on the north side of the square there is a good view of the harbour inlet. The east side of the square is dominated by the imposing façades of the Palacio del Conde de Torre Saura (left) and Palacio Salort (right: see below). At the south-east corner of the square is a small church, originally Gothic but remodelled in Neo-classical style, with a new façade, dome and chancel.

Plaza del Borne

From the north-east corner of the Plaza del Borne a short street leads to a broad flight of steps running down to the harbour, above which tower the massive fortress-like substructures of the Casa Consistorial, now occupied by discothèques. The harbour quay (Muelle) is lined with restaurants, with tables and chairs set out in the open. The harbour is occupied by many

Harbour

Cala Blanca, Cabo d'Artrutx

fishing-boats as well as a multitude of sailing craft and motor-boats. Here, too, particularly on the north quay, fishermen can still be seen mending their nets. In the outer harbour is the clubhouse of the Club Naútico (with a winch and a station for refilling compressed-air cylinders), and opposite this a slipway capable of taking boats of some size.

Palacio Salort

The Palacio Salort (open Mon.–Sat. 10 a.m.–2 p.m.; admission charge) is a handsome and well-preserved mansion in Early Neo-classical style. The entrance is in Calle Mayor del Borne, which runs east from the Plaza del Borne into the older part of the town. A magnificent staircase hung with 18th c. French tapestries leads up to the first floor, with handsome apartments containing inlaid furniture, crystal chandeliers and early 19th c. ceiling-paintings. From the open columned loggia there is a view of the Plaza del Borne.

Facing the picturesque little inner courtyard is the large kitchen of the palace with its tile-clad three-part fireplace. From the kitchen a narrow outside staircase descends to ground-level. Opening off the courtyard, below, are the old stables and the garage, still housing a 1920s car which was one of the first motor vehicles on Minorca. In another courtyard is a small open-air café.

In Calle San Jerónimo, which crosses the Calle Mayor a few yards farther on, is another fine old mansion, the Casa de Sintas.

Cathedral

The Calle Mayor del Borne joins Plaza Pio XII, on the left-hand side of which stands the Gothic Cathedral (granted the status of a basilica in 1953), a hall church without transepts which was built between 1287 and 1362. The west front, with the main

Ciudadela: the narrow harbour inlet ▶

Ciudadela de Menorca

Palacio Salort

Ciudadela Cathedral

doorway, is Neo-classical (1813); there is another doorway on the south side. Built on to the north side is a domed side chapel in Neo-classical style – a feature frequently found in Spanish churches of this period. Over the High Altar hangs a tall neo-Gothic canopy. The stained glass dates mainly from the 19th c. The south doorway was altered in the 19th c. but retains some Gothic decorative elements.

From the Cathedral Calle del Obispo Torres leads north, passing the large Palacio Episcopal (Bishop's Palace), into Calle San Sebastián, in which can be seen another handsome old mansion.

*Capilla del Rosario

A few yards to the right of the Cathedral in the little Plazuela del Rosario is the Capilla del Rosario (Chapel of the Rosary), with a fine Churrigueresque façade (best light from early afternoon onwards). The interior of the chapel is Baroque.

There are other handsome façades in Calle del Obispo Vila, the next on the right off the main street of the old town. A deconsecrated Baroque church in this street, now housing the studio of Radio Popular, has a doorway with rocaille decoration (worn by wind erosion) surmounted by a Virgin and Child. Farther along (No. 9) the old Augustinian house of El Socós now houses the Seminario Conciliar (a seminary for priests; not open to the public).

Market

A few yards east of the Seminary is the Plaza de la Libertad, with arcades housing the stalls of the town market. In the centre of the square is the fish-market.

Calle Santa Clara

On the north side of the main street of the old town (here Calle José María Quadrado) in Calle Santa Clara, stands the Church of Santa Clara, with a plain Gothic doorway, a coat of arms on the façade and a small rose-window; here, too, is the Palacio de los Barones de Lluriach, seat of Minorca's oldest noble family.

From Plaza Pio XII Calle José María Quadrado, a narrow arcaded street, leads to the attractive Plaza de España, with pavement cafés.

Plaza de España

The line of streets running through the old town ends in Plaza Alfonso III. In this square is the bus station for services into the surrounding countryside.

Plaza Alfonso III

A10

*Cala Blanes

Immediately west of Ciudadela lies the new development of Cala Blanes, with a hotel and numbers of holiday homes lining a long narrow rocky inlet which offers ample scope for snorkellers and subaqua divers. At the head of the inlet is a beautiful little sandy beach, which, with a large hotel in the vicinity, tends to become overcrowded.

A10

Cala Forcat

To the west of Cala Blanes we come to the large hotel and holiday colony of Cala Forcat. The beach here is rocky, with only one small stretch of sand. Large hotels, apartment blocks and detached houses huddle closely together. With its numerous shops Cala Forcat is better equipped to cater for the needs of holiday-makers than some other new developments.

Capilla del Rosario

Calle Quadrado

Cala Morell

Situation
10 km (6 miles) NE

A11

The road to Cala Morell (poorly signposted) runs north-east from Ciudadela, passing through flat country with fields bounded by stone walls. Cala Morell is a new development on a virgin site, with an uncrowded layout and buildings which fit well into the landscape. The only sandy beach is in a small cove sheltered by rocks which have been fashioned by erosion into bizarre shapes and have only the sparsest vegetation cover. Farther inland are gorges with prehistoric cave-dwellings hewn from the rock. The plateau above the resort is partly covered with pines, partly eroded by karstic action.

Punta Nati

Situation
7 km (4½ miles) N

A10

The road to Punta Nati, an exposed headland 7 km (4½ miles) from Ciudadela, is not signposted. It starts from the far end of the harbour and runs north, enclosed by stone walls, through a lonely and barren region which provides only sparse grazing for cattle. Scattered about in this area are a number of round towers and stone huts. On the cape is a lighthouse (public not admitted; no room to turn a car). From the iron gate on the right there is a beautiful view of the coastal cliffs.

Cabo d'Artrutx

Situation
9 km (6 miles) S

B10

The road south from Ciudadela runs at some distance from the west coast of the island, and after passing side roads to Santandría and Cala Blanca (both with small sheltered sandy beaches in rocky coves) comes to Cabo d'Artrutx, the most south-westerly point on Minorca, with a lighthouse situated on the bare eroded limestone plateau.
Near here is the large Tamarinda colony of holiday homes, with a rocky beach.

Cala 'n Bosch

To the east of the cape extends the Cala 'n Bosch development, with a sheltered boating harbour, large hotels and apartment blocks, restaurants and shops. A footbridge spans the narrow harbour entrance. Beyond the large hotel is a cove with a sandy beach. The hinterland is flat and partly overgrown with reeds.

Son Catlar

B11

From Ciudadela a narrow but scenically charming road leads south to the Playa de Son Saura. After 6 km (4 miles) the visitor will come to the Talayot settlement of Son Catlar.

*Naveta d'es Tudóns

Situation
6 km (3½ miles) E

B11

The Naveta d'es Tudóns, the best-known and best-preserved *naveta* on Minorca and the oldest building in Spain, lies a little way south of the main road from Ciudadela to Mahón. It is reached by turning off the main road through a gateway (signposted to the site) and continuing on the stony access road. The apse of the naveta is at the east end; a narrow passage in the west wall gives access to the two-storey chamber in the interior.
The naveta (on which minor restoration work was carried out in

Cala Blanca: good snorkelling waters

Naveta d'es Tudóns

Colonia de San Pedro

Naveta d'es Tudóns (Ground-plan)

1960) is built of large cyclopean blocks of stone and measures 14 m (46 ft) by 6·50 m (21 ft). It stands in open country near the old Roman road, here clearly traceable. A small opening on the flat west side of the structure, originally closed by a stone slab (cavities for housing it visible in framing of entrance), leads into a rectangular antechamber, from which another doorway, also once closed by a stone slab, gives access to the main chamber, 9 m (30 ft) long by 2–3 m (6½–10 ft) wide. Over this, divided up by stone arcades, is an upper chamber also communicating with the antechamber.

The human remains and other objects found in the naveta point to four periods of use and give information about changing burial practices during the Talayot period. The lowest level of remains shows that in the earliest period the naveta was used for the burial of clan chieftains and their close relatives. A later phase of liberalisation, during which anyone could be buried here, was followed by a period of declining interest in this form of burial. In a final phase the only people buried in the naveta were those whose ancestors already rested there.

The feelings of awe and apprehension inspired in the popular mind by these strange and lonely funerary monuments have evidently helped to secure them from demolition.

Torre Trencada
Torre Llafuda

South-east of the Naveta d'es Tudóns are the taulas of Torre Llafuda and remains of the prehistoric settlement of Torre Trencada, where there is also a taula. Both sites lie in fields at some distance from the narrow country road, here running between enclosing walls, and are quite difficult to find, since the walls prevent an over-all view. The best plan is to return from the Naveta d'es Tudóns to the main road and take the next turning to the right. The excavations are on the right of this little road.

Colonia de San Pedro
C7

Island: **Majorca**
Altitude: sea-level

Situation

The developing seaside resort of Colonia de San Pedro, on the south side of the Bahía de Alcudia, is reached on a side road off the main road from Artato Ca'n Picafort.

The resort

Colonia de San Pedro, once a fishing village and now a small holiday resort with a particular appeal to families, lies at the foot of the barren Mount Faruch (Ferrutx: 510 m (1673 ft)) on a predominantly rocky stretch of coast, with only one small sandy cove. The hills to the east of the town are much eroded by karstic action. There is some wine production in the surrounding area.

Colonia de Sant Jordi
F5

Island: **Majorca**
Altitude: sea-level

Situation

The resort development of Colonia de Sant Jordi lies south-west of Ses Salines near the southernmost tip of Majorca.

The resort

Colonia de Sant Jordi, a little town catering almost exclusively for the tourist and holiday trade, clusters round the small sheltered harbour of Puerto de Campos, from which there are boat trips to the island of Cabrera, visible offshore to the south, and other places of interest in the area. It is smaller than some more recent developments and has perhaps a rather antiquated atmosphere, but this in fact gives it a certain charm of its own. The beaches within the resort area are shelving and rocky. There are large sandy beaches extending north-west to Ses Covetes, and to the south-east are the beaches of Es Carbó and Sa Roquetas.

Costa de los Pinos   D8

Island: **Majorca**
Altitude: sea-level

The resort of Costa de los Pinos lies in the Bahía de Artá, near Majorca's most easterly point. | Situation

The resort

This modern development extends along the Playa d'es Rivell (beach of fine sand) between Port Vey and Cabo d'es Piná, below the south side of Mount Jordi (315 m (1034 ft)).

See Arta | Cuevas de Arta

Ermita de Nuestra Señora de Bon Any   D6

Island: **Majorca**
Altitude: 317 m (1040 ft)

The Monastery of Nuestra Señora de Bon Any is situated almost exactly in the centre of the Llanura del Centro. It lies a little way north of the Palma–Manacor road, although there is no direct access to the monastery from that road. | Situation

The monastery is dedicated to Our Lady of the Good Year. The "good year" was 1600, which saw the end of a severe drought that had brought failed harvests and famine. | History

The monastery

The monastery, prominently situated on a hill, is reached on a beautiful little country road which runs south-west from Petra (see entry), starting just to the south of the town centre.

From the terrace in front of the church there is a magnificent panoramic view extending over the Sierra del Norte (with the little town of Petrá in the foreground), the Bahía de Alcudia and the central plain to the south. | **View

91

San Pau

San Antonio Abad

From the forecourt we pass through a narrow gateway into a road which leads up to the church. On either side of the gate are majolica panels, the one on the left depicting the finding of the church's wonder-working image of the Virgin, the one on the left representing the legendary "good year" of 1600. On the inner sides of the door jambs can be seen majolica images of St Paul of Thebes, the first Christian hermit, and St Anthony Abbot (with his attribute, a pig).

The pilgrimage church, originally built in the 17th c. but dating in its present form from the first third of the 20th c., is of no great interest in itself, but it has one notable feature – the "Bethlehem Grotto" to the left of the entrance, with miniature landscapes and scenes from country life which are viewed through two large magnifying glasses. The Virgin behind the High Altar – an early medieval figure of rather rustic type – is accessible from both arms of the transept on short flights of steps.

From the topmost terrace there are good views of the Sierra del Norte (Serra de Tramuntana) to the north-west and the Serranía de Levante to the south-east.

Ermita de San Salvador

E7

Island: **Majorca**
Altitude: 509 m (1670 ft)

Situation

The Ermita de San Salvador lies in south-eastern Majorca, in the Serranía de Levante range which runs parallel to the coast.

*The sanctuary

The Ermita de San Salvador, an important Majorcan place of pilgrimage, is magnificently situated near the summit of the Puig de San Salvador. The origins of the hermitage go back to the mid 14th c., when the first church was built. The present structure dates from the 16th–18th c., since damage caused by corsair raids had frequently to be made good.

The sanctuary is reached from Felanitx, 6 km (4 miles) away, on a road on which the latter part is particularly beautiful. Leaving Felanitx on the road which runs south-east to Porto Colóm, we take a side road on the left which soon begins to wind its way uphill, passing on the right a small wayside chapel. On a spur of hill below the summit is a stone cross, and just before the sanctuary is reached a conspicuous 19th c. figure of Christ, 7 m (23 ft) high, stands on a massive substructure. From the base there is a superb view of the coast, with the modern developments of Calas de Mallorca and Porto Calóm.

The sanctuary is entered through a massive gatehouse. On the left-hand wall of this is a Late Gothic wood-carving of the Last Supper. The gatehouse has a number of pictures of no particular quality, together with jerseys presented by racing cyclists as *ex votos*. It also contains a restaurant. Adjoining the small square in front of the church is a vaulted room with votive plaques.

In the church (18th c.), immediately to the right of the entrance, is one of the "Bethlehem grottoes" commonly found in Majorcan churches. In the right-hand transept a Gothic limestone altar-piece shows remains of colouring. Behind the High Altar is the much-venerated image of the Virgin, which can be reached from the transept, and behind this again is a High Baroque alabaster altar-piece, also with remains of its original polychrome colouring.

Esporlas (Esporles)   C/D3

Island: **Majorca**
Altitude: 46 m (151 ft)
Population: 3000

The little town of Esporlas (Majorcan Esporles) lies in the Sierra del Norte 15 km (9 miles) north-west of Palma.

Situation

**La Granja

The handsome old country house of La Granja stands in a wooded valley 1·5 km (1 mile) west of Esporlas. There was a house here in Moorish times which was later occupied by Cistercian monks and finally passed into the hands of the Fortuny family, who still own the property. La Granja is now open to the public. It is still largely unrestored, and in consequence conveys an impression of unspoiled authenticity. Many rooms were until quite recently in everyday use and have been preserved without alteration or refurbishment.

Opening times
daily, until sunset

The tour of the house (route indicated by signposts) begins in the large forecourt with its plane trees. Here, in addition to the ticket office, are old-style potter's and turner's workshops

Tour

and stalls selling (and offering samples of) local delicacies (pastries, pressed figs and almonds, etc.) and wines. Folk-dances are performed at 3.30 p.m. on Wednesdays and Fridays; a brochure can be obtained from the ticket office.

From here we go up a ramp to see various outbuildings and offices containing agricultural equipment (harness, a wine-press, etc.), and then continue round the house into the Renaissance gardens higher up; the irrigation channels for watering the gardens can still be seen, although they are no longer in use.

We then enter the main buildings from a small courtyard with a Baroque fountain. In the first room are a number of pictures and Baroque cupboards containing collections of fans. Beyond this are a series of apartments, largely preserved in their original state. They include a small theatre, a games-room and several bedrooms containing 16th–18th c. paintings, musical instruments and folk-costumes, together with beautiful glass and majolica chandeliers. We then emerge into the Renaissance loggia, on the lower side of the inner courtyard, with fountains which draw their water from a mountain stream. To the left of the loggia is a glassed-in gallery, on the walls of which are beautiful majolica panels, mostly depicting scenes of everyday life (see picture on page 21). Here, too, is the former office with some old furniture, including an Art Nouveau cupboard and telephone switchboard, and the children's nursery with all kinds of old toys, including model trains.

The gallery takes us back to the dining room.

Particularly notable is the kitchen, which is partly faced with tiles and contains some handsome domestic glassware. Adjoining the kitchen is the bakery, also faced with tiles. We

La Granja: a country-house museum

then pass down some stairs to the plumber's workshop, alchemist's laboratory and oil-mill (with explanation of the purpose and operation of the equipment) and the wine-cellar containing large barrels and presses. The long corridor which follows includes the old workshops once used by basket-makers, sail-makers, shoemakers and jewellers.

Further rooms contain a series of weaving looms of different sizes, with tapestries and specimens of embroidery hanging on the walls. Also of interest is a large built-in cabinet faced with blue, yellow and white tiles.

We then come on to the terrace, from which there is a view of the fountains mentioned above. From here a short footpath leads up the stream, crosses it and comes to a number of enclosures containing sheep, goats, etc., and a small aviary. We then return across the stream and enter the basement of the house, entering first a kitchen and then a room containing an open hearth surrounded by benches. Then follow a series of vaulted cellars (bottle stores; large larders and store-rooms with old swords on the walls). We then emerge from the cellars at a large basin with a fountain. From here a short flight of steps brings us back to the forecourt where a number of old coaches stand. In the entrance is the former chapel with majolica floors. Beyond the building complex, near the bottom of the valley, lies the somewhat overgrown park with a large fountain, old trees and shady pergolas.

Estellencs (Estallenchs)

D2

Island: **Majorca**
Altitude: 150–300 m (490–980 ft)
Population: 500

The village of Estellencs (Majorcan Estallenchs) lies in western Majorca on the road which winds its way along the much-indented north coast from Andraitx towards Esporlas.

Situation

The village

Estellencs lies some distance above the coast on the steep flank of the hills. To the east rises Mount Galatzó (1026 m (3366 ft)), which can be climbed with the help of a guide. On both sides of the village are terraced fields, mainly devoted to tomato-growing. This is a picturesque old-world little village of narrow winding lanes, with a fine parish church (San Juan Bautista; built in 1422, renovated in the 17th c.) and an old watch-tower. From the village a steep and narrow road winds its way down to a rocky cove with moorings for small fishing-boats. Here there are a number of small bars, open only during the season. Since there are few passing-places on the road it is preferable, during the main holiday season, to walk rather than drive down.

There is a very attractive view of Estellencs from the Coll d'es Pí (with restaurant), beyond the valley to the west.

Coll d'es Pí

The Mirador de Ricardo Roca, 6 km (3½ miles) south-west of Estellencs, is one of the most impressive viewpoints on the north-west coast. Beyond a short tunnel cutting through a spur of rock is a parking-place (on the left). From here a stepped path

**Mirador de Ricardo Roca

Coastal scenery at the Mirador de Ricardo Roca

Estellencs

Felanitx

leads up to the viewpoint, some 400 m (1300 ft) above the sea, with the remains of an old watch-tower. There are breathtaking views on both sides of the rugged and much-indented coast and of the sea, which can often be quite rough.

Felanitx   E6

Island: **Majorca**
Altitude: 108 m (354 ft)
Population: 14,000

The lively little town of Felanitx lies on the south-eastern edge of the Llanura del Centro, here bounded by the Serranía de Levante.
Felanitx was the birthplace of Guillem Sagrera (c. 1380–1454), who built the Lonja (Stock Exchange) in Palma de Mallorca.

Situation

The town

The market town of Felanitx, with pottery and glass manufacture, wine production and spirit distilling making major contributions to the economy, occupies four hills, once crowned by numerous windmills. The stumps of a number of windmills can be seen on one of the hills (now slashed by a quarry) when approaching the town from the east.
The large and handsome Parish Church of San Miguel (13th c.) has a Renaissance doorway; the Churrigueresque façade dates from the Baroque period. It bears a memorial tablet commemorating the 414 people who were killed by the collapse of a wall in 1844. The single-aisled interior is flanked by chapels; on the left wall of the nave is a small chapel with a round dome. 19th c. stained glass windows can be seen in the clerestory. From the church a broad flight of steps descends to the main square and continues to a fountain on a lower level. To the left of the church are the presbytery and another fountain with the figure of a Majorcan peasant woman. In the square is the Caso de Cultura (temporary exhibitions).
To the east of the town in a Calvario (Mount Calvary), from which there is a fine view.

*Castillo de Santueri   E7

6 km (3½ miles) south-east of Felanitx, on the main ridge of the Serranía de Levante, stands the Castillo de Santueri, which ranks after the Castillo del Rey (see Pollensa) and Castillo de Alaró (see Alaró) as the most important and best preserved of Majorca's medieval castles. Originally a Moorish stronghold, it was largely destroyed by Jaime I but was rebuilt and enlarged in the 14th c. to secure the island against attack.
The winding but very beautiful road up to the castle ends in a car park, from which a stepped path leads up to the castle gate. The interior can be seen on payment of an admission fee.
From here there are magnificent views to east and south. The most prominent feature on the coast is the little port of Porto Colóm. In good weather the view extends as far as Minorca to the north and Ibiza to the south.

Castillo de Santueri

Ermita de San Salvador   See entry

Fornalutx   C4

Island: **Majorca**
Altitude: 99 m (325 ft)
Population: 500

Situation   Fornalutx lies north-east of Sóller at the foot of the Sierra de Torrellas, 40 km (25 miles) north of Palma.

*The village

This is a typical old mountain village with picturesque stepped lanes and a handsome parish church (1680).
4 km (2½ miles) north is the Mirador de Ses Barques, from which there are fine views of the nearby coast, in particular of the almost completely enclosed harbour bay of Puerto de Sóller.

Gorch Blau   C4

Island: **Majorca**

Situation   The Gorch Blau Reservoir lies north-west of Palma (60 km (37 miles) via Sóller, 45 km (28 miles) via Inca) in the saddle between the Puig de Massanella to the east and Puig Mayor to the west.

*The setting

The stream which has formed the gorge, the Gorch Blau (see below), has been dammed higher up to provide a reservoir, the Embalse del Gorch Blau. If you are approaching by car from an easterly direction (Lluch), it is advisable to slow down in the road tunnel, as it is necessary to turn sharp left at the exit into the car park.

Between the road and the reservoir, near the car park, stands a roughly hewn monolithic column, probably from an ancient temple; the column was moved to its present position in order to preserve it from being engulfed by the rising water.

Embalse del Gorch Blau

The Gorch Blau (blue gorge) is a romantically wild and rocky ravine at the foot of Puig Mayor, it is 500 m (550 yd) long and up to 100 m (330 ft) deep. Until recently the gorge was one of the finest scenic attractions of Majorca, but as a result of the erection of a power station the gorge is no longer accessible to the public.

Near here the road is spanned by an aqueduct which was originally constructed by the Romans. Here, too, the "Snake" road (see La Calobra) branches off the main road and runs down to the Cala de la Calobra.

Gorch Blau

To the west of the reservoir is Majorca's highest summit, Puig Mayor (1443 m (4734 ft)), topped by a prominent radar mast.

The reservoir

Gorch Blau, a reservoir in a mountain setting

The whole hill is a closed military area (access only with special permission).

*Puig de Massanella

To the east of Gorch Blau rises the Puig de Massanella, the island's second-highest mountain (1348 m (4423 ft)), famed for its magnificent panoramic view. It is best climbed from the road leading south over the Sierra del Norte to Inca (time taken, approximately four hours), or from Lluch Monastery (see Lluch). The summit is noted for a maginificent panorama.

Embalse de Cúber

About 3 km (2 miles) along the road to Sóller is the Embalse de Cúber, a reservoir for drinking-water.

Inca

C5

Island: Majorca
Altitude: 121 m (397 ft)
Population: 20,000

Situation

The busy industrial and commercial town of Inca lies 30 km (19 miles) north-east of Palma on the edge of the Llanura del Centro.

Economy

Inca's most important industry, and the one most obvious to the visitor, is the manufacture of leather goods. Leather articles are sold all over Majorca, but most of the factories are in Inca. Almost all of them are open to the public and have showrooms in which their products can be seen and purchased.
Other industries which contribute to the economy of Inca are textiles, furniture and foodstuffs.

Ermita de Santa Magdalena, on the Puig d'Inca

Sights

In the Plaza Santa María la Mayor, in the centre of the town, stands the Parish Church of Santa María la Mayor (13th c., rebuilt in the 18th c.), which has in the sacristy a fine 14th c. figure of Santa María d'Inca (by J. Dourer).
Other features of interest in the town are the two Baroque monasteries of San Francisco and Santo Domingo, both with beautiful cloisters, and the Monasterio de las Jerónimas, an enclosed Hieronymite nunnery with a Gothic belfry.

To the east of the town rises the Puig d'Inca (304 m (997 ft)), on which is the Ermita de Santa Magdalena. This modest little hermitage is reached by leaving on the Alcudia road and at km 32, in a left-hand bend, taking a narrow side road on the right. On top of the hill are the small pilgrimage chapel, with a hospice for pilgrims, and a restaurant. From the terrace there are magnificent views over the whole island.
High up on the wall near the convent door (porteria), inscribed on ceramic tiles, is the poem "Peregrinacio Pollensina" (1891) by Miquel Costa i Llobera.

Puig d'Inca

Isla Dragonera   D1/2

The Isla Dragonera is a rocky island off the western tip of Majorca, separated from it by a cliff-fringed arm of the sea 600 m (650 yd) wide, with the little resort of San Telmo in a bay. 4 km (2½ miles) long by 700 m (765 yd) wide, it rises to a height of 310 m (1017 ft). On Cabo Tramontana at the north end of the island and on Cabo Llebeix at the south end are important lighthouses. The island is now a nature park.
There are boat trips to Dragonera from Puerto de Andraitx (see Andraitx) and from San Telmo (see entry).

Situation and characteristics

Lloseta   C5

Island: **Majorca**
Altitude: 152 m (499 ft). Population: 5000.

Lloseta lies 25 km (15 miles) north-east of Palma to the left of the road to Inca, in the foothills of the Puig de Sa Creu (672 m (2205 ft)). The main industry is the manufacture of leather goods.

Situation

The town

The parish church is modern but contains a Romanesque image of the Virgin. Adjoining the church stands the Ayamans Palace (rebuilt in the 17th c.), in a beautiful Italian garden (visits by prior arrangement only: tel. 51 96 74).

Llubí   C5/6

Island: **Majorca**
Altitude: 73 m (240 ft). Population: 2500.

Lloseta: church and Ayamans Palace

Lluch Monastery: Majorca's most important place of pilgrimage

The little town of Llubí lies in the Llanura del Centro 40 km (25 miles) north-east of Palma and 8 km (5 miles) south-east of Inca, off the main through roads.

Situation

The town

This quiet little country town largely depends for its subsistence on the growing of capers in the fertile and gently rolling countryside surrounding the town. The Parish Church of San Feliu dates from the 17th–19th c.

On a hill 2 km (1¼ miles) outside the town (signposted) we come to Ermita de Santo Cristo de la Salud y del Remedio or Ermita Remei (19th c.). The fine panoramic view from here has increasingly been blocked in recent years by the growth of trees.

Lluch Monastery

C5

Island: **Majorca**
Altitude: 400 m (1300 ft).

The great Monastery of Lluch lies in a wide valley in the Sierra del Norte, some 16 km (10 miles) north of Inca.

Situation

The Monastery of Nuestra Señora de Lluch was founded about 1250, but legend gives it a much earlier origin. The story goes that a Moorish shepherd boy, who, with the rest of his family, had become a Christian after the Reconquest and had been given the name of Lluc (Luke), found in the forest one day a dark-coloured wooden figure of the Virgin. He took it to the priest of his parish who set it up in the church, but three times the Virgin disappeared from the church and returned to her original place in the forest. The priest recognised the will of God, and built a church on the spot which attracted large numbers of pilgrims. The Virgin is still known to the local people as "La Morenta", the Dark-Skinned One.

History

*The monastery

Lluch Monastery, the most important place of pilgrimage on Majorca, lies off the main road in the remote mountain valley of the Torrente de Lluch. The present buildings date from the 17th and 18th c. The monastery now houses a boys' music and choir school; the choir ("Escolanía") sings Mass at 11.15 a.m. every day.

Foreign visitors may have difficulty in finding their way about the monastery, since all signs and notices are in Majorcan.

The monastery precincts are entered through a double gateway. Along the right-hand side of the spacious forecourt extends a long covered passage, once occupied by stables for visitors' horses and various workshops. On the axis of the forecourt stands a column with a representation in relief of the Death of the Virgin, and beyond this is a fountain with three basins. On the hill behind the monastery is a large cross, to which leads a Way of the Cross (see below).

After passing through the main doorway of the conventual buildings (museum on first floor, open 10 a.m.–5.30 p.m.) we

La Moreneta

103

come into an inner courtyard with a bronze memorial (1920) to Bishop Pedro Juan Campins y Barceló. To the right can be seen the large plain Baroque façade of the church. The interior (aisled, with short transepts and a dome over the crossing) is dark. The aisles are continued by short flights of steps which lead up to a small chapel beyond the High Altar, in which, on the wall behind the altar, is the much revered image of La Moreneta. An alabaster relief depicts the monastery's famous boys' choir; around the walls are the coats-of-arms of the Majorcan municipalities.

Museum

On the first floor of the monastery a museum (open daily 10 a.m.–6 p.m.) house prehistorical and Roman finds, medieval manuscripts, naive paintings, religious art and folk-costumes; a special department shows paintings and drawings by the artist Coll Bartollet (19th/20th c.).

To the left of the conventual buildings is the beginning of the Way of the Cross, the various stations of which have richly carved reliefs and Latin inscriptions. The Way goes up under shady trees and below a steep rock face, affording beautiful views of the fertile valley and the hills beyond. A few yards off the path is a small cemetery with walled-up columbaria (niches for the reception of funerary urns).

Beside the large car park in front of the monastery is an attractive restaurant, as well as picnic areas and play areas.

Lluch is a good base from which to climb the Puig de Massanella (see Gorch Blau), Majorca's second-highest peak (1348 m (4423 ft)).

Monument to the shoemakers of Lluchmayor

Lluchmayor (Llucmajor)   E5

Island: **Majorca**
Altitude: 143 m (469 ft)
Population: 15,000

The town of Lluchmayor (Majorcan Llucmajor) lies 25 km   Situation
(15 miles) south-east of Palma in the Llanura del Centro, on the
road to Santaňy.

The town

The trim and friendly town of Lluchmayor is the market town
and administrative centre of the largest rural district on
Majorca. Near the west end of the town can be seen a monument to the shoemakers to whom Lluchmayor owes its
prosperity.

The Neo-classical Parish Church of San Miguel has a plain
Renaissance doorway on the south side. The interior (aisleless)
has a dome baptistery on the north side and other chapels
along both sides.

The Franciscan Friary of San Buenaventura dates from the
17th c. The church has fine Baroque doorways.

North-east of the town is the scene of the battle in 1349 in which
Jaime II was killed fighting his cousin Pedro IV of Aragon.

See Algaida.   Puig de Randa

Mahón (Maó)   B13

Island: **Minorca**
Altitude: sea-level
Population: 25,000

Mahón (Minorcan Maó), Minorca's capital and principal port,   Situation
lies at the east end of the island on steep cliffs above the south
side of the long inlet which forms its famous harbour.

Mahón has perhaps the best natural harbour in the whole of the
Mediterranean – sheltered from wind and weather, strategi-
cally situated and easily defended. Accordingly it became a
source of dispute between the European Powers, particularly
during the 18th c. It is now a Spanish naval base, a quarantine
station and the island's principal commercial port. Mahón can
also claim to have given mayonnaise (from *salsa mahonesa*) to
the world. It was first made here by the French and thereafter
introduced into the international cuisine.

According to legend the town was founded and given its name   History
by Mago, Hannibal's brother. It is certainly the case that Mago
came to Minorca about 205 B.C. to recruit Balearic slingers for
the Carthaginian Army, but this derivation of the town's name
seems doubtful. Probably the Carthaginians established a military station here on the site of an earlier megalithic settlement.
The name of Maghen by which is was then known has been

variously interpreted, but it seems most probable that it came from a Semitic word for "fortress".

In Roman times it became a thriving commercial port under the name of Portus Magonis, linked with the town of Iamnona (Ciudadela) by a metalled road which can still be traced at many points. In Byzantine and later in Moorish times Mahón was a port of call and entrepôt on the Mediterranean shipping routes. In 1287 Alfonso III of Aragon occupied the Isla del Rey, in the harbour inlet, and expelled the Arabs from Minorca. In 1535 it was briefly recovered for Islam by Khaireddin Barbarossa after half the population had been slaughtered. Thereafter, in order to provide protection against the repeated raids by Moorish and Turkish corsairs, the Emperor Charles V built the Fort of San Felipe on the Punta de San Carlos, on the south side of the harbour entrance; the architect was Calvi, who also designed the fortifications of Ibiza town.

In 1708, during the War of the Spanish Succession, Minorca was occupied by British forces, and in 1713 it was annexed to the British Crown. The island's new masters improved the harbour, strengthened its fortifications still further and established a lazaretto (hospital) on the Isla del Rey. The British influence on Minorca's architecture (interior arrangement of houses, sash-windows) and way of life (golf, gin) is still unmistakable; the temporary French occupation from 1756 to 1763 has left no traces.

Mahón was the birthplace of Mateo José Bonaventure Orfila (b. 1787, d. in Paris 1853), the founder of experimental toxicology, who became Professor of Forensic Medicine in Paris in 1819 and Professor of Chemistry in 1838; he developed a

Mahón harbour

number of procedures for the identification of poisons (particularly arsenic).

**The harbour inlet

Mahón's famous harbour inlet (Spanish Puerto de Mahón, Catalan and Minorcan Port de Maó) extends inland for some 5 km (3 miles), ranging in width between 300 m (330 yd) and 1200 m (1300 yd), and is defended by a number of forts. Although nowadays the easiest and quickest way to get to Mahón is by air, it is well worth while – if, for example, you are coming from one of the other islands in the group – to arrange to arrive by sea, for the approach to the town along the much-indented fjord-like inlet with its strong defences and ever-changing views, is a memorable experience.

Coming from the south-east, the ship sails between the Punta de San Carlos to the south, with a lighthouse and the remains of the Castillo de San Felipe, and the Cabo de la Mola to the north, with the Fortaleza de Isabel II (fort and military prison). Projecting into the inlet is the long Isla del Lazareto, a peninsula which was separated from the mainland in 1900 by the construction of the Canal de Alfonso XIII, now generally known as the Canal de Sant Jordi; the old lazaretto and quarantine station is now a convalescent home for Spanish Health Service staff. The coves of Cala Pedrera, Cala Fons (fishing harbour) and Cala Corb are passed on the left, and beyond these, above the left bank, can be seen the light-coloured houses of Villa Carlos (see below), built in the 18th c. as a British military cantonment.

Opposite the northern tip of the Isla del Lazareto lies the Isla de la Cuarantena or Isla Plana, with various buildings connected with the old military hospital on the Isla del Lazareto. Beyond this point the inlet opens out; on the right are the Cala Llonga, lined with holiday homes, and beyond this the Cala de San Antonio (Cala de Sant Antoni), with the landing-stage for the magnificent colonial-style mansion of San Antonio (Sant Antoni), known as the Golden Farm (see below), higher up the slope.

The boat then sails past the Isla del Rey (formerly called the Isla de los Conejeros or Rabbit Island), which was captured by Alfonso III of Aragon on 17 January 1287 and served as a base for his reconquest of Minorca. North-west of this was the Isla de la Ratas (Rat Island), now removed.

Beyond this, on the left, is the Cala Figuera, lined with wharves (textile factory); on the right is the Cala Rata. The boat now enters the innermost part of the harbour, the Cala Serga. To the right is the small Isla Pinto (submarine base), now linked with the mainland by a bridge; on the left are the quays of the commercial harbour and, high above them, the picturesque upper town of Mahón.

Just off the landing-stage used by the ferries and passenger ships is the Aquarium (Acuario de Menorca; open Mon.–Fri. 9.30 a.m.–1 p.m. and 4–7.30 p.m., Sat. 9.30 a.m.–2 p.m.; admission charge), with numerous tanks displaying Mediterranean marine fauna (primitive creatures, crabs, cephalopods, fishes, etc.). The labelling is rather inadequate but accurate.

Around the harbour are numbers of restaurants and shops selling craft products.

Aquarium

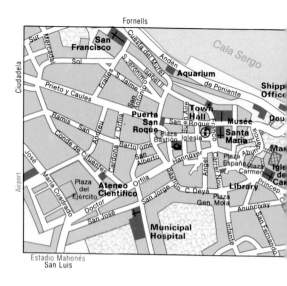

The town

In the town centre (largely pedestrianised) there is little room for parking; it is best, therefore, to leave your car in the harbour area and explore the town on foot. If you are travelling by bus you will normally arrive in the Plaza de la Explanada (see below), on the south-west side of the old town centre.

From the harbour the winding Rampa de la Abundancia (one-way traffic, downhill only) and a stepped lane flanked by gardens lead up to the town. On the steps is a monument to Admiral Miranda.

Iglesia del Carmen

The ramp ends in Plaza de España, above which is Plaza del Carmen. In Plaza del Carmen stands the Iglesia del Carmen, originally Baroque but much altered in the 19th c.; on the main front, which has four stumps of columns arranged in pairs, is the date 1751. The interior (domed) is of no great artistic interest.

To the left of the church is the cloister of the old Carmelite convent, now deconsecrated and occupied by the stalls of the market; in the centre is the small fish-market. In the part of the cloister facing Plaza Miranda (below) is the municipal exhibition hall (Sala d'Exposiciones), which from time to time puts on art shows.

*Plaza Miranda

A narrow and little-used branch of the stepped lane mentioned above leads direct from the harbour to the Plaza Miranda, on the east side of the cloister. From this square there is a good view of the inner harbour, with the landing-stage used by passenger ships and car ferries.

Pedestrian zone

From Plaza de España the narrow Calle Cristo leads past the Plaza Real to the Carrer Nou, the town's main shopping and commercial street, flanked on both sides by arcades. This street continues north into Plaza de la Constitución, at the far end of which stands the handsome Town Hall (Ayuntamiento).

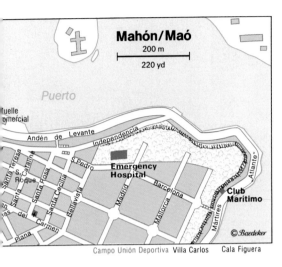

Mahón/Maó

200 m

220 yd

Puerto

Muelle comercial

Andén de Levante

Independencia

Santa Teresa

S. Catalina

S. Roque

Santa Rosa

Santa Cecilia

Bellavista

del Carmen

Plana

S.Pedro

Madrid

Mallorca

Emergency Hospital

Barcelona

Mártires

Atlante

Club Marítimo

© Baedeker

Campo Unión Deportiva   Villa Carlos   Cala Figuera

The east side of Plaza de la Constitución is dominated by the west front of the massive Church of Santa María (which, unusually, is oriented from north to south), founded by the Catalans in 1287 and rebuilt between 1748 and 1772 as an aisleless hall church in Neo-classical style. Particularly notable is its great organ, with 3006 pipes, 51 stops and 4 manuals, made in 1810 by the Swiss organ-builder Johannes Kiburz. It is now used for organ recitals as well as for services. It was presented to the church by a wealthy merchant in thanksgiving for his preservation from peril on the sea.

Santa María

In the corner building opposite the church is the Tourist Information Bureau (open Mon.–Fri. 9.30 a.m.–1 p.m. and 5–7 p.m., Sat. 9.30 a.m.–1 p.m.).

Leaving the church either by the doorway on the east side or taking a little street to the right of the Town Hall, we come into the little Plaza de la Conquista, in the centre of which can be seen a monument to Alfonso III of Aragon set up here in 1950. On the west side of the square is the Public Library (Biblioteca Publica del Estado; with museum). To the right of the Library, at the end of a narrow lane which passes through a building, is a viewpoint affording a prospect of the Rampa de la Abundancia and the east end of the harbour.

Plaza de la Conquista

From the Town Hall, Calle de San Roque runs west to Plaza Bastión, in which is the Puerta de San Roque, one of the old town gates, with scanty remains of the old walls. From here Calle San Bartolomé and Calle Cardona y Orfila continue southwest to the Ateneo Científico, Literario y Artístico (founded 1905), with a museum of natural history, archaeology and art.

Beyond the Ateneo can be seen the spacious Plaza Explanada, with parking, bus stops and a taxi rank. On the far side of the square stands a large war memorial in the form of an obelisk and beyond this a large barracks (military area, closed to the public).

Plaza Explanada

109

Cabo Gros

Golden Farm

San Francisco

Calle Isabel II leads north-west from the Town Hall, passing the Gobierno Militar (headquarters of the Military Governor), to the Parish Church of San Francisco in Plaza del Monastir. Over the round-arched doorway is a Baroque carving of the Annunciation. The church, built between 1719 and 1792, originally belonged to a Franciscan friary. From the nearby outlook point a fine view of the harbour can be enjoyed.

Cap La Mola

B13

The harbour inlet is bounded on the north by Cap La Mola, which extends east to end in Punta Espero. The road to the cape runs north-east from the head of the inlet and then bears east, passing through hilly country with a low cushion-like growth of macchia.

Cala Murtar

Some 4 km (2½ miles) from Mahón a side road goes off on the left of the road to the cape and in another 3 km (2 miles) comes to a fork. The right-hand road leads to Cala Murtar, a small fishing harbour in a rocky cove, with a headland reaching out to sea on its south side. There is only very limited scope for bathing on this coast with its dark-coloured slaty rocks.

Cala Mezquida

The left-hand fork leads to the small coastal village and holiday resort of Cala Mezquida.
Immediately beyond the junction with this side road the asphalt surface comes to an end and the road continues towards Cabo Gros as a gravel track, passing on the right, at some distance from the road, a 16th c. watch-tower. The road ends at a beautiful bay with a large sandy beach. From here the

rocky hill of Cabo Gros should be climbed for the sake of the superb views – southward over the bay within its sheltering cliffs, northward over a beach of coarse shingle facing the open sea, often covered with flotsam and jetsam.

A short distance beyond the side road to Cala Mezquida, to the right, is the handsome colonial-style mansion of San Antonio (Minorcan Sant Antoni), better known as the Golden Farm, in which Nelson and Lady Hamilton stayed in 1799 and 1800. The property is not open to the public.

Golden Farm

To the south-east of the Golden Farm lies the Cala Llonga development, a colony of holiday homes beautifully situated immediately above the harbour inlet. It was originally planned on a considerably larger scale, hence the extensive system of development roads, some of them running through areas at present without buildings.

Cala Llonga

From the road which continues from here to Cap La Mola there are charming glimpses to the right of Mahón and its long harbour inlet. The end of the peninsula, beyond a narrow isthmus, is military territory closed to the public. On the hill is the Fortaleza de Isabel II.

Mahón to Fornells

B13–A12

The route suggested here follows the much-indented north-east coast of Minorca with its numerous little coves. Including detours, the total distance is just under 70 km (45 miles).
From the head of the harbour inlet take the road signposted to Fornells, and in about 1 km (¾ mile) turn right into a road which runs north-east through hilly country to the coast.

The road passes the modern development of Shangri-La and comes to Es Grao, an older and more modest holiday resort, originally a fishing village, which has a sandy beach in a sheltered bay. Here a stream flows into the sea from S'Albufera d'Es Grao, a small lake to the west of the village. Boats sail from the little harbour to the Isla d'en Colóm, at the mouth of the bay (information from the Can Bernat bar, on the beach).

Es Grao

From here the road to Fornells continues past the Ermita Mare de Déu de Fátima (Hermitage of Our Lady of Fátima), above the road on the right.

The next turning on the right after the hermitage leads to the Favaritx Lighthouse (10 km (6 miles)). The vegetation becomes increasingly sparse as the road approaches the coast, and is finally reduced to a scanty growth of reddish sedums clinging to the blackish rock. The area around the lighthouse on the headland is closed to the public, as is the military area on the north coast of the peninsula. The rocky and inhospitable terrain is very different from the normal idea of a Mediterranean landscape.

Faro de Favaritx

From the cape we go back the same way to the Fornells road.

7 km (4½ miles) farther on another road branches off on the right. At the next crossroads an access road on the right descends to the holiday settlement of Addaya, most of which lies on high ground above two long narrow inlets. There is a good view of the two inlets and of the new boating harbour (winch and slip), well sheltered by offshore islands.

Addaya

Faro de Favaritx

Macaret

Near the harbour is Macaret, which is reached by returning to the crossroads and continuing north-east on the line of the access road. Macaret is a new development centred on an old fishing village, its holiday homes extending on to the (relatively low) plateau above the sea. The village with its low houses has an attractively old-world air. The coast here is rugged and much indented, with cliffs and reefs reaching out into the sea. At the innermost point of the harbour is a small sandy beach. Inland there are large areas of rather sparse pine woods.

Arenal d'en Castell

From Macaret we continue, either direct or by way of the crossroads on the main road, to the lively seaside resort of Arenal d'en Castell, with a number of the tall hotel blocks which are not particularly numerous on Minorca. Arenal lies in a very beautiful and almost completely enclosed bay with a broad beach of fine sand, but its proximity to the large hotels means that during the main holiday season it tends to be overcrowded. Apart from this the coast is rocky and much indented. The resort was planned on a much larger scale than the actual development, with a road system which extends for a considerable distance over an undeveloped area of the karstic plateau.

*Son Parc

Returning to the main road and continuing for another 3 km (2 miles), we come to another junction where a road goes off on the right to the large and ambitiously planned development of Son Parc, laid out on a grid plan around a golf-course. Beautifully maintained, it consists mainly of privately owned holiday homes (sales office in the town centre) and a number of apartment blocks. It has a sheltered bay with a magnificent beach of fine white sand fringed by dunes and dense pine woods. Here, too, apart from the bay, the coast is rugged and rocky. The resort has facilities for a variety of sports – golf, tennis, a diving school, etc.

5 km (3 miles) farther on the road joins that from Mercadal to Fornells. Turning right, we come to Fornells (see Mercadal).

**Talatíde d'Alt B13

A little way south of the main road which runs from Mahón by way of Alayor to Ciudadela, at the west end of the island, is the Taula of Talatí de d'Alt, perhaps the most finely situated monument of the kind on Minorca. A narrow side road (signposted "Taula de Talatí") flanked by stone walls leads to a small parking area where there is another signpost. From here, crossing the low wall on a stile, we follow a clearly visible track through pastureland (at the near end, on right, a typical Minorcan drawwell) and in 5 minutes we reach the site. The main taula stands in a field enclosed by walls, planted with olive and carob trees and partly overgrown by scrub. Leaning against it is a smaller taula. On the north side of the stone enclosure wall can be seen a hypostyle chamber roofed by a thick stone slab supported by a central monolith. Immediately adjoining the taula are the remains of a talayot.

Situation
5 km (3 miles) W of Mahón

3 km (2 miles) north-west, to the right of the road to Alayor, lies the Naveta de Rafal Rubí Nou, one of the best-preserved navetas on Minorca.

2 km (1¼ miles) farther on, also near the road, is the Taula de Torralba, which is most easily reached from Alayor (see entry).

Naveta de Rafal Rubí Nou

Talatíde d'Alt

Mahón to Cala'n Porter
B13–B12

By the direct road it is 15 km (9 miles) from Mahón to Cala'n Porter. It is well worth while, however, to make detours to Binidali, Cala Canutells and Cala Coves.

Leave Mahón on the road which runs south-west to the airport.

Aeropuerto de Menorca

Minorca's international airport lies to the left of the road, which runs immediately past the end of the runway. The airport handles more than 500,000 passengers a year.

Torelló

On the other side of the turn off to the airport there is a path leading to the Torelló archaeological site. On the extensive site stands a talayot; a little to the north (Es Fornás de Torelló) are remains of the floor of an Early Christian basilica.

Binidali

At San Clemente (Minorcan Sant Climent) a side road on the left leads to the resorts of Binidali and Cala Canutells, on the south coast. At a fork keep straight ahead for Binidali. The road goes through the centre of the development, ending at a turning-point just above the shore. Here a beautiful little cove thrusts its way into the limestone rocks, which consist almost wholly of fossil shells.

From here the coast road runs east via the coastal villages of Cap d'en Font and Binisafúa (both with rocky coasts) to the picturesque holiday resort of Binibeca Vell (p. 115).

Cala Canutells

The road to the right at the road fork leads to the small holiday development of Cala Canutells, beautifully situated on the gentle slopes above a small inlet, here divided into two, which as it approaches the sea is caught between high cliffs. Below the car park is the rocky section of the inlet, with moorings for sailing craft; to the right a short flight of steps leads down to the sandy part of the inlet, with a small bathing beach.

Returning to San Clemente and continuing west, we pass on the left the chalet development of Binixica, built for no obvious reason at some distance from the beach. Beyond this, also on the left of the road, is the unfinished development of Son Vitamina.

*Cala Coves

Beyond Son Vitamina the road degenerates into an unsurfaced gravel track of reasonable width which runs down a valley edged by sheer cliffs to end in the charming little bay of Cala Coves. In the rocks are many caves which served, probably in prehistoric times, as troglodytic dwellings (*cuevas troglodi-tas*); some of the entrances are framed in structures painstakingly hewn from the rock. On the left-hand side of the little cove is a spring of fresh water which supplies the needs of visitors and the backpackers who install themselves in the caves. This is a favourite haunt of naturists, and also offers good diving-grounds. The surrounding countryside is covered with a dense growth of macchia and coniferous woodland.

Cala'n Porter

The holiday resort of Cala'n Porter is situated 5 km (3 miles) west of the turning for Son Vitamina. It extends rather untidily over the plateau, with no particular plan, and, lacking any obvious centre, it has no real atmosphere of its own and it is difficult for visitors to find their way about. There are no tall apartment blocks; most of the buildings are of one or two storeys. The beach of fine sand, enclosed by rocks at the mouth of the valley, is short but quite broad; there are a number of

Cala Coves

restaurants, and pedalos and rowing-boats can be rented. Stepped paths lead up from the beach to the houses on the plateau above.

The road to the Cueva d'en Xoroi leads through the resort to a large car park on the edge of the coastal cliffs. The entrance to the cave (open 11 a.m.–1 p.m. and 4–9.30 p.m.; discothèque from 10 p.m.; admission charge) is in the sheer cliff face, reached by a stepped path. The bar and discothèque installed in the cave do good business, thanks to the fantastic situation. The dance floor extends through an opening in the cliff face into the open air, and the surf can be seen breaking against the rocks far below. The passages in the rock are low and dimly lit, and tall visitors will be well advised to keep their heads down.

*Cueva d'en Xoroi

**Binibeca Vell

C13

The road to Binibeca Vell runs south from Mahón, passing the Talayot de Trepucó (p. 118), and reaches the long straggling little town of San Luis (Minorcan Sant Lluis; bypass), where it turns west. Soon afterwards a side road branches off on the left to the imaginatively planned holiday resort of Binibeca Vell (which can also be reached on the coast road from Binidali: see above). Designed in the image of an old fishing village, Binibeca creates a striking impression, with dark stained wood standing out against the dazzling white of its walls and roofs. Its little houses are packed closely together, with lanes which are often only just wide enough for two people to pass, creating a pleasant coolness even when the sun is at its height. The resort

Situation
10 km S

115

The Stone Age settlement of Trepucó

is well provided with facilities for visitors – swimming-pools, restaurants, a shopping centre and much else besides. The sea-bathing is not particularly good: the beach is rocky, and the nearest sandy beach, to the east of the resort, is also used by holiday-makers from other large developments and tends to be overcrowded. If you go to Binibeca for a bathing holiday, a car is almost essential.

Biniancolla
Punta Prima

Biniancolla, the next resort to the east of Binibeca, also has a rocky beach. The nearest sandy beach of any size is at Punta Prima; but here, too, the sand soon gives place to rock. Offshore is the Isla del Aire (lighthouse).

Cala Alcaufar

Going inland from Punta Prima and taking a road to the right, we come to Cala Alcaufar. At the tip of the promontory is an old round watch-tower. The very beautiful rocky coast, much undermined by the sea, offers good diving-grounds. A narrow fjord-like inlet winds its way inland, with a small sandy beach at its head; bathing is also possible from the lower shelves of rock along its shores. Cala Alcaufar lies at the foot of a valley, with arable land higher up the valley. The bridge over the valley was intended to serve a new holiday development which has never been built, and now serves no purpose.

S'Algar

To the north, approached by a private road, is S'Algar, a development of hotels and apartment blocks dominated by the massive bulk of the Hotel San Luis. Along the beach are small blocks of holiday flats; the better villas lie inland. On the rocky

Binibeca Vell, a holiday settlement in traditional Majorcan style ▶

beach is a landing-stage with a winch and a slipway; ladders lead down into the water for the convenience of bathers. There is also a large open-air swimming-pool, reserved for hotel residents and the occupiers of holiday flats. Near the beach is a holiday settlement (no cars) which, like Binibeca, is modelled on a traditional Minorcan village, but is more regularly planned and more conventional in style than Binibeca.

Villa Carlos

B13

Situation
2 km (1½ miles) SE

Above Mahón's harbour inlet is Villa Carlos, a settlement established by the British in the 18th c. under the name of Georgetown which still preserves a British atmosphere. In the centre of the little town, which is laid out on a rectangular grid, lies the spacious Plaza Explanada, surrounded by handsome military and administrative buildings. In the bay is the Club Náutico.

* * Trepucó

To the south-west, near the road from Mahón to San Luis, can be seen the remains (excavated 1928–30) of the prehistoric settlement of Trepucó. The massive taula (vertical monolith 4·2 m (14 ft) high, 2·75 m (9 ft) wide, 406 mm (16 in) thick; capstone 3·45–3·65 m (11–12 ft) long, 1·5–1·6 m (5–5¼ ft) wide, 0·4 m (2 ft) thick) is the largest and best preserved of its kind. Around the nearby talayot (restored) are numerous prehistoric dwellings.

Manacor

D7

Island: Majorca
Altitude: 110 m (360 ft)
Population: 25,000

Situation

Manacor, the second largest town in the Balearics, lies on the eastern edge of the Llanura del Centro, 47 km (29 miles) east of Palma.

History

Manacor occupies the site of Roman Cunici or Cunium, a site which has been occupied since the period of the talayots. The remains of an Early Christian basilica (4th c.) and the cemetery associated with it were excavated in 1912. The present town, however, is of Arab origin. During the period of Moorish rule, which lasted until the 12th c., Manacor was the most important place on Majorica, known for its fine harbour (on the site of present-day Porto Cristo). In the 14th c. a royal palace was built here, of which nothing survives but the remains of a tower.

Sights

* Manufacture of artificial pearls

Manacor has a reputation extending far beyond the bounds of Spain for its artificial pearls, manufactured by a number of specialised factories in the town. Manacor pearls are so deceptively similar to natural pearls that an ordinary person cannot distinguish an artificial pearl of reasonable size from the genuine article. There is room for argument, of course, whether imitation pearls are in good taste, but they can be enjoyed for their own sake as high-quality fashion jewellery. Majorcan artificial pearls are not cheap, but they are said to be more durable than genuine pearls and to preserve their lustre even when they are not worn.

Majorica pearls, made by hand

The oldest and best-known factory producing artificial pearls is the Majorca firm, established in 1890. It has a well-arranged showroom and shop at the west end of the town, on the main road from Palma, and visitors who want to see the process of manufacture will be piloted to the factory in the town centre. During the tour of the factory visitors can observe the various stages in the process. The core of the pearl, formed by a globule of glass, is covered with many coats of a mother-of-pearl solution (made from the finely ground scales of a particular species of Mediterranean fish mixed with synthetic resin) which hardens when exposed to heat. The colours most favoured are the slightly yellowish natural tone and an iridescent metallic grey. The pearls are then carefully polished, threaded into necklaces or otherwise assembled, carefully checked for quality (defective specimens being destroyed with a hammer) and finally incorporated in various types of jewellery (necklaces, armlets, ear-rings, brooches, etc.). The various stages in production are numbered in sequence, with brief explanations for the benefit of visitors.

Outside the factory, on the opposite side of the street, is another showroom and shop.

A prominent landmark in the town is the slender tower of the parish church (Virgen de los Dolores; 14th c.), built on the site of an earlier mosque which had served for a short time as a church. Originally in severe Gothic style, the church was enlarged in the late 19th c., and this has detracted from its stylistic unity.

Parish church

Outside, in the Torre dels Enegistes, stands the Archaeological Museum (open Tues.–Thur. 9 a.m.–1 p.m.), founded after the

Museo Arqueológico

excavation of the Early Christian Basilica of Son Peretó (6 km (4 miles) from Manacor on the road to Artá) in 1912. Among the museum's principal treasures are mosaics from Son Peretó and a variety of Late Roman finds (coins, terra sigillata, bronze objects). It also contains some prehistoric material.

Convento San Vicente Ferrer

North-west of the parish church, in the town centre, can be found the Convento San Vicente Ferrer, a Dominican house founded in 1576 and dedicated to St Vincent Ferrer (1346–1419). Notable features of the church are a beautiful Baroque retablo in Churrigueresque style and the Capilla del Rosario (Chapel of the Rosary). There is a fine Baroque cloister with two-storey arcades.

Torre del Palau
Torre de Ses Puntes

The Torre del Palau and Torre de Ses Puntes, on the south side of the town centre, are 14th–15th c. towers which once formed part of the town's defences. The Torre de Ses Puntes contains a small local museum.

In the surroundings of Manacor are the remains of cyclopean structures, burial caves and the stumps of a number of windmills.

Mercadal (Es Mercadal)   B12

Island: **Minorca**
Altitude: 60 m (200 ft)
Population: 3000

Situation

The little country town of Mercadal (Minorcan Es Mercadal) lies almost exactly in the centre of Minorca on the main road from Mahón to Ciudadela.

The town

This little town of whitewashed houses lies at the foot of Monte Toro at an important road junction, the intersection of the main roads from east to west and north to south. The major local industries are building and woodworking. Minorca's main east–west road runs to the south of the town centre.

**Monte Toro

The road to the top of Monte Toro, Minorca's highest hill (357 m (1171 ft)), is signposted from the town centre. It runs east and – well engineered, with many narrow bends – comes in 3·4 km (2 miles) to the summit, on which are radio aerials and a large 19th c. figure of Christ on a high base. From the various outlook terraces there are superb views extending over the whole island and on a clear day as far as the east coast of Majorca. Immediately adjoining the statue of Christ is the entrance to the Santuario de Nuestra Señora de El Toro (with the inscription on the gate, Casal de El Toro), a place of pilgrimage built by Augustinian monks in the 17th c. This is a picturesque complex of buildings grouped around a courtyard, with the stump of an old square tower, a restaurant (*pousada*; outlook terrace) and a church. The church, in Neo-classical style, is aisleless, domed and flanked by chapels. On the massive Baroque High Altar can

A bird's-eye view of Minorca from Monte Toro

be seen a small image of the Virgin, Patroness of Minorca, which is revered as wonder-working. As in many Spanish churches, there are steps leading up to the image from the transepts. There are pilgrimages to Monte Toro throughout the year, with a particular celebration on the first Sunday in May, when the Bishop blesses the land. On the way down there is a good view, to the right of the road, of a handsome farmhouse, El Péu de Toro, with the characteristic circular threshing-floor.

Fornells

A12

From Mercadal the road to Fornells runs almost due north through hilly country. After a road junction a large and almost totally enclosed inlet (Minorcan Port de Fornells) comes into view on the right. To the south of the village, at Ses Salines d'es Fornells, are long beaches of ochre-coloured sand, with excellent facilities for surfing and sailing small boats.

Situation
10 km (6 miles) N

Fornells itself is a long straggling settlement of whitewashed houses with a good harbour (slipway, with cradle for large boats; restaurants, etc., on quay), finely situated at the narrow mouth of the inlet. Many of the inhabitants still earn their living as fishermen.

It is well worth while to climb up from the turning-point at the end of the road to the massive old watch-tower (passing on the way a Lourdes Grotto), from which there is a view of the whole inlet, extending to its mouth, and of the rocky coast to the west. The rocks around the tower have been carved into curious shapes by wind erosion.

From Fornells there is a rewarding boat trip to the caves in the peninsula on the east side of the inlet. The most striking, with

Cova Na Polida

its stalactitic formations, is the Cova Na Polida (accessible only from the sea), near Punta Na Guiemassa.

Cala Fornells
(Playas de Fornells)

The road to Cala Fornells goes off on the right (west) from the Mercadal road immediately south of Ses Salines, affording good views (to left) of the barren hill country approximately parallel to the coast. The development at Cala Fornells has been limited to a reasonable size, and the architecture and layout make this a very attractive resort. The central part of this chalet settlement is laid out with pretty little squares, stepped lanes and unusually designed houses. Building is still actively proceeding on the east side of the inlet.

There is a small bay of ochre-coloured sand in the inlet, with a diving club and a swimming-pool near the beach. There are other little coves on the rocky and much-indented coast.

Cala Tirant

On the opposite side of the inlet, visible from Cala Fornells, lies the small and compact development of Cala Tirant.

Binimel-La

From Cala Tirant a narrow road shut in between stone walls leads inland to a junction where a broad but rather dusty road, finally degenerating into a very poor track, branches off to Binimel-La. A large holiday development was planned here but never carried out. There is a beautiful sandy beach at the mouth of a stream which flows down to the much-indented and mainly rocky coast.

*Cabo de Cavallería

There is a strenuous but rewarding walk to Cabo de Cavallería, the most northerly point on Minorca. Half-way along the road from Cala Tirant to Binimel-La a side road (negotiable by a car for a short distance, but no room to park or turn at the end) leads north. From the cape (lighthouse) there are impressive views. Offshore, to the north-west, is the little Isla d'els Porros. At the little port of Sa Nitja (which can also be reached by boat from Fornells) can be seen the remains of a prehistoric settlement.

Minorca

Area: 700 sq. km (270 sq. miles)
Population: 56,000

Situation

Minorca (Menorca), the second largest and perhaps the most characteristic of the Balearic islands, lies north-east of Majorca between latitude 40°5′ and 39°48′ N and between longitude 7°28′ and 8°0′ E. The two islands are separated by an arm of the sea which narrows to 34 km (21 miles) between Cabo Capdepera on Majorca and Cabo d'Artruch on Minorca.

Characteristics

Minorca is 48 km (30 miles) long, from Cabo de Menorca in the west to Punta Esperó in the east, and 20 km (12½ miles) wide, from Punta Na Guiemassa in the north to Cala'n Porter in the south. It is traversed by a long range of limestone hills running broadly from east to west and cut by numerous fertile valleys and depressions, which rise to 357 m (1171 ft) in Mount Toro, in the centre of the island, and fall away gradually from north-east to south-west. On the north coast, which is rugged and broken up by numerous fjord-like inlets, there is little tourist

The holiday village of Cala Fornells

The sheltered harbour of Fornells

development, but the south coast and the southern parts of the east and west coasts are gentler and less indented, with beautiful sandy beaches. Most of the recently developed holiday settlements and hotel colonies (Spanish *urbanizaciones*) are on these coasts.

The island is covered by a dense network of high stone field walls, which provide protection from the prevailing strong north winds and preserve the soil from drying-out and erosion.

Population

Some 60 per cent of the island's total population of some 56,000 (Menorquines), including 1500 British, are concentrated in and around the two main centres of population, Mahón and Ciudadela; the remaining 40 per cent are dispersed over the island in rural communities and individual farms. As fellow Catalans the people of Minorca are closely related – ethnically, linguistically and culturally – to their Majorcan neighbours; but as a result of the geographical separation of the two islands Minorca has preserved distinctive customs of its own, such as the playing of the pipes of Pan and a folk-dance with hobby horses. Characteristic features are the white-rimmed roofs and enclosure walls of the country houses and the circular threshing-floors which are still in common use.

Economy

The people of Minorca still mainly depend, as in the past, on agriculture to provide them with their modest degree of prosperity. It supplies not only the island's principal exports but also the raw materials for industry and craft production. In recent years tourism has increased considerably in importance, but there is now an increasing feeling against over-development and the selling-off of land for the provision of tourist amenities. This is vividly illustrated in some of the new tourist resorts, with elaborate systems of development roads, reflecting the original ambitious plans, which far outrun the actual development. A pleasant feature of the new resorts is the relative absence of high tower block hotels.

History

Although Minorca has large numbers of astonishingly well-preserved remains dating from the prehistoric and early historical periods – some 300 talayots (round or square towers), 64 navetas (boat-shaped chamber tombs) and more than 30 taulas (table-like stone structures) – the history of these early times is totally obscure. All that is known with certainty is that from about 1000 B.C. Phoenicians and from about 800 B.C. Greeks were visiting the island, known to them as Noura or Melousa, and trading with the farming population. Considerably more intensive were the contacts and influence of the Carthaginians, who in the 3rd c. B.C. established military bases at Jamma (Ciudadela) and Maghen (Mahón). With the coming of the Romans in the 2nd c. B.C. we get the first reliable accounts of the island. Thereafter, until the 18th c. A.D., the destinies of Minorca were closely bound up with those of its larger sister island of Majorca. Harassed from the 7th c. onwards by repeated raids by Arab corsairs, the island was occupied by the Moors at the beginning of the 10th c., and after the conquest of Majorca by Jaime I in 1229 was the only Balearic island still in Moorish hands. In 1287 Alfonso III recovered Minorca for the Crown of Aragon, although the inhabitants still suffered from repeated raids by bloodthirsty Moorish and Turkish corsairs. The period of Arab rule, when the island was known as Minûrqa, has left its mark in many place-names (Al . . ., Bini . . ., Rafal . . ., etc.) and a very few architectural remains.

A valley on Minorca

Minorca is a quiet and unspoiled island which has much of historical and artistic interest to offer in addition to its good beaches and excellent facilities for all kinds of water-sports. Those who are particularly interested in the megalithic monuments should consult the books and maps (see Practical Information: Books and maps) which give their exact situation, since many of the sites are difficult to find, with inadequate signposting or none at all, and accessible only on rough tracks. Moreover most of the remains are on cultivated land, where the high stone walls make it difficult to see and reach them.

The main sights and features of interest on Minorca are described in the entries on Alayor, Ciudadela, Mahón and Mercadal.

Miramar

C3

Island: **Majorca**

The large estate of Miramar lies between Valldemosa and Sóller on the north-west coast of Majorca, some 30 km (19 miles) north of Palma.

Situation

*The estate

The estate, which once belonged to the Austrian Archduke Ludwig Salvator (1847–1913), is magnificently situated high above the steep and rugged stretch of coast known as the Costa Brava Mallorquina (Majorca's "Wild Coast").

The house (19th c.) occupies the site of a missionary school founded by Ramón Llull and incorporates architectural elements from various older buildings. From the nearby Mirador del Portalet and from the gallery 500 m (550 yd) lower down there are superb panoramic views.

Son Marroig

2 km (1¼ miles) north-east of Miramar, below the road on the left, stands the mansion of Son Marroig, once the residence of Archduke Ludwig Salvator. Near the house is an outlook terrace from which there is a good view of the curiously shaped promontory of Sa Foradada, the "rock with a hole in it", where the Archduke's yacht used to be moored. Below the terrace is the Mirador de Sa Foradada bar and restaurant.

The palatial mansion is open to the public (admission charge). On the first floor are numerous mementoes of Ludwig Salvator, including many manuscripts and pen drawings in his hand, together with a number of pictures by local artists. From the long window front of the principal apartment there is a fantastic view of the sea. There is also an attractive little garden overlooking the nearby terraced fields with their plantations of silver-grey olive trees. On a projecting spur of land can be seen a small round marble temple copied from antique models.

Sa Foradada

To the left of the side of the building which faces uphill is the road which descends to the promontory of Sa Foradada. A toll is payable for its use; tickets are issued in the house.

Son Marroig, Archduke Ludwig Salvator's country house

Sa Foradada, the "rock with a hole in it"

Deya (Deiá)

C3

The charming village of Deya (Majorcan Deiá), much favoured by artists as a place of residence, lies at a height of 220 m (720 ft) at the foot of Mount Teix, huddled around a hill which is flanked by terraced fields and crowned by the village church. It has long been a favourite subject for landscape-painters. It is said that Pablo Picasso lived here for some time, and that in order to persuade him to stay a bathroom was specially installed in the house – a great luxury in a village which because of its elevated situation was otherwise without running water. For many years Deya was the home of the poet Robert Graves.

In the lower part of the village is a small archaeological museum (usually open only at the week-end). The parish church (San Juan Bautista), on the highest point in the village, has a Baroque altar.

North of the village is the Cala de Deya, bounded on the west by the promontory of Punta de Deya.

Situation
3 km (2 miles) E

Montuiri

D5

Island: Majorca
Altitude: 188 m (617 ft)
Population: 3000

The little town of Montuiri lies almost in the centre of the Llanura del Centro, some 30 km (19 miles) east of Palma.

Situation

127

Montuiri

Deya

Montuiri

The town

This picturesque old town is situated on a low hill, dominated by its 13th c. Gothic Parish Church of San Bartolomé. The main doorway, which is relatively plain, is usually closed, and the church is entered by the Baroque doorway (1643) on the south side. The church has two fine retablos. From its south side a flight of steps leads down to the town's little main square, the Plaza Mayor. A walk through the narrow lanes of the old part of the town is a fascinating experience.

2 km (1½ miles) east of the town is the Ermita de San Miguel (19th c.). From the top of the hill there are fine panoramic views.

San Miguel

Muro

C6

Island: **Majorca**
Altitude: 73 m (240 ft)
Population: 7000

The little country market town of Muro lies a short distance inland from the Bahía de Alcudia in north-eastern Majorca. Between the town and the coast extends the fertile plain of La Albufera. The origins of the town are believed to go back to Roman times.

Situation

The town

The Parish Church of San Juan Bautista, in Plaza Conde Ampurias Hugo IV, was founded in the 13th c. and largely rebuilt in the 16th. Above the main doorway (normally closed) in the west front is the date 1828, and above this again a rose window. Particularly notable are the arcades above the aisles – a feature found in many Majorcan churches. Over the doorway in the south aisle can be seen a relief of the Virgin as Queen of Heaven. The High Altar dates from the 17th c., the Altar of San Miguel from the 14th. There is a free-standing belfry, linked with the church by a single arch. Over the doorway of the belfry is a fine coffered ceiling; from the top of the tower there are splendid panoramic views.

Parish church

A handsome old building in the Calle Mayor (No. 15) houses the Folk Museum (officially the Ethnological Section of the Museo de Mallorca; open Tue.–Sat. 10 a.m.–2 p.m. and 4–7 p.m., Sun. 10 a.m.–2 p.m., closed Mon.; admission charge). The museum contains – among much else – old pictures, furniture, craftsmen's tools and traditional costumes. A particularly interesting exhibit is an old country kitchen with an open hearth and old utensils and equipment; a few steps down is the bakehouse. On the first floor are agricultural implements and equipment (ploughs, saddles, harness) and pottery (including the characteristic Majorcan *siurels*, archaic figures painted green and red, and 19th c. ware from Felanitx, some of it rather over-decorated). In an adjoining room is a small but appealing collection of Nativity figures. Beyond these are collections of painted domestic pottery and painted tiles with symbols designed to bring good fortune and avert evil. Passing through an attractive courtyard with a draw-well, winepresses and a noria (water-wheel of Moorish type), we come

*Museo de Mallorca

Parish church, Muro

into the rear part of the building. It contains a smithy, with a large bellows, tools and iron fittings; a second kitchen, with an open hearth and handsome earthenware vessels; a cobbler's workshop and a small weaving shop. On the first floor are a carpenter's, a wood-carver's, a stonemason's, and goldsmith's and silversmith's workshops.

Santa Ana

In Plaza José Antonio Primo de Rivera stands the 16th c. Church of Santa Ana, which belonged to a Minorite convent. It is a relatively plain building with arcading of archaic type under the roof and a Baroque doorway on the east side. Outside the church is a small modern fountain with a statue of a Majorcan peasant woman holding a water-jug.

The road to La Puebla (see entry) runs north-west from Muro, cutting through an old quarry, now disused, just outside the town. It can be seen how large cube-shaped blocks were sawn out of the soft stone. The main crops in the surrounding area are capers, artichokes, potatoes, citrus fruits, olives and figs; little wine is produced in this area.

Playa de Muro

To the north-east on the Bay of Alcudia lies the holiday area of the Playa de Muro.

Orient

C4

Island: **Majorca**
Altitude: 455 m (1495 ft)
Population: 100

Valle de Orient

Situation

The little hamlet of Orient lies north-east of Palma in the Sierra del Norte, on the beautiful but very narrow mountain road (not recommended for caravans/trailers) from Buñola to Alaró.

The village

This old mountain village nestles in a high but fertile basin in the idyllic Valle de Orient, mainly devoted to the growing of olives and almonds. It is a good base from which to climb the Castillo de Alaró (see Alaró).

East of the village, in beautiful gardens, is the Hermitage Hotel.

A little way south of Orient on the narrow country road to Santa María del Cami we come to the country house of Son Pou, in the immediate vicinity of which is S'Avenc de Son Pou, a cave chamber up to 50 m (165 ft) high (partly collapsed).

S'Avenc de Son Pou

Paguera

D2

Island: **Majorca**
Altitude: sea-level

Paguera lies in western Majorca on the Playa de Paguera, a beach with a southern exposure some 20 km (12½ miles) south-west of Palma.

Situation

The resort

This lively seaside resort and its bay are surrounded by wooded hills. The life of Paguera is almost exclusively centred on the tourist and holiday trade, but it is free of the tower blocks which are all too often found elsewhere on Majorca.

Fornells
*Cala Fornells

3 km (2 miles) west lies the quiet little resort of Fornells, with the holiday village of Cala Fornells, excellently designed and laid out in the manner of a typical Majorcan fishing village, its Moorish-style houses climbing up the steep slopes above the bay.

Camp de Mar

In the next bay to the west (with a largely rocky beach) is Camp de Mar, another holiday village. From here there is a beautiful scenic road to Puerto de Andraitx (see Andraitx).

Costa de la Calma

See Santa Ponsa

Palma de Mallorca (Ciutat)   D3/4

Island: **Majorca**
Altitude: sea-level
Population: 300,000

Situation

Palma (Majorcan Ciutat), capital of Majorca and of the Spanish province of the Balearics, is picturesquely situated on the Bahía de Palma, which reaches inland for some 20 km (12½ miles) on the south-west coast of the island.

Tip

The descriptions of the individual sights and places of interest are listed in the order in which they will be seen when taking the tours which are recommended. The Cathedral is the suggested setting-out point for all the tours of the inner city district.

In the whole of the Old town the "ORA" (*Ordenación Regulación Aparcamiento*) system applies to the parking of vehicles; it allows parking for a limited time only on weekdays between 9.30 a.m. and 1.30 p.m. and between 5 p.m. and 8 p.m. Parking permits (*tarjetas de estacionamiento*) can be obtained from all tobacconists' shops (*estancos*).

Palma in its large and beautiful bay is an important Mediterranean port and has grown into a lively modern city which now extends far inland. It is both the economic centre (commerce, banking, industry, craft production) and the cultural focus (high educational establishments, technical colleges, scientific institutes; see of a bishop; literary and artistic activities) of the Balearics and the Islas Pityusas. The population of the city includes considerable numbers of foreigners, and about a third of the native population consists of Chuetas (i.e. originally of Jewish origin).

With its busy central area (palaces, late 19th c. and Art Nouveau buildings), once surrounded by walls which have now mostly given place to a ring of boulevards, its historic old town (palaces, churches) and the extensive beaches surrounding the whole of the bay, Palma is one of the most popular holiday resorts in Spain. It is a good base from which to explore the rest of the island, since Majorca's whole road network is centred on the city, with main roads radiating in all directions.

View of Palma from Bellver Castle

Palma's most prominent landmarks are the Cathedral and Bellver Castle, high above the city.

To the east of Palma extends the wide Llanura del Centro (Central Plain), in which the city's airport is located; on the west the foothills of the Sierra del Norte reach to the boundaries of the city.

Excavations at Son Sunyer, Es Vincle, Son Oms and other sites (all near the airport) have yielded evidence of prehistoric occupation.

History

The Romans established the military post of Palmaria, probably on the site of a fishing village. The first town walls were built in the 4th c. A.D.

Periods of Vandal and Byzantine rule in the 5th and 6th c. were followed by the Moorish occupation, which lasted until the 13th c. During this period the town, known as Madîna Mayûrqa, was surrounded by a triple circuit of walls. The population included many Jews.

On the last day of 1229 King Jaime (in Majorcan Jaume) I of Aragon recaptured Palma from the Moors. From 1276 to 1349, under the name of Ciutat (the City), it was capital of the kingdom of Majorca, and from then until the 15th c. it enjoyed a great period of prosperity. In 1375 and 1384 the city was ravaged by plague. In 1391 there were great pogroms directed against the Jews, in the course of which the ghetto of El Call was sacked.

In 1401 a great spate on the River Riera caused 5000 deaths. Between 1450 and 1452 there were peasant uprisings.

The Universidad Literaria, an academy of the liberal arts, was founded in 1483. Two years later the first books printed on Majorca were published.

In 1562 new town walls were built, in 1571 the Real Audiencia (Law Courts).

The island's saint, Catalina Thomás, spent most of her life in the Convent of the Magdalene, where she died in 1574.

During the 17th c. the town was struck by famine (1648) and plague (1652). In the second half of the century the Inquisition held numerous autos-da-féin which heretics (mainly Jews) were burned at the stake.

The name Palma came into use about 1700. In 1745 a great epidemic claimed some 10,000 victims. The Jesuits were expelled from the island in 1767.

In the 18th c. the island aristocracy reached the peak of their power. Handsome palaces were built, and there was a great flowering of the silversmith's arts.

The first newspaper was published in Palma in 1808. In 1851 the island was devastated by a severe earthquake.

The population of the city has increased rapidly since 1900, rising from 64,000 in that year to 137,000 in 1950 and some 300,000 today.

▼ *Modern Palma, overlooked by Bellver Castle*

* Cathedral

Above the Old Harbour and a stretch of the old town walls
which has been preserved in this area rises the Cathedral (La
Seo), a massive structure of mellow golden-brown sandstone,
begun in 1230 in Early Gothic style but not completed until the
16th and 17th c., with three doorways, a beautiful south front,
two 19th c. towers (each 67·50 m (221 ft) high) and a bell-tower
of 1270 (47·80 m (157 ft) high; nine bells). Built on to the
bell-tower is the Casa de la Almoina (Chapter Library).
From the terrace on the south side of the Cathedral there is a
view of the Parque del Mar (below), with its large ornamental
pond, and beyond this the wide bay of Palma.

Open
Mon.–Fri. 10 a.m.–12.30 p.m.
and 4–6.30 p.m.,
Sat. 10 a.m.–2 p.m.
Closed Sun. and holidays.
(museum and treasury)

Admission charge

We enter the Cathedral through a side doorway in the north
aisle and come first to the Cathedral Museum. In the antechamber are a number of large manuscript books of plainsong. The
central feature of the first room beyond this, the Sacristía de
Vermells, is a Late Gothic monstrance with a Baroque cover. In
cases in this room are caskets, reliquaries and liturgical utensils. Other items of interest include a beautiful Annunciation
group (14th c.), manuscripts and hour-glasses. The next room,
the Old Chapter House (view of cloister), contains a fine Altar-
piece of St Eulalia (c. 1335), a St Sebastian (1488), a portrait of
Pope Silvester (14th c.) and a large altar-piece with a figure of St
Francis and scenes from his legend.
From this Gothic room we pass through a Renaissance
doorway into the New Chapter House, in a style strongly influenced by Mannerism, with an oval dome. In cases around the
walls are reliquaries, a number of silver figures of saints

* Museum

and two ivory crucifixes. The room is dominated by a gilded High Baroque altar.

Interior of the Cathedral

We now enter the Cathedral proper. With its aisled nave rising to a height of 44 m (144 ft), it covers an area of 6600 sq. m (7900 sq. yd). The interior was remodelled at the beginning of the 20th c. by the celebrated Spanish architect Antonio Gaudí. The vaulting is borne on fourteen massive columns. There are seven impressive rose-windows; the largest (1370), in the apse, has an interior diameter of 11·15 m (36½ ft). The aisles, which are surprisingly high, are flanked by a series of chapels with massive Baroque altars. They end in two subsidiary choirs, which are structurally separate from the nave.

The stained-glass windows are of different dates and varying quality.

In the Capilla Real (presbytery) is the High Altar, over which is suspended a gigantic canopy by Antonio Gaudí, in the form of

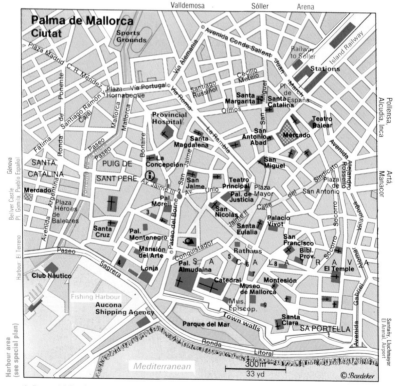

1 Fuente del Sepulcro
2 Fuente de la Princesa
3 Casa Belloto

4 Consulato del Mar
5 Casa Oleo
6 Almudaina Arch

7 Casa Oleza
8 Casa del Marqués de Palmer
9 Arab Baths (Casa Font y Roig)

Palma Cathedral and Harbour

a Crown of Thorns, surrounded by a ring of lamps. At the end of the presbytery stands the bishop's throne. On the side walls are the monuments of Berenguer Batle (bishop 1332–49) and Guillem de Vilanova (bishop 1304–18), who made major contributions to the construction of the Cathedral.

Beyond the Capilla Real we come to the Capilla de la Trinidad (Trinity Chapel), with the sarcophagi of Kings Jaime (Jaume) II and III.

To the left of the presbytery is the massive stone pulpit (1531), in Plateresque style, which is a little out of keeping with the general Gothic aspect of the church.

Cathedral

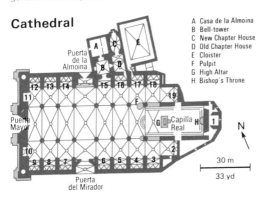

A Casa de la Almoina
B Bell-tower
C New Chapter House
D Old Chapter House
E Cloister
F Pulpit
G High Altar
H Bishop's Throne

CHAPELS (Capillas)
1 Trinidad (sarcophagi)
2 San Pedro
3 San Antonio de Padua
4 Nuestra Señora de la Corona
5 San Martin
6 San Bernardo
7 Nuestra Señora de la Grada
8 Santo Corazón de Jesús
9 San Benito
10 Baptistery
11 Almas (Animas)
12 Purisima
13 San Sebastián
14 San José
15 Todos los Santos
16 Piedad (with organ above)
17 Santo Cristo
18 San Jerónimo
19 Corpus Christi

137

In the north choir are a large silver retablo and two silver candelabra. Adjoining is the entrance to the cloister, by which we leave the Cathedral.

In the streets immediately north of the Cathedral are numerous shops selling craft goods and souvenirs of varying quality.

Diocesan Museum

Immediately opposite the choir of the Cathedral stands the Bishop's Palace (1616), now occupied by the diocesan offices and archives. In the centre of the inner courtyard is a 19th c. statue of Christ and on the wall to the left is a handsome escutcheon with a sundial. Off the courtyard opens a staircase with fine wrought-iron banisters. To the right of the large doorway is the entrance to the Diocesan Museum (open daily 10 a.m.–1 p.m. and 3–7 p.m.), with a collection which includes liturgical utensils, incunabula, architectural fragments, coins and ceramics.

Almudaina Palace

Opposite the west doorway of the Cathedral stands the Palacio de la Almudaina, once the seat of the Moorish Viziers and from 1230 a royal stronghold. It is now occupied by the military, but there are conducted tours of some of the state apartments. In the courtyard can be seen the Gothic Chapel of Santa Ana.

Below the Almudaina Palace, particularly at its west end, a small park is laid out in the Moorish style with fountains. It contains a number of modern works of sculpture, including a mobile by Calder (1971).

Parque del Mar

Below the Cathedral and the Almudaina Palace lies the Parque del Mar, recently redesigned and reopened to the public in October 1984. At the foot of the steps leading down to the park is a bronze figure of one of the legendary Balearic slingers. The park has a large ornamental pond, in and around which are a number of pieces of modern sculpture as well as a small open-air theatre and restaurants. On the south wall of the park, bordering the through road along the coast, can be seen a tiled panel with a picture by Joan Miró (1983). A pedestrian underpass under the main road gives access to the sea.

From the Parque del Mar we come into the palm-shaded Paseo Sagrera. At its near end is a monument (1967) to Ramón Llull (Latinised as Raimundus Lullus), the great Majorcan scholar. Beyond the square above the harbour is the naval headquarters.

*Lonja

The Lonja (originally the Commercial Exchange) on the right of the Paseo Sagrera, was built in the 15th c. by Guillermo Sagrera. In the tympanum of the main doorway, which is in pure Gothic style, is a figure of an angel. Particularly notable are the tall windows with their rich tracery; the large arched doorways leading into the hall which occupies the whole area of the building, its roof supported only by a few columns, are glazed to their full height. The Lonja is now used as an exhibition hall.

Opposite the main entrance, in Plaza de la Lonja, stands a fine but now rather dilapidated building in Art Nouveau style.

Consulado del Mar

Adjoining the Lonja is the Consulado del Mar, once the seat of the Admiralty Court, with a beautiful Renaissance gallery on

Ceramic painting by Miró

the first floor and a small clock-tower. Flanking the entrance are two old naval guns and an anchor.

To the north of the Lonja stands the Church of Santa Cruz (Holy Cross), with a fine 13th c. crypt.

Santa Cruz

Harbour

Palma's harbours begin below the Alumdaina Palace and extend westward to the Cala Mayor. At the east end the fishing harbour lies within the shelter of a long breakwater. On the harbour is the Lonja del Pescado (Fish Exchange). From this part of the harbour there is a particularly good view of the Cathedral.

Fishing harbour

Beyond the fishing harbour are the Club Náutico and the large boating harbour, with many luxury yachts. At the west end of the harbour area is the passenger harbour (Porto Pí), with the

＊Boating harbour
Passenger harbour

The Lonja (Stock Exchange)

A baker's shop, Palma

Estación Marítima (Marine Station), used by the car ferries and the regular boats to the neighbouring islands and mainland Spain. Near by can be seen a lighthouse and the Torre de Pelaires, an old defensive tower (15th c.).

Paseo del Borne

From the Old Harbour the Avenida Maura runs north by way of the Plaza de la Reina (fountains) and joins the Paseo del Borne, Palma's principal promenade. On the west side stands the large Palacio Morell (Palacio Sollerich; 1763), with elegant arcades on the upper floor and a beautiful inner courtyard. It now houses the Exhibition and Documentation Centre of Contemporary Art (temporary exhibitions; closed Sun., Mon. and public holidays).

From the north end of the Paseo del Borne (Plaza Pio XII) Avenida Rey Jaime III, a wide avenue lined by arcades, goes north-west.

La Concepción

A little way north of Avenida Rey Jaime III is the Convent of La Concepción.

Plaza Catalina Thomás

To the east of Plaza Pio XII is Plaza Catalina Thomás, in which is the Palacio Berga (Law Courts). In this beautifully laid out square, under a large rubber tree, stands a monument in Art Nouveau style to the Palma-born politician Antonio Maura (1852–1925), who was several times Prime Minister of Spain in the early years of the 20th c. Around the square are a number of Art Nouveau buildings.

Rambla

Continuing from Plaza Catalina Thomás into the adjoining Plaza Weyler (from which a wide stepped street leads up to the Plaza Mayor) and turning north past the Theatre (Teatro Principal; 1860), we come into Via Roma, commonly known as the Rambla. Palma's flower-market is held under the plane trees in this avenue. At the near end of the street, opposite the entrance to an underground car park, are two Classical-style statues of Caesars. A magnificent flight of steps leads up from here to the Plaza Mayor (see below).

Santa Magdalena

Off the west side of the Rambla is the Church of Santa Magdalena, built in the 18th c. for the convent (originally founded in the 14th c.) in which Catalina Thomás, Majorca's saint, was a nun. Her glass sarcophagus is in the church.

Plaza Weyler

Plaza Weyler lies to the west of Plaza Mayor. The art collection owned by the "Caixa" (Savings Bank) was put on display here in an Art Nouveau building in 1993.

Plaza Mayor

The Plaza Mayor (pedestrians only), Palma's handsome principal square, stands above the surrounding area, amid fine arcaded houses. Lining the square are pavement cafés, restaurants and shops. There is a large underground shopping arcade. The streets around the square are partly pedestrianised, with some good shops.

Palma de Mallorca
Ciutat

Harbour area

300 m
330 yd

© Baedeker

Leisure time in the Plaza Mayor

Collección March

To the north of Plaza Mayor, on the left side of Calle San Miquel, stands the March Bank building, with an art collection and temporary exhibitions of contemporary Spanish art.

San Miguel

To the north of the Plaza Mayor stands the Church of San Miguel, originally a mosque, which has preserved a 14th c. façade. It boasts a superb Baroque altar with rich gilding.

San Antonio

On the right near the northern end of the pedstrian zone will be found the cloister of the former San Antonio Hospital, built in 1768. In 1979 the building was purchased by the Banco de Bilbao and restored. The very interesting arcaded courtyard is often the site of various temporary art exhibitions.

Market Hall
Plaza de España

Immediately north-east of San Antonio we reach the Mercado del Olivar, Palma's large market hall. Beyond this is the spacious Plaza de España, a busy traffic intersection, with an equestrian statue of King Jaime II. On the north-east side of the square is the railway station (service to Sóller).

*Old town

To the north-east of the Cathedral lies the old town of Palma, a maze of narrow lanes and flights of steps, with few streets of any great width, all bustling with life and activity. All over this part of the town are doorways, windows, roof ornaments and inner courtyards which are well worth examination.

Town Hall

In Plaza Cort stands the Baroque Ayuntamiento (Town Hall), an imposing three-storey building with a richly decorated façade.

North-east of the Town Hall is the Church of Santa Eulalia, in
High Gothic style. Notable features of the dimly lit interior
(aisled) are a large Baroque altar and a few old stained-glass
windows (though most of the glass is 19th c.). The façade,
much restored, is very obviously 19th c. work.

*Santa Eulalia

In Calle de Almudaina are the Casa Oleo (No. 8), with a fine
patio (inner courtyard), an art collection, and a Moorish arch,
the Arco de Almudaina. Near by, in Calle Morey, can be seen a
handsome Renaissance mansion, the Casa Oleza (No. 9 –
though, confusingly, the house next door is numbered 33/I),
also with a fine patio.

In the narrow Calle San Bernardo, which runs west to the
Cathedral, is the Confradrería de San Pedro y San Bernardo
(No. 13), with an imposing Baroque façade and a beautiful
patio.

On San Francisco Square, to the east of Santa Eulalia, stands
the Gothic church of San Francisco. The building was begun in
1281, but the door betrays the plateresque style of the Spanish
Baroque; between the arch and the rose-window stands a
statue of St George. In front of the doorway will be seen a statue
of the Indian missionary Junipero Serra; inside the church, in
the second chapel on the left in the ambulatory, is the alabaster
tomb of Raimon Lullus. Note also the Late Gothic cloister
(14th c.; access through the small building on the right) with its
slender pillars.

San Francisco

Patio of Casa Oleza

Palma de Mallorca

San Francisco

Arab Baths

Art Nouveau architecture

In the Pueblo Español

*Museo de Mallorca

The Museo de Mallorca is housed in the excellently restored Palacio Ayamans (Casa Desbrull, Calle Portella 5). On the ground floor can be seen engraved stone tablets and decorative woodcarvings from the Moorish period, as well as partly painted wooden ceilings (some from the Almudaina), and Pre-Talayot and Talayot finds. A staircase (note the sculpture of St Michael from the Lonja) leads up to rooms containing the large art gallery. Special mention should be made of the Romanesque and Gothic tablets; there is also a small lapidarium and a collection of china. Founded in 1976, the museum is still in course of development and further departments are gradually being opened.

Open:
Tue.–Sat. 10 a.m.–2 p.m. and 4–7 p.m., Sun. and pub. hol. 10 a.m.–2 p.m.; closed Mon.

Admission charge

In Calle Serra, which adjoins the east side of the museum stands the Casa Font y Roig (No. 7), in the garden of which are the remains of a 10th c. Arab bath-house (Baños Arabes; open daily 10 a.m.–1.30 p.m. and 4–7 p.m.).

Arab Baths

The street which runs north from the Arab Baths leads to the Church of Montesión, built by the Jesuits in the 16th and 17th c. It has a massive Baroque doorway and a fine interior, with a 15th c. altar dedicated to the Virgin.

Montesión

Palacio de Congresos

A Teatro Romano
B Temple
C Colonnade
D Palace of Congresos (Imperial Hall)

Pueblo Español

© Baedeker

REPRODUCTIONS OF OLD BUILDINGS IN PUEBLO ESPAÑOL

1 Puerta de Bisagra (Toledo)
2 Cristo de los Faroles (Córdoba)
3 Casa Canaria (La Laguna)
4 Court of Myrtles, Alhambra (Granada)
5 Arab Baths (Baza)
6 Ermita de San Antonio (Madrid)
7 Casa de Melibea (Toledo)
8 Casa El Greco (Toledo)
9 Church from Castle of Torralba de Ribota (Zaragoza)
10 Tower and façade of Church of Santa Catalina (Valencia)
11 Palacio de la Diputación (Barcelona)
12 Town Hall, Vergara (Guipúzcoa)
13 Patio Cervantino
14 Puerta de Toledo (Ciudad Real)
15 Ermita del Cristo de la Luz (originally a mosque; Toledo)
16 Andalusian quarter
17 Entrecastillos (metalworking craftsmen)
18 Torre de Oro (Seville)

Es Jonquet

To the west of the Torrente la Riera (here canalised), which bounds the old town at this point, is the former fishermen's quarter of Es Jonquet. Standing above the Paseo Marítimo are four old windmills. In these, and in the neighbouring streets, are a variety of night-spots and bars.

Above the Paseo Marítimo and roughly parallel to it is a broad street which passes through the entertainments quarter around Plaza Gomila, where heretics were burned in the time of the Inquisition, to the suburb of El Terreno, a district of villas and hotels.

**Pueblo Español (Poble Espanyol)

Open:
daily 9 a.m.–8 p.m.

Admission charge

The Pueblo Español (Majorcan Poble Espanyol, Spanish Village) lies on higher ground to the west of the town centre. The "village", excellently designed and laid out, consists of faithful reproductions of important and characteristic old buildings from all parts of Spain. In the buildings are numerous craftsmen's workshops and shops selling their products (glass, enamel, pottery, leather goods, paintings, knotted and woven carpets, etc.).

Palace of Congresses

To the north-east of the Pueblo Español is the Palace of Congresses, a large complex of buildings modelled on a Roman forum, with an open colonnade, a small temple and an amphitheatre as well as the congress hall itself. The interior is normally not open to the public.

**Castillo de Bellver

Open:
April–Sept. 8 a.m.–8 p.m.
Oct.–Mar. 8 a.m.–6 p.m.

Above the city to the west, at a height of 113 m (370 ft) above sea-level, stands Bellver Castle, a circular Gothic structure of the 13th c., once a royal stronghold. From 1802 to 1808 the Spanish politician and writer G. M. de Jovellanos was imprisoned here.

Bellver
Castle

The road up to the castle (signposted) passes through a large wrought-iron gate into an extensive area on top of the hill planted with pines. There is a large car park just outside the castle. From the summit plateau there is a fantastic view over the whole area of the city; the best light is in the afternoon.

Bellver Castle, surrounded by walls and a moat, is a formidable stronghold on a circular plan (pointing to the influence of Eastern models), with one free-standing round tower and three others built into the main structure. The twin-arched Romanesque windows belong to the residential apartments.

(after a plan by
Archduke Ludwig
Salvator)

The castle is entered on a bridge (formerly a drawbridge) spanning the moat. It encloses an inner courtyard, the Patio de Armas, surrounded by arcades, Romanesque on the lower tier and Gothic on the upper tier, with a well in the centre. The flat roof is so constructed that rainwater can be collected and directed into a cistern, which occupies almost the whole area under the courtyard.

*Fundación Pilar y Joan
Miró

Near Cala Mayor (Calle Saridakis 29) the Fundación Pilar y Joan Miró has recently been opened in the artist's former residence. Painting, drawings and sculptures are exhibited, many of them for the very first time.

Bellver Castle

Huerta de Palma

D4

The fertile Huerta (Garden) de Palma, to the west of the city, is dotted with numerous villages, estates and country houses.

One of the best-known country houses in this area is Son Vida, 5 km (3 miles) north-west of Palma, once the seat of the Marqués de la Torre and now converted into a luxury hotel (18-hole golf-course, tennis-courts, etc.).

Son Vida

6 km (3½ miles) north of the city we come to Son Berga, a mansion built in 1776, the main attraction of which is its magnificent gardens.

Son Berga

North of Palma, on the road to Indiotería (Son Fusteret), is the Krekovic Museum (closed on Sun. and public holidays), which specialises in Inca and Peruvian art.

Museo Krekovic

5 km (3 miles) west of Palma lies the village of Genova, an artists' colony. There is an interesting little stalactitic cave here with colourful sinter formations. From the hill of Na Burguesa, to the east of the village, there are fine views of Palma and its bay.

Genova

Bahía de Palma (west side)

The Paseo Marítimo joins a well-designed road which continues along the south-west side of Palma Bay, not much above sea-level for most of the way and passing through the resorts of Cala Mayor (beach of fine sand), Sant Agusti, Illetas (small sandy cove between rocks), Portals Nous and Cala d'en Blanes. Parallel to this road and a short distance inland a motorway runs as far as Palma Nova.

Marineland

Open: daily from 9.30 a.m.

Admission charge

At Cala d'en Blanes, just off the beach of fine sand, is Marineland, with a dolphinarium, an aquarium, a seal-pool, a tropicarium and other marine features; there are also some monkeys and reptiles. There are displays by various kinds of animals daily (parrots 11.30 a.m., 2.15 and 4 p.m.; dolphins and sealions 10.30 a.m., 12.30, 3 and 5 p.m.).

Palma Nova
Magalluf

The coast road continues to the resorts of Palma Nova (sandy beach; gaming casino) and Magalluf (beach of fine sand). Magalluf was developed in the early days of the tourist boom and illustrates some of the planning errors which were avoided in later developments, with tower blocks, souvenir shops, bars and fast-food establishments packed closely together. Magalluf's golf-course lies between Palma Nova and Santa Ponsa.

Portals Vells   E3

From Magalluf a narrow minor road runs south through pleasant and varied scenery, with expanses of macchia and dwarf pines. A side road on the left leads to Portalls Vells in its little bay, with a small restaurant. From here visitors can explore the coastal waters in glass-bottomed boats.

Cave church

In the cliffs on the right-hand side of the bay, reached by a footpath, is a cave church. Note particularly the altar and holy-water stoup, both hewn from the soft rock. The church is said to have been established by Genoese seamen in thanksgiving for their preservation from peril on the sea. Having come ashore in the bay, they set up in the cave a small figure of the Virgin from their ship. The figure is now in the church at Portals Nous.
The southern tip of the peninsula, around Punta Mula, is a military area closed to the public. The road comes to a dead end, with no room to park or to turn.

Castillo de Bendinat   D3

From Porto Pí a motorway runs above the coast road and parallel to it, passing close to Bendinat Castle (on the left; no admission). The castle was built in the 13th c. and enlarged in the 18th. The popular explanation of its name is that after his victory over the Moors in 1229 King Jaime I, having shared a modest meal of bread, garlic and wine with his soldiers, exclaimed "Havem ben dinat" ("We have dined well").
At Palma Nova the motorway crosses the Coll de Sa Batalla (Pass of the Battle), the scene of Jaime I's victory in 1229.

Bahía de Palma (east side)

San Juan Airport

The motorway (Ronda Litoral) runs east from Palma to the airport of Son San Juan (10 km (6 miles)), the principal airport in the Balearics, and then continues parallel to the coast, some distance inland, to El Arenal (below).

Marineland

The cave church of Portals Vells

Portals Vells

*Playas de Palma

A road (mainly one-way in the Palma direction) runs parallel to the motorway along the south-east coast of Palma Bay by way of the former fishing villages of Portixol and El Molinar, the Coll d'en Rebassa (a little way inland), Ciudad Jardín (Garden City, in Cala Gamba; sandy beach) and Cala Estancia to Ca'n Pastilla. It then continues as a four-lane highway along the Playas de Mallorca (Beaches of Majorca; sandy beach 6 km (3½ miles) long and up to 40 m (45 yd) wide) to Las Maravillas and El Arenal (small harbour). This stretch is now an almost continuous tourist resort, with numerous hotels, restaurants, shops and places of entertainment.

El Arenal

At the eastern end of the Playa de Palma lies the well-known seaside resort of El Arenal, with its closely-packed high-rise apartments, which developed in the very early years of the tourist boom. The main attraction is "Aquacity", a swimming and leisure centre near the junction with the motorway, said to be the largest of its kind in the world. It boasts a number of pools and flumes, children's playgrounds, a typewriter museum and a parrot-show, as well as a large choice of restaurants and cafés.

Cala Blava

From Aquacity the road continues to Cala Blava, with a commanding view of the whole of the Bahía de Palma.

Petrá

D6

Island: Majorca
Altitude: 105 m (345 ft)
Population: 4000

Situation

Petrá lies in the eastern part of the Llanura del Centro some 50 km (30 miles) from Palma, a few kilometres north of the road to Manacor.

The town

This ancient little country town, which can probably trace its origins back to Roman times, is an important market centre. It was the birthplace of the Franciscan friar Junípero Serra (1713–84), who went to North America as a missionary and founded many mission stations and towns in what is now the State of California.

Parish church

In the lower part of the town stands the Parish Church of San Pedro (16th c.), which has a badly weathered but very beautiful façade with a large rose-window and an arched doorway (no figural ornament: even the tracery is missing). Over the south aisle are large open arcades. Outside the church is a monument (1976) to the Majorcan peasant woman.
The church, with a richly furnished interior, is entered by a 19th c. neo-Gothic doorway, to the right of which is a tablet commemorating Junípero Serra, set up in 1963.

San Bernardino

In the upper part of the little town the Oratorio de San Bernardino (17th c.) was originally a monastic church. The main front with its weathered Renaissance doorway faces on to the narrow Calle Mayor. At the east end of the church, reached

Fra Junípero Serra's mission station in San Francisco

by a side street on its south side, a four-sided monument to Junípero Serra, with majolica panels on all four sides depicts his life and missionary activity. Farther along the street, on both sides, are majolica panels in wrought-iron frames depicting his mission stations in California.

At the end of the street, beyond a narrow cross street, we come to the Museo Serra, and a few paces to the left (No. 6) is the Casa Serra, the modest house in which the missionary was born, with a commemorative tablet on the façade. For admission to the museum and the house apply to No. 2, Calle P. Miguel de Petra (to the right of the entrance to the museum: route shown in plan on museum door).

Museo Serra
Casa Serra

Pollensa (Pollença)   B6

Island: Majorca
Altitude: 200 m/655 ft
Population: 10,000

The town of Pollensa (Majorcan Pollença) lies near the northern tip of Majorca in the foothills of the Sierra del Norte.

Situation

The low-lying country around Pollensa was one of the earliest areas on Majorca to be settled by man. The town was founded by the Catalans during the Reconquista and was given the name of Majorca's old Roman capital, Pollentia, which was actually at Alcudia (see entry).
Pollensa was the birthplace of the priest and lyric poet Miguel Costa i Llobera (1854–1922).

History

The town

Pollensa, with its winding lanes and severe houses built of natural stone, is attractively situated on the edge of a fertile huerta looking on to the Bahía de Pollensa, bounded on the north by the Sierra de San Vicente and on the south by the Sierra de Sa Coma. The town's main sources of income are shoemaking, textile industries and the making of basketware.

Nuestra Señora del Rosario

Just off the road from La Puebla can be found the recently restored Church of Nuestra Señora del Rosario, which is basically a Baroque church. In front of the doorway stands an ancient olive tree and an interesting modern sculpture, consisting of a block of limestone with a hollowed-out square in which stand ceramic "books", on the backs of which are inscribed the names of numerous artists. In a short side wing is the entrance to the cloister and museum.

In the square on the north side of the church are a square tower and an old noria (water-wheel)

Jesuit church

The church of the former Jesuit house of Montesión dates from the 17th c. Miguel Costa i Llobera was priest here, and the church was restored during his time (1891).

To the left of the church stands the imposing Casa Consistorial, a 17th/18th c. building.

From here, following the signpost to the Calvary (Calvario), we come to the parish church.

Nuestra Señora de los Angeles

The Parish Church of Nuestra Señora de los Angeles, in the centre of the town on the colourful Plaza Mayor with its pavement cafés, was built in the 13th c. and renovated in the 18th. It

Farmhouse near Pollensa, under the Sierra del Norte

has wall-paintings by Boveri, an Argentinian artist, and Mosgraber, a German.

From the parish church there are two ways up the Calvary hill: to the left a flight of 365 shallow steps lined by cypresses, to the right the motor road. The ascent on foot is much the more attractive. Notable features of the Baroque pilgrimage chapel (1794) at the top are its fine façade and the doors, studded with ornamental nails. On the pillars flanking the entrance are coloured majolica panels (unfortunately damaged) depicting on the left the Raising of Lazarus and on the right the Mater Dolorosa. The chapel has a Crucifix which may date from the 13th c. A path to the right of the chapel leads to an outlook terrace with a good view to the north-east of Cap Formentor and the bays of Pollensa and Alcudia. | *Calvary

3 km (2 miles) south-east of Pollensa rises the Puig de María (320 m (1050 ft)), reached on a side road which leaves the main road just before km 52. On the hill is the Ermita Nuestra Señora del Puig (13th–16th c.), with a hospice for pilgrims. The refectory has Gothic panel-paintings. | Puig de María
There are sweeping views from Puig de María.

*Castillo del Rey

6 km (3½ miles) north of Pollensa (road closed to traffic; 4–5 hours' walk), on a crag 500 m (1640 ft) above the sea, stands the Castillo del Rey, a stronghold and place of refuge of the Majorcan kings. Magnificent panoramic views.

See Cabo Formentor | Puerto Pollensa

Porreras (Porreres) | D6

Island: **Majorca**
Altitude: 120 m (395 ft). Population: 5000

Porreras (Majorcan Porreres) lies in the heart of the Llanura del Centro, between the roads from Palma to Manacor and to Campos del Puerto. To the south-west rises the Sierra de Montesión (294 m (965 ft)). | Situation

The town

The handsome 17th c. Parish Church of Nuestra Señora de la Consolación contains a number of beautiful majolica pictures and a silver processional cross by A. Oliva (c. 1400). | Parish Church

3·5 km (2 miles) south, in the Sierra de Montesión, is the Santuario de Nuestra Señora de la Visitación, once part of the Jesuit house of Montesión. | Nuestra Señora de la Visitación

---

Porto Colóm | E7

Island: **Majorca**
Altitude: sea-level. Population: 500

Felanitx

Porto
Cólom

Port de
pêche

Club
Náutico

Port de
plaisance

Felanitx

Port de
commerce

Sa Punta

HOTELS
1 San Francisco
2 Vista Mar
3 César

Rade

Diving and
Surfing Club

3

2

1

Lighthouse

P

Cala Marsal

200 m
220 yd
© Baedeker

| Situation | The little port of Porto Cólom lies near Felanitx at the south end of Majorca's east coast. |

The village

Porto Cólom, situated on a shelving bay, has remained an attractive and relatively unspoiled fishing village. In front of the church (which has no particular features of interest) is a beautiful little square shaded by pine trees.

*Harbour

Below the church lies the pretty little harbour, the older part of which is lined with boat-sheds. To the south is the modern boating harbour, with a new development growing up around it. The sheltered and almost totally enclosed bay has only a very narrow entrance from the open sea.

There is good bathing in Cala Marsal to the south and Cala S'Algar to the north-east. A few kilometres away is a golf-course.

Porto Cristo   D7/8

Island: Majorca
Altitude: sea-level
Population: 800

Situation

The attractive little port town of Porto Cristo lies half-way along the east coast of Majorca, 13 km (8 miles) from Manacor.

**The town

The centre of Porto Cristo lies off the main road, linked with it by a very beautiful avenue of old pines. The harbour is particularly

Porto Colóm: the fishing harbour

Porto Cristo's narrow harbour inlet

well sheltered. A monument on the pier commemorates those who died in the Civil War. Nearer the sea is a 17th c. watchtower, with the little Cueva des Colóms a short distance away. Near the the harbour is a small beach of fine sand. There are a number of restaurants on the seafront.

**Cuevas del Drach   D7/8

Open:
daily from 9.30 a.m.

Admission charge
(conducted tours, with
commentary in English)

The Cuevas del Drach (Dragon Caves), explored by the French speleologist Edouard Martel in 1896, are one of Majorca's major tourist attractions, with four huge chambers containing fantastic stalactitic formations and a large lake.

The road to the caves, 1·5 km (1 mile) south of the village, is well signposted. There is a large parking area, shaded by pines, with a restaurant, souvenir shops, etc., as well as the ticket office. The entrance to the caves (from which there is a fine view of the sea) is a short walk away through the park-like grounds.

A steep flight of steps leads down into the caves, with passages running down on either side. The tour comes first to Diana's Bath, an underground lake up to 3 m (10 ft) in depth; on the roof of the chamber are numerous stalactites, set close together. Beyond this, to the left, is the Enchanted City, with a large group of stalagmites in the centre and shorter stalactites hanging in dense formations from the roof. From here the concrete path continues past a group of pure white stalagmites known as the Montaña Nevada (Snowy Mountain).

Then follows the large Hall of Columns, with another large sinter mass in the centre. To the left, some distance away, is a formation which with a little imagination can be identified as a figure of Buddha. Beyond this, also to the left, is the Blue Canal,

The play of light and colour in the Cuevas dels Hams

some 5 m (16 ft) deep. Other groups of stalagmites resemble candles. On some columns running from floor to ceiling can be seen horizontal fractures, the result of earth movements at some time in the past.

We now enter the gigantic hall containing the Lago Martel, a large underground lake named after the first explorer of the caves. Lying 39 m (128 ft) under the surface, it is 177 m (194 yd) long by up to 40 m (44 yd) wide, with a depth of 29 m (87 ft). The water has a constant temperature of about 18–20 °C (64–68 °F) and is slightly saline as a result of the infiltration of sea-water. Here a *son et lumière* performance is laid on for visitors, with a torchlight procession of boats carrying musicians and singers. From here the tour continues along the right bank of the lake (with transport by boat available at extra charge) and up stepped paths to the exit, near the restaurant.

Near the car park is the Aquarium, a two-storey building with both freshwater and sea-water tanks (Mediterranean fauna).

Aquarium

5 km (3 miles) south-west is Cala Anguila, with the Porto Cristo Novo development (excellent tourist infrastructure; sailing school, wind-surfing, etc.). Beyond this is Cala Estany.

Porto Cristo Novo

6 km (3½ miles) south of Porto Cristo on the road to Santañy, at the junction with a country road coming from Manacor, stands Son Forteza Vey (the Old Fortress), a handsome and strongly fortified medieval house (private property; no admission). On the opposite side of the road is an old fountain.

Son Forteza Vey

*Cuevas dels Hams

D7

2 km (1½ miles) west of Porto Cristo are the Cuevas dels Hams (Caves of the Fish-Hooks; so called because some of the stalactites are curved into the shape of fish-hooks). The caves, which are accessible for a distance of 350 m (380 yd), were formed by an underground river. The entrance to the caves (with car park) is a little to the south of the Manacor road (signposts). There is a self-service restaurant.

Open:
daily from 9.30 a.m.

Admission charge
(conducted tours, with
commentary in English)

The stalactites and stalagmites grow at the rate of about a centimetre (just under two-fifths of an inch) every thirty years. The varying colours of the formations are due to the admixture of salts of iron and copper. The temperature of the caves remains almost constant at 20 °C (68 °F). Dramatic effects are produced by coloured artificial lighting. At a depth of 30 m (100 ft) is an underground lake known as the Lake of Venice; it is linked with the sea by channels through the rock, and its water has a salt content of some 2 per cent. As in the Cuevas del Drach (above) the lake provides the setting for an underground concert.

In the next chamber, known as Paradise Lost, the pure white sinter formations bear a remote resemblance to a petrified town. To the rear, higher up, is a formation that can be recognised, with some imagination, as a castle; in front, to the right, is a stalagmite resembling the celebrated Virgin of Montserrat (province of Barcelona, on the Spanish mainland).

In the next chamber, on the right, is the Crib (Nativity group). The stalactites hanging from the roof are hollow and yield an abundant supply of water in winter. The stalactitic formations extending from roof to floor in this part of the caves show horizontal cracks like those in the Cuevas del Drach, caused by earth movements in the past.

The next chamber, the Angel's Dream, contains the famous Excentriques – stalactitic formations which grow in all directions, in seeming defiance of the law of gravity, including in particular the hook-like formations from which the caves take their name. This is a particularly fascinating part of the caves, with its stalactites of filigree-like delicacy set closely together hanging from the roof.

In the last chamber shown to visitors are stalagmites (on left) resembling a group of elephants.

S'Illot

D8

Situation
5 km (3 miles) N

The large – and still growing – hotel colony of S'Illot lies in a sheltered inlet on the Cala Moreia, which has a beach of fine sand. Farther south, on the rocky parts of the coast, are good diving-grounds. To the north of the resort, on the south side of the Punta Amer Peninsula (ruined castle), is the sandy Playa de Sa Coma.

La Puebla (Sa Pobla)

C6

Island: **Majorca**
Altitude: 24 m (79 ft). Population: 12,000

Situation

La Puebla (Majorcan La Pobla) lies on the northern edge of the Llanura del Centro, near the Bahía de Alcudia.

The town

The little country town of La Puebla (formerly called Sa Pobla de Huyalfas), on a low hill on the western edge of the plain of

The country house of Son Forteza . . .   *. . . and its old aqueduct*

La Albufera, was founded after the Reconquista on the site
of a Moorish country estate and laid out on a regular plan. The
17th c. Parish Church of San Antonio Abad still preserves the
altar and some architectural remains of an earlier 14th c.
church. Near the church is the Casa Consistorial (Town Hall).
There are a number of handsome old burghers' houses in the
town.

On Calle Antonio Maura stands the Museum of Contemporary
Art (Museo de Arte Contemporáneo; open Thur.–Sat. 11
a.m.–2 p.m. and 6–9 p.m., Sun. 11 a.m.–2 p.m.

Museum

La Albufera

The Albufera is a fertile plain with some areas of bog. Water
was distributed with the help of windmills but nowadays elec-
tric pumps are used. The winning of salt from the sea in the
local salt-pans and the eel fisheries also make a contribution to
the economy of the town. Large crops of vegetables, particularly beans and potatoes, are grown in the Huertas de la Puebla.
A wetland area, extending over some 800 ha/1977 acres, was
recently placed under legal protection.

Puigpuñent (Puigpunyent)   D3

Island: **Majorca**. Altitude: 240 m (790 ft). Population: 5000

The little town of Puigpuñent (Majorcan Puigpunyent) lies in
the Sierra del Norte in western Majorca, some 15 km (9 miles)
north-west of Palma.

Situation

The town

Puigpuñent is situated in a wide valley flanked by terraced
fields, with Mount Galatzó rising to a height of 1026 m (3366 ft)
above it. The parish church (Iglesia de la Asunción) dates from
the 17th and 18th c.

North of Puigpuñent, to the left of the road, lies the large Son
Forteza estate (17th c.; not open to the public). The handsome
house is surrounded by plantations of citrus fruits and olive
groves.

*Son Forteza

At the last sharp bend before the house, below the road on the
right, is the source of the Torrente Sa Riera, which flows
through Palma. The bed of the stream is spanned by a picturesque old aqueduct.

Galilea

From Puigpuñent a very beautiful road runs south-west for
4 km (2½ miles) through orchards of citrus fruits and terraced
fields of olive trees to the old-world village of Galilea (alt. 455 m
(1495 ft)), which in recent years has become an artists' colony.

The parish church (Iglesia de la Inmaculada Concepción) was
built in the early 19th c. on older foundations. From the square
in front of the church (Plaza Pio XII) there is a wide-ranging view

Church

Galilea's terraced fields, with the sea in the background

north-westward over the terraced fields to the sea. The church has two sundials, one over the principal doorway, the other on the south wall. The nave (without aisles) is spanned by a barrel-vaulted roof and flanked by chapels; the only light comes from the rose-window over the organ-gallery.

Sancellas (Sencelles)   D5

Island: **Majorca**
Altitude: 118 m (387 ft)
Population: 2500

Situation

Sancellas (Majorcan Sencelles) lies in the north-western part of the Llanura del Centro, 25 km (15 miles) north-east of Palma.

The town

This old-world little country town is situated on a low hill. The fine 13th c. Parish Church of San Pedro has a small doorway in the aisle which already shows Renaissance influence. The main doorway is in a narrow lane at the east end; in the tympanum is a Baroque figure of St Peter. In the small square in front of the church stands a monument (1955) to a nun named Francina Aina. On the base of the tower is a beautiful majolica representation of the Entombment, with the date 1712 in the vaulting above it. Some frescoes have been preserved in the domed side chapel of the church.

To the left, at right angles to the façade of the church, can be seen an attractive old house with a majolica panel depicting

Christ before Pilate and a loggia on the first floor. It is linked with the church by a small masonry arch.

San Juan (Sant Joan) D6

Island: Majorca
Altitude: 143 m (469 ft)
Population: 2000

The village of San Juan (Majorcan Sant Joan) lies in the Llanura del Centro 35 km (22 miles) east of Palma, on a secondary road which turns left off the road to Manacor at Montuiri.

Situation

The village

The parish church was built in the 13th c. but altered in later centuries. It has a richly furnished interior, with a fine pulpit and frescoes.

Church

To the south of the village, on high ground, stands a pilgrimage chapel with a beautiful Way of the Cross, the Oratorio de Nuestra Señora de la Consolación (17th and 18th c.). From the chapel there is a fine view.

Nuestra Señora de la Consolación

San Lorenzo del Cardessar (Sant Llorenç d'es Cardessar) D7

Island: Majorca
Altitude: 203 m (666 ft)
Population: 4000

The village of San Lorenzo del Cardessar (Majorcan Sant Llorenç d'es Cardessar) lies in eastern Majorca on the road from Manacor to Artá.

Situation

The village

San Lorenzo lies in an area, inhabited by man since prehistoric times, with many talayots. The 19th c. parish church has a fine Romanesque figure of the Virgin, the Mare de Déu Trobada.

Santa Margarita (Santa Margalida) C6

Island: Majorca
Altitude: 92 m (302 ft)
Population: 5000

Santa Margarita (Majorcan Santa Margalida) lies in the north-eastern part of the Llanura del Centro, almost exactly half-way between Inca and Artá.

Situation

The town

This attractive little town lies on a hill rising above the wide fertile plain, on a site which was already inhabited in ancient times. Its major sources of income are farming (mainly vine-growing) and leather-working.

Church

The parish church (13th c., rebuilt in 17th c.) stands on the highest point of the hill, with good views to north and west. It has a fine Baroque south doorway, above which is a rose-window, and notable wall-paintings in the interior.
South-west of the church, on the edge of the main square, is a monument to Catalina Thomás, erected on the 400th anniversary of her death (1 September 1974).

Santa María de la Salud

6 km (3½ miles) south-west is the straggling village of Santa María de la Salud (usually abbreviated to María), with the parish church rising above the village.

Santa María del Camí   D4

Island: **Majorca**
Altitude: 130 m (425 ft). Population: 4000

Situation

Santa María del Camí (Our Lady of the Way) lies in the west of the Llanura del Centro, 14 km (9 miles) north-east of Palma.

The town

This little market town (vine-growing, craft products) occupies the site of the Moorish settlement of Canarrosa and probably also of an earlier Roman settlement.

Santa Margarita

Santa Maria del Camí

To the south of the main road from Palma to La Puebla stands the handsome 18th c. Parish Church of Santa María del Camí, the most notable feature of which is its belfry, clad with deep blue tiles. The interior is in Churrigueresque style (a Spanish development of Baroque).

Parish church

North-west of the parish church, on the main road from Palma to Inca, is a former Minorite friary, the Convento de los Mínimos, also known as "Nuestra Señora de la Soledad" (17th c.). There is a very beautiful Renaissance courtyard surrounded by arcades.

Convento de los Mínimos

On the first floor of the convent building on the far side of the courtyard there is a small museum (not signed), with a wide range of exhibits including fossils, stuffed animals, coins and seals, religious art, books and documents.

Museum

3 km (2 miles) north of the town is a fine country house, Son Torrella, with a beautiful patio,

Son Torrella

Marratxi

The village of Sa Cabaneta, 6 km (3½ miles) south of Santa María, is noted for the manufacture of *siurels*, the naïve little white pottery figures painted red and green which are a favourite souvenir of Majorca.
The Parish Church of San Marcial, which dates in its present form from 1699, has a Gothic retablo.
Sa Cabaneta is the administrative centre of the large commune (rural district) of Marratxi, formed by the amalgamation of a number of small villages.

Sa Cabaneta

Santañy (Santanyi)

E6

Island: **Majorca**
Altitude: 70 m (230 ft). Population: 6000

The little country town of Santañy (Majorcan Santanyi) lies in the Llanura del Centro, a few miles north-east of the southern tip of Majorca.

Situation

The town

Santañy has preserved one of its old town gates, the Porta Murada, and scanty remains of its medieval walls.
The Parish Church of San Andrés Apostol was built on to the Iglesia del Roser, a fortified 13th c. church, in the 18th c. Its organ came from the Monastery of Santo Domingo in Palma.

Oratorio de la Consolación

5 km (3 miles) north of Santañy, reached on a cart track from Alquería Blanca, can be found the little 16th c. Oratorio de la Consolación, a pilgrimage chapel on a low hill to the east of Puig Gros (270 m (886 ft)). It has a 17th c. retablo (restored) of St Scholastica (Santa Escolástica). From the top of the hill there are fine views.

Monument commemorating the Catalan landing in 1229

Santa Ponsa: new holiday development around the bay

Santa Ponsa

Island: Majorca
Altitude: sea-level

The resort of Santa Ponsa lies in western Majorca on the penin-   Situation
sula which bounds the Bahía de Palma on the west.

The resort

This large holiday centre is still growing; its centre is grouped
around a well-protected, sandy bay.

On the rocky promontory of Sa Caleta, 2 km (1¼ miles) west   Sa Caleta
of the centre of Santa Ponsa, is a cross commemorating the
Catalan landing in 1229. On the base are reliefs depicting this
historic event.

Visitors to Santa Ponsa should not miss the drive up the hill   *La Cima
(signposted "A la Cima"), on a road which ends in a wide loop
through the complex of villas and apartment blocks, with
extensive panoramic views.

Costa de la Calma

On the steep slopes on the opposite (north-west) side of the
bay, above the Punta d'es Castell, is Costa de la Calma, a colony
of apartment blocks.

San Telmo (Sant Telm)

Island: Majorca
Altitude: sea-level

The former fishing village of San Telmo (Majorcan Sant Telm)   Situation
lies on the western tip of Majorca, opposite the Isla Dragonera.

The town

San Telmo, now a rising holiday resort, is situated in a small
rocky bay. There is a new development extending along the
bay to the north, but otherwise the village has not expanded
greatly beyond its original bounds. There are two small
beaches in the bay, separated by the Aquamarin Hotel. The
rocky parts of the coast are a good area for subaqua divers.
Offshore lies the rocky islet of Pantaleu, from which Jaime I
launched his victorious campaign for the reconquest of
Majorca, and beyond this the long Isla Dragonera (see entry).
On a steep crag to the south-east of the town are the ruins of the
Castillo de San Telmo (14th c.).

Selva

Island: Majorca
Altitude: 202 m (663 ft). Population: 3000

The Isla Dragonera, sheltering the bay of San Telmo

Selva, dominated by its church

Selva lies below the south-east side of the Sierra del Norte, 4 km (2½ miles) north of Inca.   Situation

The town

Standing above this trim little town and visible from some distance away is the Parish Church of San Lorenzo, originally built in the 14th c. and altered in the 19th. A stepped path flanked by cypresses leads up to the main doorway. On the High Altar can be seen a 14th c. figure of the Virgin. Church treasury.

S'Estanyol   E5

Island: **Majorca**
Altitude: sea-level

The simple little holiday resort of S'Estanyol lies on the south coast of Majorca, due south of Lluchmayor.   Situation

The resort

This small and in some respects antiquated development has an excellent boating harbour (with Club Náutico). There are good views of the southern tip of Majorca and of the opposite side of the bay, with Colonia Sant Jordi.
The beach is rocky, with only limited scope for bathing.

La Rápita

To the east is the resort of La Rápita, which is rather larger but, like S'Estanyol, is not ultra-modern and has few buildings higher than three storeys. Beyond the boating harbour stretches a beach of fine sand. The road to the east of the resort soon turns inland.
The beach of Arenal de la Rápita, to the east, extends to Ses Covetes.

Sineu   D6

Island: **Majorca**
Altitude: 144 m (472 ft)
Population: 4000

The old-world little country town of Sineu lies in the geographical centre of Majorca, 30 km (19 miles) east of Palma. Recognising the importance of its situation, Jaime II built a royal palace here.   Situation

The town

In Plaza de San Marcos, in the centre of the town, stands the Parish Church of Nuestra Señora de los Angeles (13th c., rebuilt in 16th c.), approached by a flight of steps.   Nuestra Señora de los Angeles

Sineu

Lion of Sineu

Outside the church is the famous winged lion of Sineu, the emblem of the town's patron, St Mark.

Above the side door of the church, in Plaza Catalina Thomás, is a sundial of 1783. The massive free-standing bell-tower is separated from the nave of the church by a narrow passage. Over the doorway of the tower, the vaulting of which has suffered badly from wind erosion, is a Baroque figure of St Barbara with her tower, also much weathered.

The passage beside the church leads to the Plaza de España (the name is partly obliterated – a sign of Balearic independence), with the beautiful, predominantly Gothic, main front of the parish church.

The church has a beautiful interior with Gothic vaulting; 15th c. altar-piece. In the sacristy is the church treasury.

Casa Consistorial

To the north of the parish church stands the Casa Consistorial (Town Hall), with a beautiful inner courtyard incorporating part of an old Franciscan friary. The Monastic Church of San Francisco dates from the 18th and 19th c.

Iglesia de la Concepción

West of the parish church, on rather higher ground, are the Church and Convent of the Concepción. On the tower of the church can be seen a handsome coat of arms. The church is aisleless and without transepts, but has two large side chapels. The entrance to the convent is in the building at right angles to the church on the left.

Art Gallery

The former railway station building now houses the "S'Estacio" Art Gallery.

In and around Sineu there are a number of old wine cellars (cellers) and windmills.

Sineu, Majorca's geographical centre

Near Sineu are the prehistoric sites of Son Creixell and Son Pere and the talayots of Sa Rixola and Sa Torre de Montornes.

Prehistoric sites

María de la Salud

The large village of María de la Salud (usually called simply María), north-east of Sineu, is dominated by its parish church (Virgen de la Salud).

Situation
6 km (3½ miles) NE

Sóller

C4

Island: **Majorca**
Altitude: 54 m (177 ft)
Population: 10,000

The prosperous little town of Sóller lies 35 km (22 miles) north of Palma on the seaward slopes of the Sierra del Norte.

Situation

**Coll de Sóller

Sóller can be reached from Palma either by car or by the charming old-fashioned railway which runs parallel to the road practically all the way.

Beyond Alfabia (see entry) where lies the entrance to the tunnel which is currently being constructed, the road climbs, with numerous sharp bends, to the wild and romantic Coll de Sóller, a pass at a height of 496 m (1627 ft). From the pass there are pleasant walks to the summer residences of Kings Jaime II and Sancho below the summit of Mount Teix (1062 m (3484 ft)) or to the Sierra de Alfabia to the north-east.

On the northern side of the pass there are fine views of the Valle de los Naranjos (Valley of Orange Trees) and the town of Sóller.

The town

Sóller nestles in the sheltered and fertile Valle de los Naranjos, enclosed by high hills, with plantations of citrus fruits extending to the outskirts of the town. Sóller claims to be the birthplace of Columbus.

In the centre of the town stands the Parish Church of San Bartolomé (originally 16th c.). There are a number of handsome 17th and 18th c. patrician houses.

Outside the town on the road to the Coll de Sóller (above) is the Convento de San Francisco, with a Baroque façade; it is now a school.

In the botanical garden on the road from Palma will be found the Natural History Museum (Museo Balear de Ciéncias Naturales; closed on Sun. afternoons and Mon.).

Museum

Puerto de Sóller

The charming little fishing village of Puerto Sóller lies in an almost exactly circular bay, sheltered on the north by the Mount de Santa Catalina (military area, closed to the public) and surrounded by hills. There is a good view of the village and

Situation
5 km (3 miles) N

*Village

169

Puerto de Sóller seen from the lighthouse

the harbour from the road which winds its way up the left-hand side of the bay to the lighthouse on Cap Gros.
Puerto de Sóller is connected with the town of Sóller by an old-fashioned tram (streetcar) system.

Lluch Alcari

Situation
10 km (6 miles) NW of Sóller

The hamlet of Lluch Alcari, reached from Sóller on the winding coast road (C710), was once a Moorish country estate. A number of artists have made their home here. The chapel has an altar-piece of 1688. There are three Moorish watch-towers in the area.

Son Servera   D8

Island: **Majorca**
Altitude: 92 m (302 ft). Population: 4000

Situation

Son Servera lies near the east end of Majorca, a little inland from the Bahía de Artá.

The town

This modest little town nestles at the foot of the Puig de Sa Font (272 m (892 ft)). The 18th c. Parish Church of San Juan Bautista has a Baroque retablo with a Virgin of the Rosary.
The bathing beaches on the nearby east coast are among the most popular on the island.

Valldemosa (Valldemossa)   C3

Island: **Majorca**
Altitude: 425 m (1395 ft). Population: 1500

The pleasant little hill town of Valldemosa, in the fertile valley of   Situation
that name, lies some 15 km (9 miles) north of Palma in the
Sierra del Norte.
It is a highly-regarded health resort and tourist centre.

**Valldemosa Monastery

The Charter House of Valldemosa (Cartuja de Jesús Nazareno)   **Open**:
was founded in 1399 on the site of a Moorish alcázar; the   daily 9.30 a.m.–1 p.m.
present monastic buildings date from the 17th and 18th c. It   and 3–6 p.m.
was here that Chopin spent the winter of 1838–39 with George
Sand, and here that he composed the "Raindrop Prelude" and   **Admission charge**
other works. George Sand wrote her account of their stay in
"A Winter in Majorca"; but not until 1842, so that it does not
reflect her immediate impressions. Apart from one or two passages the book is not particularly flattering to Majorca and its
inhabitants.

The church is a large and solid building. The main doorway,   Church
with a large round-headed arch, is now walled up; above it are
a rose-window and a Baroque pediment. In front of the west
front and the south side is a square shaded by plane-trees.
The church is entered by the doorway on the south side (tickets
for admission to church and monastery issued outside). On the

Valldemosa

171

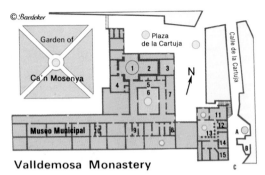

Valldemosa Monastery

MONASTERY	7 Monks' cloister	13 Cloister of the
1 Church	8 Prior's cell	Virgin
2 Monks' choir	9 Cell No. 2	14 Refectory
3 Lay brothers'	10 Cell No. 4	15 Tower
choir		
4 Sacristy	PALACE OF KING SANCHO	A Plant garden
5 Pharmacy	11 Church	B Old pharmacy
6 Myrtle Cloister	12 Porter's lodge	C Miranda balcony

right of the doorway is a coloured majolica panel with a representation of Catalina Thomás and the inscription in Majorcan
"Blessed Catalina Thomás, intercede for us". The interior,
aisleless, with short transepts, is very dark; the recently restored furnishings and ceiling-paintings in the crossing cupola
are High to Late Baroque. To the left of the chancel is the
sacristy, with richly embroidered vestments, missals, etc. In the
wall is a holy-water fountain (coloured marble inlay work; in
the centre the IHS monogram).

Monastic buildings

Passing through a doorway in the north transept, we come into
the picturesque but rather neglected cloister with its old trees
and, going parallel to the north wall of the nave, enter the
pharmacy, with a notable collection of old glass and majolica
drug-jars, artistically designed and painted. In the adjoining
room is a small souvenir shop.

Continuing through the cloister, we reach the monks' cells.
Notices on the walls (in English and other languages) explain
the function and furnishings of the various rooms and the main
provisions of the Rule of the Carthusian Order. The first cell to
be entered is that of the prior, the Celda Prioral, to which is
attached a small chapel with a polychrome wood figure of the
Virgin. In this chapel Gaspar Melchor de Jovellanos heard
Mass daily during his imprisonment in 1801 (commemorative
tablet). Here, too, is a small collection of mementoes of Majorca's own saint, Catalina Thomás, who was born in Valldemosa
(in a house in Calle Rectoría).

Beyond this is the Library, a picturesque vaulted room with
bookcases around the walls; in addition to the books, these
also house a collection of china and pottery. Note the fine ivory
triptych (on the wall to the right of the door into the garden) and
the picture of the marriage of Marie de Montpellier and Pedro
of Aragon (their son Jaime was later to win Majorca back from
the Moors).

Then follows the Audience Chamber, with many 17th and
18th c. pictures. In the centre of the room stands a showcase

The monastic pharmacy, Valldemosa

containing early prints and the prior's chair of office. The adjoining banqueting room was used only for official functions, as the monks normally ate in their cells. In the faithfully restored abbot's cell will be found a small collection of monastic utensils and equipment.

Visitors are also shown the cells occupied by Chopin and George Sand. These contain many mementoes of the couple, including the piano which – as George Sand relates in her book – was brought from France and hauled up to the monastery with immense difficulty. From the little walled garden outside the cells there is an enchanting view of the valley to the south.

The Municipal Museum is also housed in the monastery. Its most notable features are a large collection of relief plates used in printing and a rich store of material on the life and work of Archduke Ludwig Salvator, including his seven-volume work on the Balearics, a compendium which is still of value. There are also a number of oil-paintings of the Balearics, including some by Santiago Rusiñol.

Museo Municipal
(closed Sun.)

The nearest door leading out of the cloister is the entrance to the new Museum of Modern Art, on the upper floor. It contains works by classical modern and contemporary painters and graphic artists, including Miró, Picasso, Tàpies and Moore. There is also an extensive collection of works by the Majorcan artist Juli Ramis (1909–90).

Museum

Palacio del Rey Sancho

Leaving the cloister by a doorway beside the prior's cell, we come out into the square in front of the church. From here the

Open: daily 9.30 a.m.–1 p.m. and 3–6 p.m.

Valley of Valldemosa

second door on the right leads into the sumptuous Palace of King Sancho, a building redolent of the atmosphere of the past. The monastery originally developed out of the palace, which was built in the mid 14th c. The massive keep was added 200 years later to provide protection against the raids by corsairs which were becoming increasingly frequent.

The building surrounds a pretty little inner courtyard. Inside the building can be seen old furniture, paintings, engravings and etchings, with collections of porcelain and silver displayed in the wall-cupboards. On Mondays and Thursdays at 10.30 a.m. there are sometimes piano concerts and also folk-dancing.

San Bartolomé

To the east of the monastery, lower down, stands the Parish Church of San Bartolomé, which dates in its present form from the 15th c., with some later alterations. It contains a marble statue of Majorca's own saint, Catalina Thomás, and a number of pictures depicting scenes from her life.

Birthplace of Catalina Thomás

A few paces north of the parish church, immediately adjoining the presbytery (Rectoría), can be seen the house in which the Saint was born, now a place of prayer and devotion.

Son Moragues

To the west of the town, on the road to Puerto de Valldemosa (below), is the country house of Son Moragues, once the property of Archduke Ludwig Salvator. The house is at present undergoing restoration.

Puerto de Valldemosa

An excursion to Puerto de Valldemosa is highly recommended to visitors to Valldemosa – provided that they are not worried about driving on narrow and winding single-track mountain roads. The road descends, with many sharp bends and magnificent views, passing the country house of Son Mas, to the little fishing village at the foot of steep wooded slopes. Here there are no facilities for tourists. The water is incredibly clear and there is a small beach of coarse shingle.

Situation
7 km (4½ miles) NW

**Scenery

Villafranca de Bonany   D6

Island: **Majorca**
Altitude: 97 m (318 ft)
Population: 3000

The village of Villafranca de Bonany lies in the Llanura del Centro, on the main road from Palma to Manacor.

Situation

The village

This trim and friendly little place grew up in the 17th c. on the site of a number of country houses, some of them of Moorish origin. The Parish Church of Santa Bárbara dates from the 17th c. but was altered in the 19th. The village takes its name from the Ermita Nuestra Señora de Bon Any (see entry), the pilgrimage chapel on a hill to the north. From here the chapel can be reached only on foot; by road it is reached from Petrá (see entry).

Practical Information

It is not always possible to give addresses and/or telephone numbers for all places listed in the Practical Information Section of these guides. This information is readily obtainable from hotel reception desks or from the local tourist office.

Accommodation

See Hotels

See Vacation Apartments

See Youth Hostels

Airlines

Scheduled services between Britain and Majorca are provided by Iberia and British Airways. Services between North America and Majorca are provided by Iberia and American Airlines.

Iberia

11–12 Haymarket
London SW1 Y4BP;
tel. (071) 830 0011

United Kingdom

Room 2, Level 5
Manchester Airport
Wythenshawe
Manchester M22 5PJ;
tel. (061) 436 6444

509 Madison Avenue
Ground Floor NY 10022;
tel. (212) 644 8830

United States

Boulevard Towers South
205 North Michigan Avenue
Chicago IL 60601;
tel. (312) 819 2900

150 SE Second Avenue
Miami FL 33131;
tel. (305) 358 8800

2020 University Street
Suite 1310
Montreal H3A 2A5;
tel. (514) 849 3352

Canada

Airport

Majorca

Iberia

Paseo del Borne 10
Palma de Mallorca;
tel. (971) 71 01 40, 72 29 43

Calle Juan March Ordinas 12
Palma de Mallorca;
tel. (971) 75 01 67 and 75 01 84

Son San Juan Airport
Palma de Mallorca;
tel. (971) 26 26 47, ext. 1229

Aviaco

Calle del Conquistador 18
Palma de Mallorca;
tel. (971) 26 02 72

British Airways

Son San Juan Airport
Palma de Mallorca;
tel. (971) 26 16 91, ext. 1162

American Airlines

Son San Juan Airport
Palma de Mallorca;
tel. (971) 29 34 94, ext. 1129

Minorca

Aviaco

Mahón Airport
Mahón
tel. (971) 36 56 73/74 (reservations)
and 36 15 77 (information)

Airport

Palma de Mallorca Airport is situated 11km (7 miles) south-east of Palma de Mallorca.

Information

Tel. 26 46 28, 26 46 66, ext. 133/6

Taxi service

A 24-hour taxi service is available at the airport. Journey time to the city centre is approximately 20 minutes.

Bus service

A bus service is available from the airport to Palma, Plaza de España, approximately every 30 minutes from 7 a.m. until midnight. Journey time is approximately 30 minutes.

Car rental

Open daily 7.30 a.m. to midnight:
Atesa, tel. 26 61 04, 26 61 00
Avis, tel. 26 09 10/1; telex 6 91 85
Europcar, tel. 26 38 11; telex 6 90 91
Hertz, tel. 26 08 09; telex 6 92 63

Open daily 8 a.m. to 11 p.m.:
InterRent, tel. 26 61 00
The car rental desks are situated on the ground floor of Terminal A.

Art Galleries

See Museums

Banks

Banks are generally open Mon.–Thur. 8.30 a.m.–4.30 p.m., Fri. 8.30 a.m.–2 p.m., Sat. 8.30 a.m.–1 p.m. From June to September Mon.–Fri. 8.30 a.m.–2 p.m., Sat. closed.

Bicycle and motorcycle rental (alquiler)

The relatively short distances on the Balearics make cycling an agreeable way of seeing the country. Bicycles, scooters and light motorcycles can be rented in all tourist resorts.

Boating harbours and anchorages

NAME	SITUATION	FEATURES	FACILITIES
		Majorca	
Arenal	E side of Palma Bay	Boating harbour	Club Náutico; lift; fuel; hotels
Bonaire	NE coast	Boating harbour	Resort development
Cala Bona	NE coast	Harbour for small boats	Water; hotels
Cala Calobra	NW coast	Long rocky inlet at mouth of Torrent de Parais; sandy anchorage; often considerable swell; small jetty in front of restaurant	Hotel; restaurants
Cala Codolar	NW coast	Small rocky creek	No supplies
Cala Deya	NW coast	Fairly sheltered anchorage	Village of Deya above anchorage
Cala d'Or	NW coast	Yacht harbour; good long-term moorings	Club Náutico, slip; lift supplies
Cala Estancia	E side of Palma Bay	Boating harbour	Bathing facilities; hotels
Cala Figuera	SE coast	Small sheltered harbour with short breakwater; fishing-boats; cliffs	Water; provisions above harbour
Cala Gamba	E side of Palma Bay	Boating harbour	Club Náutico; hotels
Cala Millor	NE coast	Harbour for small boats	Hotels
Cala Murta	N tip	Quiet anchorage, open to E and SE	No supplies
Cala Pi	N	Anchorage in lee of Isla Formentor	Formentor Hotel
Cala Pi	S coast	Quiet anchorage; cliffs	Hotels
Cala Ratjada	NE tip	Sheltered harbour with high breakwater	Water; fuel; slip; boatyard; restaurants; hotels
Cala Santafly	SE coast	Beautiful anchorage; many small boats	Hotels
Cala Santa Ponsa	SW coast	Sheltered anchorage	Club Náutico; hotels
Cala San Vicente	N coast	Open to NE; stony bottom	Bathing facilities; hotels
Cala Tuent	NW coast	Fairly sheltered; fishing-boats	Holiday development

Boating harbours and anchorages

NAME	SITUATION	FEATURES	FACILITIES
Ca'n Pastilla	E side of Palma Bay	Boating harbour	Holiday development
Ca'n Picafort	NE coast	Boating harbour	Holiday development
Isla Dragonera	W tip	Island fringed by cliffs; three *calas* in SE	No supplies
Isla Ravena	Centre of Alcudia Bay	Holiday development (not an island) boating harbour	Club Náutico
Molinar	E side of Palma Bay	Boating harbour	Club Marítimo; hotels
Palma	SW coast (Palma Bay)	Yacht harbour immediately below old town; moorings on Paseo Marítimo Porto Pi marina, SW of El Terreno distict	Club Real Náutico; Club de Mar; slip; winch; boatyard and all supplies
Palma Nova	W side of Palma Bay	Yacht harbour	Club Náutico; winch; hotels
Portixol	E of Palma	Boating harbour	Club Náutico; hotels
Port Nou	NE coast	Harbour for small boats	Bathing facilities; hotels
Porto Colóm	E coast	Sheltered fishing and boating harbour	Club Náutico; water, fuel
Porto Cristo	E coast	Sheltered fishing harbour in a rocky river valley; jetty	Club Náutico; boatyard slip; winch; restaurants
Porto Petro	SE coast	Small sheltered fishing harbour with angled breakwater; moorings; yachts anchor in Cala	Water; provisions
Port Vey	NE coast	Harbour for small boats	Bathing facilities; hotels
Puerto Alcudia	N	Quiet harbour; not particularly attractive moorings on fishing pier; outer pier reserved for ferries and cargo ships	Water; fuel; provisions; restaurants
Puerto Andraitx	SW tip	Fine fishing and yacht harbour with three piers; moorings on N side (Club de Vela), also for short periods on fishing quay; best anchorage for yachts in centre of harbour	Club Náutico; slip boatyard; water; fuel, provisions; restaurants
Puerto Campos	S tip	Small fishing and boating harbour	Loading of salt
Puerto Pollensa	N	Majorca's principal yacht harbour after Palma; good jetty; moorings always difficult to get	Club Náutico; water and power on piers; boatyard, slip, boat supplies; provisions; fuel at Pollensa (7 km/4½ miles SW)
Puerto Sóller	NW coast	Completely sheltered bay; quiet inner harbour (fishing boats); some moorings on angled breakwater; naval vessels on N side	Boatyard, slip, fuel; provisions; water on naval quay
La Rápita	S coast	Boating harbour	Club Náutico; winch; lift; hotels
Sa Foradada	NW coast	High natural breakwater (hole half-way up) with two fairly sheltered coves; secluded	No supplies
San Telmo	W tip	Anchorage between village and islet of Pantaleu	Off tourist track
S'Estanyol	S coast	Jetty	Club Náutico; water; hotels
Minorca			
Cala Addaya	NE coast	Lonely fjord, completely sheltered	Boating harbour
Cala Alcaufar	SE coast	Beautiful anchorage, open to E	Holiday village

NAME	SITUATION	FEATURES	FACILITIES
Cala Arenal d'en Castell	NE coast	Spacious anchorage	Bathing facilities
Cala Binibeca	S tip	Harbour for small boats	Club Náutico; bathing facilities; holiday village
Cala Bosch	SW tip	Boating harbour	Holiday development
Cala Canutells	SE coast	Inner part of cove, very beautiful, but shallow	Holiday village
Cala Coves	SE coast	Plenty of room in outer part; romantic backwater in right-hand arm	Spring of fresh water at head of inlet
Cala Galdana	S coast	Beautiful sheltered anchorage; limestone cliffs	Good sandy beach; hotels
Cala Grao	E coast	Large completely sheltered anchorage	Fishing village
Cala Macarella	S coast	Spacious, fairly open	No supplies
Cala Moli	NE coast	Spacious; cliffs; rocky islets out to sea	Addaya holiday development
Cala Morell	NW coast	Fairly sheltered anchorage	Holiday development
Cala'n Porter	S coast	Spacious anchorage; steep coast (built on), with Bronze Age caves	Bathing facilities; hotels, cave bar
Cala Pregonda	N coast	Beautiful anchorage open to N	No supplies
Cala Pudent	NE coast	Secluded and unfrequented anchorage	No supplies
Cala Rafalet	SE coast	Anchorage in a picturesque rocky setting	No supplies
Cala Santandria	W coast	Inlet in low cliffs	Bathing facilities
Cala Son Saura	S coast	Spacious and lonely bay	No supplies
Cala Turqueta	S coast	Beautiful anchorage	Holiday development
Ciudadela	W coast	The island's second most important port; sheltered natural harbour at the end of a long fjord; on the N side quays for cargo ships and ferries; many fishing boats; moorings on S side. Beware of sudden changes in water-level (with currents); about 3 times weekly, with WS wind, variations of 50–75 cm (20–30 inches), every 10 minutes	Club Náutico; slip; water, provisions; town immediately above the harbour; bathing beaches to NW and SE
Isla Aire	S tip	Bare island with lighthouse; concrete pier in NW cove	No supplies
Isla Colóm	E coast	Anchorage at Los Llanes, on NW side of island (little shelter)	No supplies
Mahón	SE coast	The island's principal port at the end of a much ramified fjord 5 km/3 miles long with forts on both sides, the large Lazareto Island and two small islets; an ideal natural harbour much fought over in the past; quay for cargo ships and ferries immediately under the old town, with naval installations on opposite side, to N; moorings 1 km/¾ mile seaward	Club Náutico; water, fuel; boatyards, slip
Puerto Fornells	N coast	The island's third largest port; a long, spacious inlet; beautiful natural harbour, with anchorages; busy fishing harbour, shallow, with long breakwater (yachts at outer end)	Water; provisions; restaurants
Puerto Nitja	N coast	Anchorage (no harbour) in W bay beyond the long Cabo Caballeria Peninsula; inner part sheltered, but shallow	No supplies

Boat Trips

NAME	SITUATION	FEATURES	FACILITIES
Cala Ganduf Cala Olla Puerto Cabrera	NW side E side W side	**Cabrera** Secluded anchorage off Cabo Azul Secluded anchorage Sheltered natural harbour; anchoring permitted; pier for regular service vessels only	No supplies No supplies No supplies

Boat Trips

Majorca

From Palma	to Portals Vells to Magalluf to San Telmo (Sats. for English, Mons. for Dutch) to San Telmo and Puerto de Andraitx (Suns.) through Palma Bay
	There are also excursions from Palma to Ibiza and cruises round Majorca.
From Puerto de Alcudia	to Formentor
From Puerto Andraitx	to San Telmo and to the Isla Dragonera
From El Arenal	to Marineland (Palma Nova, with visit to dolphinarium) to Portals Vells through Palma Bay
From Cala d'Or	to beaches in surrounding area (Cala Figuera, Porto Petro)
From Cala Millor	to Cala Ratjada to Cañamel to Porto Cristo
From Cala Ratjada	to beaches in surrounding area to Cala Millor to Cañamel to Porto Cristo
From Ca'n Picafort	to Cabo de Menorca (north side of Bahía de Alcudia) to Cabo Farrutx
From Cañamel	to surrounding beaches to Cala Millor to Cala Ratjada to Porto Cristo
From Colonia de Sant Jordi	to Cabrera (once a week)
From Magalluf	to Palma Nova and Portals Vells via Palma Nova and Portals Vells to Cala Figuera to Palma Nova and Palma de Mallorca through Palma Bay
From Paguera	through Paguera Bay
From Porto Colom	to Cala Figuera and Cala d'Or
From Puerto Pollensa	to Cabo Formentor to Formentor to Pollensa Bay

to beaches in surrounding area	From Porto Cristo
to Cala Millor	
to Cala Ratjada	
to Cala Varques	
to Cabo Pinar	From Puerto Alcúdia
to Cala Tuent	From Puerto de Sóller
to the Cala de la Calobra and to the Torrente de Pareis	
to Sa Foredada	
to the Cala de Deya	
to Puerto de Valldemosa	
to San Telmo	
to Isla Dragonera	From San Telmo

Minorca

along the harbour inlet and to the Isla del Rey and the Isla del Lazaretto	From Es Castell (south-east of Mahón)
to beaches at southern end of west coast	From Ciudadela
to beaches on south coast (boats also available for rental)	From Cala Galdana
Since timetables are liable to change, departure times should be checked in advance. Detailed information on the current excursion programme can be obtained from regional and local information offices (see Information) and from hotel reception desks.	N.B.
See entry	Excursions

Camping and Caravanning

Top category site. Open all year. Platja Blava, at km 8 between Alcudia to Arta. Bookings (971) 203861.
There are very few official camp sites on Majorca – at Muro and at Colonia de San Pedro, both on Alcudia Bay. There is one site at Son Bou on the south coast of Minorca. Under Spanish regulations camping is only allowed for one night in any one place apart from an official camp site and, therefore, there is little point in planning an extended camping holiday. It should also be borne in mind that the roads on the islands, apart from the main trunk roads, are mostly very narrow, with many bends in the hilly regions, and will often not be negotiable by trailer caravans or motor caravans any bigger than the Volkswagen Microbus.

Car ferries

See Getting to Majorca/Minorca
See Inter-island transport

Car Rental (Coches de alquiler)

Majorca

Calle Vicealmirante Moreno 50   Avis
Alcudia; tel. (971) 54 54 68

183

Avenida Casino
Puerto de Alcudia;
tel. (971) 89 19 12

Calle Maria Antonio Salva 14
El Arenal;
tel. (971) 26 62 25

Avenida Fernando Terrago 9
Cala d'Or;
tel. (971) 65 75 69

Son Corp
Cala Millor;
tel. (971) 58 58 69

Calle Leonor Servera 19
Cala Ratjada;
tel. (971) 56 56 38

Avenida Notario Alemany
Magalluf;
tel. (971) 68 07 88

Avenida Paguera 36
Paguera;
tel. (971) 68 78 10

Paseo Marítimo 16
Palma de Mallorca;
tel. (971) 23 07 20

Avenida Joan Miró 326
(in the western part of San Agustin district)
Palma de Mallorca;
tel. (971) 79 00 00

Aeropuerto Son San Juan
Palma de Mallorca;
tel. (971) 26 09 10

Avenida Joan XXIII 80
Puerto Pollensa;
tel. (971) 53 13 94

Calle Ramón de Moncala 20
Santa Ponsa;
tel. (971) 69 29 32

Beta Cars

Paseo Marítimo 20
Palma de Mallorca;
tel. (971) 45 52 00 and 45 24 62

Budget

Calle de Manacor 40
Palma de Mallorca;
tel. (971) 77 07 00

europcar

Paseo Marítimo 19
Palma de Mallorca;
tel. (971) 45 48 00

Aeropuerto Son San Juan
Palma de Mallorca;
tel. (971) 26 38 11

Paseo Marítimo 62
Puerto de Alcudia;
tel. (971) 54 59 22

c/o Viatges Arenal
Calle Amilcar 6
El Arenal;
tel. (971) 26 66 73

Calle Antonio Costa 7
Cala d'Or;
tel. (971) 64 33 16

Urbanización Son Bon Temps
Cala Millor;
tel. (971) 23 47 37

Calle Pedro Vaquer Ramis 2
Magalluf;
tel. (971) 23 47 37

Paseo Marítimo 13
Palma de Mallorca;
tel. (971) 23 47 37

Aeropuerto Son San Juan
Palma de Mallorca;
tel. (971) 26 08 09

Hertz

Minorca

Plaza Ses Palmeres
Arenal d'en Castell
tel. (971) 37 98 59

Urbanisación La Serpentona
Cala Galdana;
tel. (971) 38 11 74 (May–Oct. only)

c/o Hotel Delfines
Cala'n Blanes (near Ciudadela)
tel. (971) 38 41 88;
(end of Mar.–end of Oct. only)

El Lago
Cala'n Bosch (south of Ciudadela)
tel. (971) 38 50 03;
(end of Mar.–end of Oct. only)

Paseo Marítimo 1
Cala'n Porter (west of Mahón)
tel. (971) 37 71 21;
(end of Mar.–end of Oct. only)

Calle Conquistador 81
Ciudadela;
tel. (971) 38 11 74 (Apr.–Sept. only)

Avis

	Aeropuerto Mahón; tel. (971) 36 15 76
	Plaza Explanada 53 Mahón; tel. (971) 36 47 78
Beta Cars	Plaza Explanada 8 Mahón; tel. (971) 36 06 20/21
Budget	Avenida de Ronda Mahón; tel. (971) 36 15 08
europcar	Aeropuerto Mahón; tel. (971) 36 64 00
	Plaza Explanada 8 Mahón; tel. (971) 36 06 20/21
Hertz	Aeropuerto Mahón; tel. (971) 36 48 81
	Carrer Gran 42 Villacarlos; tel. (971) 36 48 81

Formentera

Avis	Puerto de la Sabina La Sabina; tel. (971) 32 21 23
europcar	Puerto de la Sabina La Sabina; tel. (971) 32 20 31
Hertz	Calle Jaime I San Francisco Javier; tel. (971) 32 22 84
	Muelle de la Sabina La Sabina; tel. (971) 32 22 23
	Avenida del Mar Es Pujols; tel. (971) 32 80 94

There are also many smaller car rental firms which frequently work in association with the large hotels and offer special terms for guests.
Credit cards are generally accepted.

Currency

The unit of currency is the Spanish peseta (pta).

There are banknotes for 1000, 2000, 5000 and 10,000 pesetas and coins in denominations of 1, 5, 10, 25, 50, 100, 200 and 500 pesetas.

Exchange rates are subject to fluctuation. Current rates can be found in the national press, or obtained from banks and tourist offices.

Exchange rates

There are no restrictions on the import of currency, but sums in excess of the equivalent of 500,000 pesetas in foreign currency should be declared on arrival. Visitors may take out a maximum of 100,000 pesetas and foreign currency up to the amount declared on entry.

Currency regulations

It is advisable to take Eurocheques or travellers' cheques rather than large amounts of cash.

Account holders of the British National Girobank, with Postcheques and a special card, can draw the equivalent of £65 at a time from Spanish post offices.

Girobank

The large hotels and better-class restaurants, car rental firms, airlines and shops usually accept the major charge and credit cards (American Express, Diners Club, Access, Eurocard, Visa, etc.).

Credit cards

Customs regulations (Reglamentos de aduanas)

As from January 1st 1993 no duty has been payable on goods passing between EU (formerly EC) member states, although maximum limits have been fixed for private individuals; details can be obtained from the customs offices. A passport is still required.

European Union

Visitors from a non-EU country may take in free of duty 200 cigarettes or 100 cigarillos or 50 cigars or 50 gr. tobacco, as well as 2 litres of wine and 1 litre of spirits above 22° proof or 2 litres below 22° proof.

Entry

Personal effects brought in must be taken out again.

Exit

On return to the UK goods bought in an EU country (i.e. including Spain) will be allowed in free of duty. Goods purchased in duty-free shops are subject to the same maximum limits as those from non-EU countries.

Diplomatic and Consular offices (Embajadas y Consulados)

Embassies

Calle de Fernando el Santon 16
Madrid;
tel. (91) 4 19 02 00

United Kingdom

Calle Serrano 75
Madrid;
tel. (91) 2 76 34 00

United States

Edificia Goya
Calle Núñez de Balboa 35
Madrid;
tel. (91) 4 31 43 00

Canada

Consulates

United Kingdom

Plaza Mayor 3
Palma de Mallorca;
tel. (971) 21 24 45

Calle Torret 28
San Luis
Menorca;
tel. (971) 36 64 39

Vice-Consulate

United States

Avda Rey Jaime III 26
Palma de Mallorca;
tel. (971) 72 26 60

Electricity

The standard electricity supply is at 220 or 225 volts AC, 50 cycles, but in a few places the voltage is 110 or 125 (plugs are two-pin).

Emergencies (Servicios de Urgencias)

Majorca

In Palma

Police (emergency calls): 091
Policia Municipal: 28 06 06
Guardia Civil: 46 51 12

Tourist Attention

Visitors who, for example, have their vehicles stolen or are involved in an accident while on holiday during the summer months can seek assistance from "Tourist Attention".

Tourist Attention
Calle Jaime III 10
Palma de Mallorca
Business hours:
Mon.–Fri. 9 a.m.–2.30 p.m. and 3–8 p.m.
Sat. 9 a.m.–1 p.m.
tel. (971) 71 22 16

Minorca

Throughout the island

Police: 091

Events

Majorca

5 January

Palma: Reyes Magos (Santos Reyes; Epiphany); ceremonial entry of the three Kings (with fireworks, ships' sirens; presents given to children).

9 January

Campos del Puerto: San Julián; church festival and fair.

16 January

Algaida: San Honorato; church festival, bonfires.

La Puebla, Lluchmayor, Manacor and Artá: San Antonio Abad (celebrated since 1365); St Anthony's fires (*foguerons*), folk music (*cançoners del camp*), masked dances (*colla de demonis*), blessing of domestic animals.	16–17 January
Palma and Muro: San Antonio Abad; St Anthony's Ride, prizes for best decorated animals.	17 January
Pollensa: San Sebastián; dances (Cavallets; l'Estandart, with the Saint as a Roman standard-bearer), collections for charity (*taules* = tables for feeding the poor).	20 January
Algaida: San Honorato; pilgrimage to chapel (consecrated on 16 January 1398) on Puig de Randa; bonfires.	21 January
Campos del Puerto: San Blas; pilgrimage to hermitage.	3 February
Oratorio de la Consolación: Santa Escolástica; rain festival, blessing of crops.	10 February
Alayor: Santa Eulalia; Saint's feast day.	12 February
Many places: San José; Saint's feast day.	18 March
San Juan: Pá i es Peix; festival in Chapel of Nuestra Señora de la Consolación.	23 March
Many places: processions on Maundy Thursday and Good Friday.	Holy Week (Semana Santa)
Pollensa and Sineu: Devallament, procession bearing Cross from Calvary to Church of Nuestra Señora de los Angeles; torchlight procession, traditional costumes.	Good Friday
Algaida: Nuestra Señora de la Paz; pilgrimage to Santuario de Castellitx. Campanet: San Miguel; procession of Santo Cristo from the chapel at the caves to Campanet and back. Lloseta: Romería del Cocó; pilgrimage in honour of the Black Virgin found here in 1233. Montuiri: Romería to Santuario de San Miguel. La Puebla: pilgrimage to chapel at Creteix.	Week after Easter
Many places: San Jorge (St George); patronal festival.	23 April
Algaida: pilgrimage to Santuario de Nuestra Señora de la Cura on Puig de Randa; blessing of crops.	End of April
Sineu: May Festival. Sancelles: May Festival.	Beginning of May
Selva: Invention (Finding) of the Cross, folk groups.	3 May
Sóller: Nuestra Señora de la Victoria; ceremonies commemorating victory over Moorish pirates on 11 May 1561; pageant play, "Moros y Cristianos".	Mid May
Manacor: Feria de Muestras; trade fair (industrial goods, furniture) and Spring Festival; sporting and folk events.	Mid to end of May

Events

Corpus Christi	Pollensa: Fiesta del Corpus; dances of the "Aguiles" ("Eagles", emblem of the Weavers' Guild), religious procession, collection for charity (*taules*).
23–24 June	Muro: San Juan (celebrated since 14th c.); on previous Sunday invitations issued by *caixers*; pilgrimage to hermitage, equestrian games, folk events, popular fiesta; end of the traditional peasant year.
29 June	Andraitx and Alcudia: San Pedro; procession of boats in harbour.
End of June	Palma: Feria oficial de Muestrass, Artesania y Turismo (trade fair; industrial products, craft articles, tourism).
15–16 July	Puerto de Sóller, Puerto de Andraitx, Cala Figuera and La Rápita: Virgen del Carmen; processions of decorated boats, sporting contests, popular entertainments, dancing.
21 July	Petrá: Santa Praxedis; patronal festival, demon dances.
25 July	Alcudia, Manacor, La Puebla, Sóller and Calviá: Santiago (St James, Spain's national saint); great fiestas, bullfights, folk dances, fireworks.
26 July (every 3 years)	Valldemosa: Santa Catalina Thomás (the popular Majorcan saint from Valldemosa); triumphal cars, scenes from the Saint's life.
30 July	Inca: Santos Abdón y Senén; popular fiesta, bullfighting.
First Sunday in August	Pollensa (on 2 August) and Petrá: Virgen de los Angeles; historical procession by children (Juan Mas, who beat off a pirate raid); pageant play, "Moros y Cristianos".
4 August	Palma: Santa Catalina Thomás (canonisation); cavalcade, with singing angels.
Sundays in August	Pollensa: Festival Internacional de Música; concerts in cloister of Santo Domingo; Lorenzo Cerdá music prize.
10 August	Lluchmayor: San Cándido; folk performances.
10–12 August	Muro: San Lorenzo; processions.
14 August	Cala Ratjada: regatta; beauty competition.
14–16 August	Capdepera: San Roque; patronal festival.
15 August	Many places: Ascension; church ceremonies.
24 August	Sóller, Consell and Montuiri: San Bartolomé; patronal festival; cavalcades. Ses Salines: folk performances, amateur drama, beauty competition, dancing.
Last week in August	Felanitx: San Agustín; exhibitions, international painting and photographic competitions, dances.
8 September	Alaró: Navidad de Nuestra Señora (Nativity of the Virgin), pilgrimage to Castillo de Alaró. Bañalbufar: water sports, folk events, dancing. Fornalutx: folk events, concerts. Galilea: singing contest.
11 September	Everywhere: Catalan National Day.
28 September	Binisalem: Vintage Festival.
12 October	Many places: Dia de la Hispanidad (Day of the Spanish Nation).

Many places, particularly Campos del Puerto, Santañy, Porreras and Inca: ferias and fiestas; church festivals and popular celebrations. Lluchmayor: Agricultural Show.	Second half of October
San Juan de la Font Santa: Butifarró Sausage Festival (sausages cooked on open fires).	30 October
Many places: Todos los Santos (All Saints).	1 November
Inca: Dijous Bó (Good Thursday); agricultural show and great fair.	Mid November
Junipero Serra (anniversary of his birth).	24 November
Many places: Inmaculada Concepción (Immaculate Conception); church festival.	8 December
Capdepera, Sineu and Santañy: local fiestas.	December
Lluch Monastery and all churches: Nochebuena (Christmas Eve) or Navidad (Christmas); church services. (Presents are not given at Christmas but at Epiphany.)	24 December
Palma: Fiesta de la Conquista (commemorating Jaime I's conquest of Majorca in 1229); celebratory service in cathedral.	31 December

Minorca

Ciudadela: conquest of Minorca by Alfonso III in 1267.	17 January
Many places: San José; patronal festival.	19 March
Many places: Semana Santa (processions on Maundy Thursday and Good Friday).	Holy Week
Many places: San Jorge (St George); patronal festival.	23 April
Mahón: Virgen del Carmen; processions of decorated boats, sporting contests, popular entertainments, dancing.	15–16 June
Ciudadela: San Juan (celebrated since 14th c.); on previous Sunday invitations issued by *caixers*; equestrian games, folk events, popular fiesta; end of traditional peasant year.	23–24 June
Alayor: San Lorenzo; Festival of Minorcan Song; parades.	10–12 August
Ferrerias: San Bartolomé; patronal festival; cavalcades.	24 August
Mahón: Nuestra Señora de Gracia; patronal festival.	1–9 September
Everywhere: Catalan National Day.	11 September
Many places: ferias and fiestas; church and popular festival.	Second half of October
Many places: Todos los Santos (All Saints).	1 November
Many places: Inmaculada Concepción (Immaculate Conception); church festival.	8 December
All churches: Nochebuena (Christmas Eve) or Navidad (Christmas); church services. (Presents are not given at Christmas but at Epiphany.)	24 December

Excursions

Many local coach firms on Majorca and Minorca run tours of the islands and other coach excursions, which enable visitors to see the main sights without the necessity of hiring a car. Some of the excursions also include short boat trips.

Information about excursions can be obtained from local tourist information offices.

Boat trips

See entry

Ferries

See Boat trips

See Getting to Majorca/Minorca

Food and Drink

Local specialities

One great speciality of the Balearics is the *ensaimada*, a spirally shaped flaky pastry made from yeast dough and lard (*saim*) which may range from the breakfast size, as big as a man's hand, to great cartwheels. They may also be stuffed.

The *sobrasada* is a highly spiced red pork sausage, which may be eaten fried on an *ensaimada* or, with honey (in Majorcan *amb mel*), on a large roll; the latter practice is probably of Arab origin. Another kind of sausage is the *butifarrón*.

Tumbet is a stew of potatoes, aubergines, peppers and pumpkin with the addition of tomato purée. It is cooked and served in a pottery casserole, the *greixonera*, which has given its name to a number of characteristic Balearic dishes, such as *greixonera de peix* (a fish soup which is particularly popular on Minorca), *greixonera d'auberginies* (aubergines cooked in the oven or under the grill), *greixonera de frare* (a stew of vegetables, minced meat and sausages), *greixonera de peus de porc* (pigs' trotters with cheese and breadcrumbs) and *greixonera d'anguila* (a tasty eel stew).

Even quite simple peasant dishes can be very appetising, such as *pa amb oli* (bread dipped in oil, and in a more refined version eaten with tomatoes and ham) or *trempó*, a refreshing salad of tomatoes, green peppers, onions, apples, pears and wild purslane, which country people eat at their second breakfast (*berenda*).

Two special Christmas dishes are *escaldums de pollastre*, a chicken fricassée, and *salsa de nadal*, a sauce made with almonds, honey, egg, pepper and cinnamon.

Among the commonest desserts, in addition to *ensaimadas*, are *flaó* (Spanish *flan*), a sweet pudding, *menjar blanc*, a milk-based dish, and the pastries known as *coques* and *rosquilies*. In the coastal towns and villages there are usually several tasty fish dishes on the menu, as well as prawns (*gambas*), squid (*calamar*) and sometimes lobsters (*langostas*). Since fish are not particularly abundant in Balearic waters, fish dishes may be somewhat expensive and will not often be included in the set menus of hotels offering half or full board.

Bars

It was formerly the practice in bars, tavernas and bodegas (originally wine-merchants' establishments, now mainly drinking-places; in the Balearics also called *cellers*) to serve with drinks the small bits and pieces known as *tapas* ("lids", since the plate on which they were served covered the wineglass). These appetisers are now usually charged separately and can sometimes cost more than a cooked meal.

While in mainland Spain the cafés are mainly patronised by men who conduct their business affairs there, the pavement cafés in the Balearic holiday resorts cater largely for tourists, with correspondingly higher prices during the holiday season. *Café solo* is black espresso coffee, *café con leche* white coffee. As an accompaniment to their coffee visitors may care to try *hierba*, a herb liqueur which may be either *dulce* (sweet) or *seca* (dry), or *palo*, a dark-brown liqueur made from carobs, which on Minorca is drunk with the excellent local gin. A popular and refreshing drink is *horchata*, made from almonds, lemonade and iced water.

Cafés

Since some visitors may find Spanish cuisine, with its abundant use of olive oil, rather heavy on the digestion, it is advisable to do as the Spaniards do and accompany the meal with wine, which may be diluted if desired with water or mineral water (*agua mineral; con gas*, carbonated; *sin gas*, still). Excellent local wine (Spanish *vino del pais*; Majorcan and Minorcan *vino pagés*) is produced at Felanitx and Binisalem, but is now seldom to be found.

A very popular drink is *sangría*, a refreshing mixture of red wine, brandy, mineral water, orange and lemon juice with fruit and ice cubes. Every bar has its own recipe, and according to the nature and proportions of the ingredients the effect can range from agreeable to fiendish – particularly since sangría tends to be consumed faster than wine by itself.

See entry

Restaurants

Getting to Majorca

Most visitors to the Balearics go by air. There are direct flights by Iberia, the Spanish national airline, from London and Manchester to Palma (Majorca) and from London to Mahón (Minorca). Iberia also flies from New York, Chicago, Los Angeles, Miami and Montreal to Palma. Alternatively it is possible to fly to Barcelona and get a local flight from there.

By air

There are also numerous package holidays using charter flights. For Majorca these are available practically throughout the year; for Minorca the holiday season tends to be concentrated in the summer.

An alternative means of transport is provided by the car ferries linking the Balearics with the mainland. There are car ferries to Palma de Mallorca from Barcelona and Valencia in Spain, Sète in France, and to Mahón (Minorca) from Barcelona.

By sea
(car ferries)

All the ferries from mainland Spain and most of those from France and Italy are run by the Spanish line Compañía Trasmediterranea.

Agents in the United Kingdom:

Compañía
Trasmediterranea

Southern Ferries Ltd
179 Piccadilly
London LW1V 9DB;
tel. (071) 491 4968

Information and reservations on Majorca:

Compañía Transmediterranea
Muelle Viejo 5
Palma de Mallorca;
tel. (971) 40 50 14

Golf courses

Majorca	Son Vida Club de Golf in Son Vida (Palma area) 18 holes
	Real Golf de Bendinat Urbanización Bendinat Calviá (Palma area) 9 holes
	Golf Poniente between Calviá and Magalluf 18 holes
	Golf Santa Ponça in Santa Ponsa 18 holes
	Golf Pollensa in Pollensa 18 holes
	Club de Golf Son Servera Urbanización Costa de los Pinos (near Son Servera) 9 holes
	Vall d'Or Club de Golf in Cala d'Or 9 holes
Minorca	Club de Golf Son Parc near Mercadel 9 holes
Information	Federación Balear de Golf Avenida Jaime III 17 Palma de Mallorca; tel. (971) 72 27 53

Hotels (Hoteles)

Spanish hotels are officially classed according to function and quality in various categories: *hoteles* (singular *hotel*, accommodation with or without meals, own restaurant); *hotelos-apartamentos* (like *hoteles*, but with apartments or bungalows only); *hostales* (singular *hostal*, more modest establishments with or without meals); and *pensiones* (singular *pensión*, guest-houses, smaller, full board only).
Hotels, apartment hotels and *hostales* may be described as *residencias* (no restaurant, but usually providing breakfast).
Many hotels, especially those in tourist centres, are closed outside the main holiday season.

On mainland Spain there are many *paradores* in tourist areas;
these are mostly in old castles, palaces and monasteries, or in
specially erected buildings. However, there are none in the
Balearic Islands.

Categories

Official classification	In this guide
Hotels	
*****	L (luxury)
****	I
***	II
**	III
*	IV
Hostales and *pensiones*	
***	P I
**	P II
*	P III

The Spanish Ministry of Transport, Tourism and Communications publishes annually a list of hotels and apartments,
which can be obtained from tourist information offices (see
Information).

Hotel list

Hotels on Majorca (a selection)

Delfin Verde, III, 171 r.   **Alcudia**
Panoramic, III, 155 r.
More, IV, 115 r.
Posada Verano, P III, 42 r.

In Puerto de Alcudia:
Bahía de Alcudia, II, 234 r.
Condesa de la Bahía, II, 491 r.
Ivory Playa, II, 152 r.
Jupiter, II, 463 r.
Nuevas Palmeras (apartments), II, 114 r.
President, II, 240 r.
Royal Fortuna Playa, II, 210 r.
Saturno, II, 315 r.
Alcudia, III, 210 r.
Astoria Playa, III, 186 r.
Condes de Alcudia, III, 238 r.
Delfin Azul, III, 270 r.
Lagomonte, III, 272 r.
Marte, III, 282 r.
Bocaccio, IV, 272 r.
Mar y Sol, IV, 47 r.
Piscis, IV, 206 r.
El Paraiso, P I, 21 r.
Calma, P III, 30 r.
Puerto, P III, 40 r.
Vista Alegre, P III, 35 r.

In Puerto de Andraitx: **Andraitx**
Mini Follies (no restaurant; also apartments), II, 96 r.
Brismar, III, 56 r.
Bellavista (no restaurant), P II, 33 r.
Moderno, P III, 39 r.

In Camp de Mar:
Club Camp de Mar, I, 416 r.

Hotels

Lido, II, 116 r.
Playa, II, 286 r.
Villa Real, II, 52 r.

Arenal See Palma de Mallorca

Bañalbufar Mar y Vent, II, 19 r.
Sa Coma, III, 32 r.
Baronia, P III, 33 r.

Cabo Formentor *Formentor, L, 127 r.

Cala Bona See Cala Millor

Cala d'Or Cala d'Or, I, 71 r.
Gran Hotel Tucán, I, 155 r.
Iberotel Cala Esmeralda, I, 151 r.
Cala d'Or Gardens, II, 296 r.
Cala Gran, II, 77 r.
Club Martha Aparthotel, II, 279 r.
Corfu Marina, II, 214 r.
Costa del Sur, II, 102 r.
Rocador, II, 95 r.
Rocador Playa, II, 105 r.
Rocamarina, II, 207 r.
Skorpios Marina, II, 163 r.
Ariel, III, 90 r.
Antares, IV, 40 r.
Delfins, IV, 37 r.
Park Air Marine (no restaurant), P I, 25 r.
Can Trujillo (no restaurant), P II, 25 r.
Club Hipico Cala d'Or (no restaurant), P II, 25 r.
Leo, P II, 26 r.
Bienvenidos (no restaurant), P III, 35 r.
El Chico (no restaurant), P III, 45 r.
Ibis, P III, 30 r.

Cala Figuera Cala Figuera, III, 103 r.
Rocamar, IV, 42 r.
Pontas, P II, 51 r.
Tomarimar, P II, 45 r.
Ventura, P II, 38 r.
Maricel, P III, 25 r.
Neptuno, P III, 27 r.
Villa Sirena, P III, 45 r.

Cala Fornells Coronado, I, 139 r.
Cala Fornells, II, 85 r.

Cala Mayor See Palma de Mallorca

Cala Millor Bahía de Este, II, 189 r.
Girasol, II, 123 r.
Hipocampo, II, 132 r.
Hipocampo Playa, II, 204 r.
Iberotel Borneo, II, 200 r.
Iberotel Flamenco Cala Millor, II, 220 r.
Iberotel Playa Cala Millor, II, 242 r.
Iberotel Sumba, II, 280 r.
Playa del Moro, II, 160 r.
Sabina Playa, II, 132 r.
Talayot, II, 95 r.
Alicia, III, 166 r.

Biniamar, III, 108 r.
Bonamar, III, 117 r.
Castell de Mar, III, 248 r.
Don Juan, III, 134 r.
Millor Sun, III, 112 r.
Morito, III, 91 r.
Osiris, III, 207 r.
Said, III, 193 r.
La Santa María, III, 99 r.
Temi, III, 80 r.
Voramar, III, 65 r.
An-Ba, IV, 75 r.
Anba Romani, IV, 80 r.
Bikini, IV, 108 r.
Don Jaime, IV, 93 r.
Goya, IV, 56 r.
La Niña, IV, 55 r.
La Pinta II, IV, 24 r.
Sur, IV, 72 r.
Universal, IV, 60 r.
Verónica, IV, 164 r.
Verónica II, IV, 27 r.
Vista Blava, IV, 136 r.
Vistamer, IV, 116 r.
Los Alamos (no restaurant), P II, 30 r.
Eureka, P II, 91 r.
Pe-Bar, P II, 40 r.

In Cala Bona:
Gran Sol, II, 58 r.
Cónsul, III, 78 r.
Levante, III, 202 r.
Levante Park, III, 105 r.
Atolón, IV, 77 r.
Cala Bona, IV, 93 r.
Capdemar, IV, 75 r.
Moreyo, IV, 68 r.
Pérgola, IV, 33 r.
Tamarell II, IV, 42 r.
Tamarell (no restaurant), P II, 46 r.

See Capdepera   **Cala Ratjada**

Molins, I, 90 r.   **Cala San Vicente**
Cala San Vicente, II, 38 r.
Don Pedro, II, 147 r.
Simar, II, 120 r.
Niu, IV, 24 r.
Mayol, P II, 40 r.
Oriola, P II, 23 r.

América. II, 344 r.   **Calas de**
Maria Eugenia, II, 203 r.   **Mallorca**
Samoa, II, 331 r.
Sol Balmoral, II, 102 r.
Sol Canarios, II, 216 r.
Sol Chihuahuas, II, 216 r.
Sol Mastines, II, 260 r.

In Cala Murada:
Cala Murada, II, 77 r.
Valparaíso, III, 39 r.

Hotels

La Calobra　　La Calobra, III, 51 r.

Calvia　　Club Galatzo, I, 198 r.
Paradise Magalluf, II, 199 r.

Ca'n Pastilla　　See Palma de Mallorca

Ca'n Picafort　　Bonsai, II, 23 r.
Clumba Mar, II, 235 r.
Concord, II, 148 r.
Exagón, II, 285 r.
Gran Vista, II, 277 r.
Janeiro, II, 211 r.
Miramar, II, 125 r.
Montecarlo, II, 169 r.
Can Picafort, III, 100 r.
Farrutx, III, 170 r.
Gran Bahía, III, 156 r.
Gran Playa, III, 156 r.
Nordeste Playa, III, 233 r.
Santa Fé, III, 144 r.
Sarah, III, 108 r.
Sol, III, 42 r.
Sol Tonga, III, 406 r.
Son Baulo, III, 251 r.
Vista Park, III, 173 r.
Yate, III, 148 r.
Africa Mar, IV, 63 r.
Galaxia, IV, 59 r.
Haiti, IV, 234 r.
Jaime II, IV, 36 r.
Mar y Paz (no restaurant), IV, 60 r.
Markus Park, IV, 83 r.
Sultán, IV, 84 r.
Embat, P II, 36 r.
Flamenco, P II, 36 r.
Horizont Blau, P III, 75 r.
Marbella, P III, 40 r.
Marisco, P III, 42 r.

Capdepera　　Aguait, II, 189 r.
Castell Royal, II, 112 r.
Playa Canyamel, II, 132 r.
Laguna, IV, 132 r.

In Cala Ratjada:
Bella Playa, II, 214 r.
Lago Playa, II, 95 r.
Na Taconera, II, 120 r.
Regana, II, 126 r.
Sol Lux, II, 238 r.
Son Moll, II, 125 r.
Cala Gat, III, 44 r.
Cala Literas, III, 149 r.
Capricho, III, 111 r.
Carolina, III, 198 r.
Clumba, III, 120 r.
Diamant, III, 124 r.
Mar Azul, III, 76 r.
Serrano, III, 52 r.
Ses Rotges, III, 24 r.
Tucán (apartments), III, 73 r.

Alondra, IV, 156 r.
Amorós (no restaurant), IV, 48 r.
Baviera, IV, 43 r.
Bella Mar, IV, 105 r.
Bellavista, IV, 77 r.
El Cortijo, IV, 38 r.
Es Viñet, IV, 85 r.
Samu, IV, 35 r.
Vaquer, IV, 35 r.
Tulipán, IV, 51 r.
Alfonso (no restaurant), P II, 39 r.
Cas Bombu, P II, 50 r.
Dos Playas, P II, 78 r.
Jumar, P II, 40 r.
Luna, P II, 70 r.
Manila, P II, 58 r.
Vista Pinar, P II, 70 r.
Alsina, P III, 63 r.
Baleares, P III, 30 r.
Casa Bauza, P III, 60 r.
Gami, P III, 72 r.
Gili, P III, 359 r.
Villa Massanet, P III, 49 r.
Vista Sol, P III, 39 r.

Cala d'En Sureda (no restaurant), P II, 14 r.   **Colonia de San Pedro**

Isla de Cabrera, II, 72 r.   **Colonia de Sant Jordi**
Marqués de Palmer, II, 211 r.
Tres Playas, II, 118 r.
Cabo Blanco, III, 68 r.
El Coto, III, 46 r.
Romántica, III, 246 r.
Sur Mallorca, III, 200 r.
Lemar, IV, 90 r.
Martorell, IV, 29 r.

Eurotel Golf Punta Rotja (apartments), I, 244 r.   **Costa de los Pinos**

Es Molí, I, 73 r.   **Deya**
La Residencia (no restaurant), I, 27 r.
Costa d'Or, IV, 42 r.
Mundial C'an Quet, P II, 17 r.

Central, P III, 10 r.   **Esporlas**

Maristel, III, 53 r.   **Estellencs**

Cala Ferrera, II, 160 r.   **Felanitx**
Playa, II, 326 r.
Ponent (no restaurant), II, 104 r.
Tamarix, IV, 40 r.

See Palma de Mallorca   **Illetas**

Victoria, P III, 17 r.   **Inca**

Cap Blanc, I, 240 r.   **Lluchmayor**
Es Pas, III, 39 r.

See Palma de Mallorca   **Magalluf**

Continental Park, II, 155 r.   **Muro**

Las Gaviotas (apartments), II, 139 r.

Hotels

Lago Park (apartments), II, 69 r.
Lagotel Club, II, 256 r.
Playa de Muro, II, 396 r.
Playa Esperanza, II, 332 r.
Los Principes, II, 220 r.
Amapola, III, 156 r.

Orient

L'Hermitage (no restaurant), I, 20 r.

Paquera

Gran Hotel Sunna Park, I, 128 r.
Villamil, I, 125 r.
Baía Club, II, 55 r.
Baney, II, 68 r.
Beverly Playa, II, 443 r.
Carabela, II, 44 r.
Cormorán, II, 112 r.
Gaya, II, 45 r.
Iberotel Reina Paguera, II, 183 r.
Lido Park, II, 320 r.
Mar y Pins, II, 148 r.
Nilo, II, 118 r.
Nova Park (apartments), II, 168 r.
Paguera, II, 247 r.
Palmira Beach, II, 240 r.
San Valentín, II, 156 r.
Solivera, II, 150 r.
Eucalipto, III, 134 r.
Linda Playa, III, 108 r.
Madrigal, III, 56 r.
María Dolores, III, 70 r.
Oberoy, III, 73 r.
Paguera Beach, III, 86 r.
Playa Paguera, III, 46 r.
Tora, III, 86 r.
Venecia (no restaurant), III, 48 r.
Carabela II, IV, 33 r.
La Cartuja, IV, 62 r.
Cupido, IV, 85 r.
Don Miguel, IV, 35 r.
Flor los Almendros, IV, 68 r.
Palmira, IV, 100 r.
Villa Font, P I, 54 r.
Es Fasset (no restaurant), P II, 36 r.
Mary Franch, P II, 38 r.
Morlans, P II, 52 r.
Arcades, P III, 50 r.
Juana María, P III, 54 r.

Palma de Mallorca

*Son Vida Sheraton Hotel, L. 170 r.
*Meliá Victoria, L, 167 r.
*Valparaiso Palace, L, 150 r.
Iberohotel Uto Palma, I, 234 r.
Racquet Club, I, 51 r.
Sol Bellver, I, 393 r.
Sol Palas Atenea, I, 370 r.
Almudaina (no restaurant), II, 80 r.
Araxa (no restaurant), II, 75 r.
Constelación, II, 42 r.
Costa Azul, II, 126 r.
Drach (no restaurant), II, 62 r.
Majorica, II, 153 r.

Mirador, II, 78 r.
Palladium (no restaurant), II, 53 r.
Reina Constanza, II, 97 r.
Rembrandt, II, 72 r.
Riu Festival, II, 216 r.
Royal Cupido, II, 197 r.
Saratoga, II, 187 r.
Sol Jaime III, II, 88 r.
Abelux (no restaurant), III, 65 r.
Bonanova, III, 80 r.
Borenco, III, 70 r.
Cannes, III, 56 r.
César, III, 100 r.
Isla de Mallorca, III, 110 r.
Jardin Playa, III, 72 r.
Kontiki-Playa, III, 318 r.
Madrid, III, 84 r.
El Paso, III, 260 r.
Porto Fino, III, 74 r.
Rex (no restaurant), III, 38 r.
Sol Horizonte, III, 199 r.
Terreno Center, III, 73 r.
El Valle, III, 79 r.
Zaida, III, 42 r.
Ayamans, IV, 197 r.

In Cala (to the west):
Nixe Palace, I, 130 r.
Playa de Cala Mayor (no restaurant), I, 143 r.
Atlas, II, 48 r.
Belvedere Park, II, 414 r.
La Cala (no restaurant), II, 70 r.
Dalí, II, 88 r.
San Agustín, II, 56 r.
Santa Ana, II, 190 r.
Vista Mar, II, 75 r.
Cala Mayor Park, III, 51 r.
Ferrari, III, 88 r.
Los Leones, III, 77 r.
Mont Blanch, III, 73 r.
Vikingo, III, 114 r.
Zenith, III, 83 r.

In Illetas (to the west):
*Meliá de Mar, L, 144 r.
Bon Sol, I, 73 r.
Bonanza Park, I, 138 r.
Bonanza Playa, I, 294 r.
Gran Hotel Albatros, I, 119 r.
Illetas (no restaurant), I, 67 r.
Sol Playa Marina, II, 172 r.

In Portais Nous (to the west):
Bendinat, II, 31 r.
Fabiola, II, 105 r.
Kasai, II, 63 r.
María Luisa, II, 89 r.
Aguamarina, III, 80 r.
Colorado, III, 93 r.
Savalón, IV, 59 r.

Tomás, IV, 25 r.
Portals, P I, 46 r.

In Palma Nova (to the west):
Comodoro Sol, I, 83 r.
Portonova (apartments), I, 101 r.
Punta Negra, I, 69 r.
Son Caliu, I, 239 r.
Aquarium, II, 109 r.
Bermudas, II, 121 r.
Delfin Playa Sol, II, 144 r.
Hawaii, II, 230 r.
Honolulu, II, 216 r.
Palma Nova, II, 210 r.
Panamá (apartments), II, 192 r.
Playa Palma Nova, II, 54 r.
Rosa de Mar (apartments), II, 182 r.
Santa Lucía, II, 332 r.
Sol Cala Blanca, II, 171 r.
Sol Mirlos, II, 336 r.
Sol Tordos, II, 312 r.
Sol Trópico Playa, II, 117 r.
Son Matias Beach, II, 135 r.
Tobago, II, 218 r.
Torrenova Marina, II, 254 r.
Treinta y Tres, II, 272 r.
Don Bigote, III, 231 r.
Morocco, III, 54 r.
Naves Blancas, III, 98 r.
Olimpic, III, 185 r.
Saint Michel (apartments), III, 62 r.
Teix, IV, 42 r.

In Magalluf (to the west):
Atlántic, I, 80 r.
Flamboyán, I, 123 r.
Forte Cala Viñas, I, 245 r.
Sol Antillas, I, 329 r.
Sol Barbados, I, 428 r.
Sol Magalluf-Playa (apartments), I, 242 r.
Barracuda Marina, II, 264 r.
El Caribe (no restaurant), II, 53 r.
Don Juan, II, 182 r.
Oasis Trópico, II, 328 r.
Pax, II, 161 r.
Samos, II, 417 r.
Sol Coral Playa, II, 184 r.
Sol Don Manolo, II, 252 r.
Sol Guadalupe, II, 488 r.
Sol Jamaica, II, 308 r.
Sol Magalluf Park, II, 404 r.
Sol Trinidad, II, 375 r.
Don Paco, III, 87 r.
Dulcinea, III, 198 r.
Florida, III, 150 r.

In Ca'n Pastilla (to the east):
Riu Grande (apartments), I, 138 r.
Almendros, II, 91 r.
Ambos Mundos, II, 96 r.
Las Arenas, II, 152 r.

Boreal, II, 64 r.
Calma, II, 190 r.
Gran Hotel El Cid Sol, II, 216 r.
Leo, II, 285 r.
Linda, II, 189 r.
Luz, II, 130 r.
Oasis, II, 110 r.
Oleander, II, 264 r.
Orleans, II, 128 r.
Perla, II, 68 r.
Playa d'Or, II, 71 r.
Riu Obelisco, II, 192 r.
Riu Playa Park, II, 373 r.
Sol Alexandra, II, 164 r.
Sol Java, II, 249 r.
Anfora, III, 61 r.
Apolo, III, 151 r.
Balmes, III, 120 r.
Brasilia (apartments), III, 83 r.
Cisne, III, 116 r.
Don Quijote, III, 94 r.
Hélios, III, 305 r.
Isla Azul, III, 51 r.
Miraflores, III, 69 r.
Riu Caballero, III, 308 r.
Riu Concordia, III, 220 r.
Rua Sofía, III, 328 r.
Balear, IV, 69 r.
Can Pastilla Playa, IV, 77 r.
Covi, IV, 98 r.
Gala, IV, 126 r.
Sant Jordi, IV, 89 r.
Volatin, IV, 55 r.
Catalá, P II, 54 r.
Marbel, P II, 66 r.

In Las Maravillas (to the east):
Metropolotan Playa, II, 104 r.
Sol Gran Fiesta, II, 241 r.
Sol Playa de Palma, II, 113 r.
Sol Timor, II, 241 r.
Sol Tropical, II, 165 r.

In El Arenal (to the east):
Delta, I, 288 r.
Garonda, I, 112 r.
Riu Bravo, I, 199 r.
Acapulco Playa, II, 109 r.
Alegría (no restaurant), II, 64 r.
Aya, II, 145 r.
Ayron Park, II, 103 r.
Bahía de Palma, II, 433 r.
Belgravia, II, 190 r.
Bella Playa, II, 88 r.
Cactus, II, 110 r.
Copacabana, II, 112 r.
Cosmopolitan, II, 227 r.
Cristóbal Colón, II, 158 r.
Dunas Blancas, II, 167 r.
Encant, II, 116 r.
Flamingo, II, 100 r.

Hispania, II, 164 r.
Honderos, II, 132 r.
Ipanema Park, II, 210 r.
Iris, II, 63 r.
Kontiki Park, II, 110 r.
Latino, II, 60 r.
Lemán, II, 98 r.
Luna Park, II, 318 r.
Luxor, II, 52 r.
Luxor Playa, II, 40 r.
María Isabel, II, 132 r.
Marina Arenal, II, 52 r.
Negresco, II, 90 r.
Neptuno (no restaurant), II, 103 r.
Olimpo, II, 90 r.
Orient, II, 273 r.
Pamplona, II, 105 r.
Paradiso Garden Hotel, II, 118 r.
Playa Golf, II, 222 r.
Riu Bali, II, 264 r.
Riu San Francisco, II, 138 r.
Riutort, II, 195 r.
San Diego, II, 179 r.
Sol Riviera, II, 74 r.
Tal, II, 198 r.
Taurus Park, II, 341 r.
Torre Arenal, II, 143 r.
Torre Azul, II, 133 r.
Tropical Park, II, 221 r.
Venus Playa, II, 83 r.
Vista Odín, II, 126 r.
Alejandría, III, 226 r.
Bahamas, III, 259 r.
Bahía Park, III, 116 r.
Europa, III, 140 r.
Geminis, III, 193 r.
Gran Bahía, III, 217 r.
Kilimanjaro, III, 142 r.
Lancaster, III, 318 r.
Los Angeles, III, 58 r.
Mallorca, III, 106 r.
El Mansour, III, 125 r.
México, III, 114 r.
Niágara, III, 140 r.
Palma Mazas, III, 108 r.
Playas Arenal, III, 90 r.
Principe, III, 87 r.
Reina del Mar, III, 180 r.
Reina Isabel, III, 180 r.
Santa Mónica (no restaurant), III, 111 r.
Sol Pinos, III, 110 r.
Arcadia (no restaurant), IV, 113 r.
Bonamar, IV, 48 r.
Carmen Playa, IV, 95 r.
Don Miguel, IV, 84 r.
Emperador, IV, 66 r.
Gracia, IV, 87 r.
Isla Dorada, IV, 125 r.
Julia, IV, 65 r.
Mallorca, IV, 106 r.

Mediodía, IV, 167 r.
Ondina, IV, 170 r.
Panorámica Playa, IV, 42 r.
Playa Grande, IV, 54 r.
El Pueblo, IV, 276 r.
Riomar, IV, 68 r.
Saga, IV, 229 r.
Solimar, IV, 135 r.
Son Duy, IV, 92 r.
Torrente, IV, 100 r.
Golondrina, P I, 59 r.

In Puerto Pollensa: **Pollensa**
Capri, II, 33 r.
Daina, II, 60 r.
Illa d'Or, II, 119 r.
Miramar, II, 69 r.
Pollensa Park, II, 316 r.
Pollentia, II, 70 r.
Sis Pins (no restaurant), II, 55 r.
Uyal, II, 105 r.
Raf, III, 40 r.
Carotti, IV, 30 r.
Romantic, IV, 78 r.
Borras (no restaurant), P II, 24 r.
Eolo (no restaurant), P II, 52 r.
Galeón, P II, 43 r.
Luz de Mar, P II, 12 r.
Singala, P II, 26 r.

Cala Marsal, II, 364 r.   **Porto Colóm**
Club Hotel Belsana, II, 70 r.
Las Palomas, II, 114 r.
Ría, III, 72 r.
Vistamar, III, 144 r.

Castell dels Hams, II, 191 r.   **Porto Cristo**
Drach, III, 70 r.
Estrella, IV, 41 r.
Felip, IV, 106 r.
Perelló, IV, 95 r.
Son Moro, IV, 120 r.
Aguamarina, P III, 67 r.

In S'Illot:
Club S'Illot, III, 59 r.
Colombo, III, 139 r.
Mariant, III, 194 r.
Punta Amer, III, 97 r.
Perla de S'Illot, IV, 188 r.
Peymar, IV, 99 r.
Playa Mar, IV, 172 r.

Picafort Park, II, 189 r.   **Santa Margarita**

In Cala Santañy: **Santañy**
Pinos Playa, II, 104 r.

Golf Santa Ponsa (no restaurant), I, 18 r.   **Santa Ponsa**
Iberotel Bahía del Sol, II, 161 r.
Jardin del Sol (apartments), II, 236 r.
Pionero, II, 310 r.

Hotels

Punta del Mar (apartments), II, 186 r.
Rey Don Jaime, II, 417 r.
Royal Jardin de Mar (apartments), II, 188 r.
Santa Ponsa Park, II, 269 r.
Casablanca, III, 87 r.
Isabela, III, 156 r.
Ofelia, III, 89 r.
Playa de Mallorca, III, 218 r.
Playas del Rey (apartments), III, 64 r.
Siesta Mar, III, 104 r.
Playa Santa Ponsa, IV, 216 r.

San Telmo   Aquamarin, IV, 116 r.

Ses Salines   Don León, I, 126 r.

Sóller   Edén, II, 152 r.
                   Edén Park (no restaurant), II, 64 r.
                   Espléndido, II, 104 r.
                   Mare Nostrum, III, 58 r.
                   Marina, III, 96 r.
                   Monte Azul, III, 109 r.
                   Porto Soller, III, 127 r.
                   Costa Brava, IV, 57 r.
                   Generoso, IV, 109 r.
                   Marbell, IV, 83 r.
                   Es Port, P I, 156 r.
                   Madrid (no restaurant), P II, 41 r.
                   Monumento (no restaurant), P II, 19 r.
                   Nadal (no restaurant), P II, 26 r.
                   Rocamar I, P III, 106 r.
                   Brasilia, P III, 47 r.
                   Brisas, P III, 47 r.

Son Servera   Melis II (no restaurant), P III, 26 r.

Valldemosa   C'an Mario, P III, 8 r.

Hotels on Minorca (a selection)

Alayor   San Valentin Menorca (apartments), I, 214 r.
                   Royal Son Bou (apartments), II, 252 r.
                   Sol Milanos, II, 300 r.
                   Sol Pinguinos, II, 300 r.
                   Playa Azul, IV, 126 r.

                   In Ferrerias:
                   Audax, I, 244 r.
                   Sol Gavilanes, II, 357 r.

                   In San Cristóbal:
                   Santo Tomás, I, 60 r.
                   Sol Cóndores, II, 188 r.

Ciudadela   Almirante Farragut, II, 472 r.
                   Cala Blanca, II, 147 r.
                   Cala'n Bosch, II, 169 r.
                   Esmeralda, II, 135 r.
                   Mediterrani, II, 180 r.
                   Prinsotel La Caleta, II, 245 r.
                   Sagitario Playa, II, 72 r.
                   Sol Club Falcó, II, 450 r.

Cala Galdana, III, 204 r.
Cala'n Blanes, III, 103 r.
Los Delfines, III, 92 r.
Ses Voltes, III, 40 r.
Alfonso III, IV, 52 r.

Port Mahón, I, 74 r.   **Mahón**
Capri (no restaurant), II, 75 r.
Noa (no restaurant), P II, 40 r.

In Cala'n Porter:
Acuarium, IV, 59 r.

In San Luis:
S'Algar, II, 106 r.
Pueblo Menorca, IV, 538 r.
Sur Menorca, IV, 238 r.
Xaloc, IV, 58 r.
Biniali, P I, 9 r.
Son Rusiñol, P II, 18 r.
Xuroy, P II, 44 r.

In Villacarlos:
Agamenon, II, 75 r.
Hamilton, II, 166 r.
Rey Carlos III, II, 87 r.
Sol del Este Mar (no restaurant), II, 96 r.
Almirante, IV, 38 r.
Miramar (no restaurant), P II, 30 r.

Aguamarina, II, 248 r.   **Mercadal**
Castell Playa Fiestas, II, 264 r.
Lord Nelson, II, 177 r.
Victoria Playa, II, 266 r.
Cap Gros Beach Club (no restaurant), III, 96 r.
Topacio, III, 276 r.

In Fornells:
Port Fornells (no restaurant), P II, 20 r.
S'Algaret, P II, 23 r.

See entry

Vacation
apartments

Information

Spanish National Tourist Office   In the United Kingdom
57–58 St James Street
London SW1A 1LD;
tel. (071) 499 0901

Spanish National Tourist Office   In the United States
665 Fifth Avenue
New York NY 10022;
tel. (212) 759 8822

845 North Michigan Avenue
Chicago 1LL 60611;
tel. (312) 944 0216

Information

A ferry in Palma harbour

In Canada

Spanish National Tourist Office
102 Bloor Street West
Toronto, Ontario M4W 3B8;
tel. (416) 961 3131

In Majorca

Conselleria de Turisme de Balears
Calle Montenegro 5
Palma de Mallorca;
tel. (971) 71 20 22/23

Oficina de Turisme (Govern Balear)
Avenida Jaime III 8
Palma de Mallorca;
tel. (971) 71 22 16

Oficina de Turisme (Consell Insular)
Aeropuerto Son San Juan
Palma de Mallorca;
tel. (971) 26 08 03

Foment de Turisme de Mallorca
Plaza de la Constitución 1
Palma de Mallorca;
tel. (971) 72 53 96

There are local tourist offices in the following places: Cala d'Or,
Cala Figuera, Cala Millor, Cala Ratjada, Ca'n Picafort, Colonia
de Sant Jordi, Illetas, Magalluf, Paguera, Porto Cristo, Puerto
de Alcudia, Puerto de Pollensa, Puerto de Soller, Santa Ponsa,
Soller and Valldemosa.

Oficina d'Informació Turistica
Plaza de la Constitución 15
Mahón;
tel. (971) 36 37 90

Foment de Turisme de Menorca
Carrer Nou 25
Mahón;
tel. (971) 36 23 77

Delegació de Turisme del Govern Balear
Plaza Explanada 40
Mahón;
tel. (971) 36 08 79

In Minorca

Inter-island transport

There are several flights daily between the airports of Palma
(Majorca) and Mahón (Minorca). The flight takes about ½ hour.

By air

There are boat services between Palma (Majorca) and Ciuda-
dela (Minorca), between Palma (Majorca) and Mahón
(Minorca) and between Palma and Cabrera.
Car ferry services between the individual islands and between
the islands and the mainland are run by the Compañía
Trasmediterranea.

By boat

Information and reservations:
Compañía Trasmediterranea
Muelle Viejo 5
Palma de Mallorca;
tel. (971) 40 50 14

London agents: see Getting to Majorca/Minorca

See entry

Boat trips

Maps and Plans

Visitors who plan to get away from the main roads on the
islands will do well to supplement the general map at the end
of this guide by maps on a larger scale. The following is a
selection:

Balearics

Firestone Mapa de Carreteras, sheet 6 (Eastern Spain and the Balearics)	1:500,000
Mapa provincial Baleares (official map)	1:200,000
Hildebrand Travel Map of Balearics	1:185,000
RV Map of Balearics (with town plan of Palma de Mallorca)	1:150,000
Firestone Map T 26 (with town plan of Palma de Mallorca)	1:125,000
Mapa Militar (official military map; 22 sheets for the Balearics)	1:50,000

Majorca

1:175,000	Hallwag Map of Majorca Clyde Leisure Map of Majorca (with town plan of Palma de Mallorca) AA Leisure Map of Majorca (with town plan of Palma de Mallorca)
1:150,000	RV Map of Majorca (with town plan of Palma de Mallorca)
1:125,000	Hildebrand Travel Map of Majorca
1:100,000	Mapa Militar (official military map; 5 sheets for Majorca)
Archaeological guide	A good survey of the prehistoric and early historical monuments of Majorca is provided in a booklet issued by the Spanish Ministry of Education and Science (Ministerio de Educacíon y Ciencia) "Monumentos Prehistóricos y Protohistóricos de la Isla de Mallorca" (1967, with large archaeological map).

Minorca

1:100,000	Mapa Militar (official military map; 2 sheets for Minorca (some of it rather old)).
1:75,000	Clyde Leisure Map of Ibiza and Minorca (with town plans) AA Leisure Map of Ibiza and Minorca (with town plans) Firestone Map of Minorca (with town plans) RV Map of Minorca
Archaeological maps and guides	Visitors who are particularly interested in Minorca's prehistoric sites should obtain the detailed archaeological map (Mapa Arqueológico de Menorca; with town plans), published by Ediciones Menorquines, Ciudadela, which can be bought anywhere on the island. Not quite so informative, but still useful, is the free map of Minorca issued by the island's tourist authorities. There is also an archaeological guide (Guía Arqueológica de Menorca; in Spanish), published by the Consell Insular de Menorca, which is of particular value for its illustrations, sketch-maps and ground-plans. This, too, can be obtained anywhere on the island as well as the brochure "Itineraris Arquelògics".

Motorcycle rental

See Bicycle and motorcycle rental

Motoring

Traffic regulations	In Spain, as in the rest of continental Europe, traffic travels on the right, with overtaking (passing) on the left. Seat belts must be worn. Children under 10 must travel in the rear seats. It is compulsory to wear a crash helmet when riding a motorcycle of any capacity. In general, traffic coming from the right has priority, and this applies even to side streets in towns. Exceptions to the rule are indicated by signs. When turning left on a road outside a built-up area drivers must pull into the right of the road and wait until the road is clear. At

junctions the road is often divided into lanes with appropriate markings.

When turning left into a road which has priority, motorists frequently enter an acceleration lane from which they bear right into the traffic flow. This may take some getting used to. When overtaking (passing), the left-hand indicator light must be kept on during the whole manoeuvre and the right-hand one operated when pulling in to the right. Drivers about to overtake, or approaching a bend, must sound their horn during the day and flash their lights at night. Beware of overtaking by heavy lorries!

On well-lit streets and roads (except expressways and motorways) driving with sidelights is permitted. A careful watch should be kept for vehicles driving without lights.

Parking on one-way streets is permitted only on the even-numbered side of the street on even-numbered days and on the odd-numbered side on odd-numbered days.

In the whole of the Old Town district of Palma de Mallorca the "ORA" (*ordenación regulación aparcamiento*) applies to the parking of vehicles, and operates on weekdays between 9.30 a.m. and 1.30 p.m. and between 5 p.m. and 8 p.m. (Sat. 9.30 a.m. to 1.30 p.m. only), and allows parking for a limited period only. Parking permits (*tarjetas de estacionamieneto*) are obtainable from all tobacconists (*estancos*).

In towns, particularly when the streets are crowded with people in the evening, pedestrians are often reluctant to give way to traffic. Even on relatively quiet country roads great care is required, since country people sometimes tend to pay little regard to road traffic regulations. Livestock, too, is often a hazard on country roads.

Foreign visitors in particular should maintain strict driving discipline – apart from anything else, for the sake of their national reputation. The instructions of the traffic police (*policia de tráfico*) in towns and the Guardia Civilo in the country must be immediately complied with; if drivers do not stop when signalled to do so the police may well make use of their revolvers, since they are not infrequently on the alert for terrorists.

Drivers committing traffic offences are liable to substantial fines; payment on the spot will reduce the fine by 20%. The blood alcohol limit is 0.8 per mille (8 milligrams per millilitre).

An accident can have very serious consequences for a foreign driver. Whether the accident is his fault or not, his car may be impounded (and may be released only after the completion of any judicial proceedings that follow), and in serious cases the driver may be arrested.

After any accident the Spanish insurance company named on the driver's "green card" must be informed without delay, so that arrangements may be made for any payment required in the way of bail.

Towing broken-down vehicles by private cars is prohibited.

In the event of an accident involving a hired car the instructions in the hire documents should be followed.

Accidents

120km p.h. (74¼ m.p.h.) on motorways (highways)
100km p.h. (62 m.p.h.) on roads with two or more lanes in each direction
90km p.h. (56 m.p.h.) on other roads
60km p.h. (37 m.p.h.) in built-up areas

Speed limits

See Travel Documents

Motoring documents

211

Museums (Museos)

Majorca

Palma de Mallorca	Cathedral Museum Religious art, liturgical utensils, etc. Mon.–Fri. 10am–12.30pm and 4–6.30pm, Sat. 10am–1.30pm; closed Sun. and public holidays.
	Diocesan Museum (in Palacio Episcopal) Medieval Majorcan painting, archaeology, ceramics Mon.–Sat. 10am–1pm and 3–6pm; closed Sun. and public holidays
	Municipal Museum (in Bellver Castle) Archaeology, history of the Moorish period Oct.–Mar. Mon.–Sat. 8am–6pm; Apr.–Sept. 8am–8pm; closed Sun.
	Museo de Mallorca (Calle Portella) Archaeology, medieval painting Tues.–Sat. 10am–2pm and 4–7pm, Sun. and public holidays 10am–2pm; closed Mon.
	National Museum (Patrimonio national; in Almudaina Palace) Furniture, tapestries, old weapons, pictures Daily 9.30am–1.30pm and 4–6.30pm; closed Sat. pm and Sun.
	Museo Krekovic (Calle Ciudad de Querétaro) Inca culture and art Mon.–Sat. 10.30am–1.30pm; closed Sun. and public holidays
Alcudia	Museo Arqueológico (Calle General Goded 7) Tues.–Sat. 10.30am–1.30pm and 3.30–6.30pm; Sun. 10.30am–1.30pm; closed Mon.
Artá	Museo Artá Mon.–Fri. 10am–noon
Deya	Son Marroig (on Valldemosa–Deiá road) Mementoes of Archduke Ludwig Salvator of Austria Mon.–Sat. 9.30am–2.30pm, 4.30–8pm in summer
Lluch	Museum in Lluch Monastery Daily 10am–5.30pm (until 7.30pm in summer)
Manacor	Municipal Archaeological Museum (in Town Hall, Calle Rector Rubí) Daily 10am–1pm and 4–7pm; Sat. 10am–1pm; closed Sun. and bank holidays
	Museo de Mallorca (Calle Mayor 15) Tues.–Sun. 9am–1pm and 4–7pm; closed Mon.
Petrá	Museo Junípero Serra Daily 9am–8pm
Pollensa	Municipal Museum (in Monastery of Santo Domingo) Seen by appointment (apply to Town Hall) Convento de Santo Domingo. Open 10am–midnight, Tues., Thur. and Sun.
Santa Maria del Camí	Museo del Traje Balear Traditional costumes

Museo Municipal	Valldemosa
Museo Chopin–George Sand	
Museum of Contemporary Art	
(all three in monastery)	
Oct.–Mar. Mon.–Sat. 9am–1pm and 3–5.30pm; Apr.–Sept. Mon.–Sat. 9.30am–1pm and 3–6.30pm; closed Sun.	

Minorca

Museo de Menorca	Mahón
History of the island	
Ateneum	
Natural history, prehistory and early historical period	
Municipal Museum (in Town Hall)	Ciudadela
Regional history	
Diocesan Museum (in Seminary, Calle Obispo Vila)	
Religious art	
Museum on Monte Toro. In course of development	Mercadal

Opening times (Horas de apertura)

The times when museums and palaces are open vary considerably. In general it may be assumed that they are closed at lunchtime (usually from 1 to 4pm) and on Sundays and public holidays. Most rural churches are open only for services.	Museums, palaces and churches
There are no statutory closing times. Shops are usually open from 9am to 1pm and from 3 or 4 to 7pm In summer shops (particularly food shops and tobacconists) often stay open until late in the evening.	Shops
See entry	Banks
See Postal Services	Post offices
Tabernas are supposed to close at midnight, restaurants at 1am.	Restaurants

Postal Services (Correos y telégrafos)

The Spanish post (correos) is usually reliable. The opening hours of post offices vary but are usually open from 9am to 2pm on Monday to Friday. The main post office is also open from 4 to 7pm. They are all closed on public holidays.	Open
Letters sent poste restante should be addressed to the "Lista de correos" in the nearest town.	Poste restante
Stamps (sellos) are sold in tobacconists (estancos) as well as at post offices.	Stamps
Surface mail to northern Europe takes at least four days.	
A letter sent by airmail (por avion) costs no extra.	

Public holidays (Dies de fiesta; dies feriados)

1 January: Año (New Year's Day)	Statutory holidays
6 January: Reyes Magos (Epiphany)	

213

Public holidays

19 March: San José (St Joseph's Day)
1 May: Dia del Trabajo (Labour Day)
24 June: San Juan (St John's Day; the King's name-day)
29 June: San Pedro y San Pablo (SS Peter and Paul)
25 July: Santiago (St James's Day)
15 August: Asunción (Assumption)
12 October: Dia de la Hispanidad (discovery of America)
1 November: Todos los Santos (All Saints)
8 December: Inmaculada Concepción (Immaculate
Conception)
25 December: Navidad (Christmas Day)

Movable feasts

Viernes Santo (Good Friday)
Corpus Christi

Rail travel

There are two railway lines still in use on Majorca. One runs
from Palma (station in Plaza de España/Plaça de Espanya; 5 or 6
trains daily) to Sóller, from which the journey can be continued
to Puerto de Sóller by a vintage tram. This trip is recommended
to all railway enthusiasts.

Majorca's other railway line runs from Palma to Inca, with
trains at approximately hourly intervals from 6am to 10pm

There were formerly rail services beyond Inca over the Llanura
del Centro to La Puebla and via Manacor to Artá, but these lines
were closed down some years ago, since the island's roads are
now much more suitable for the conveyance of both passengers and freight.

Tram, Sóller

There are no trains on Minorca.

Restaurants (Restaurantes)

As in all Spanish tourist regions, the needs of holidaymakers
are catered for by a wide range of restaurants, from the rustic-
style beach restaurant, by way of the *fonda* (a modest country
eating-house), the *casa de comida* and the *méson* to high-class
establishments with an international cuisine. All restaurants
are required to offer a fixed-price menu of three courses,
though this frequently falls short, both in quantity and quality,
of a meal chosen from the *à la carte* menu at a somewhat higher
cost.
The times of meals in Spain are one or two hours later than in
more northerly countries, though hotel restaurants with a cli-
entele predominantly from northern and central Europe have
to a large extent adapted their meal-times to conform to the
habits of their customers. Unfortunately this is frequently also
the case with their menus, on which tasty local specialities are
increasingly giving place to ordinary and insipid dishes which
are thought to appeal to the taste of visitors. Good local cook-
ing, however, can still often be found in country restaurants
away from the tourist haunts on the coast.

Glass horse

A siurel

Cakes and sweets, popular since Moorish times

Roads (Carrecteras)

Majorca

The main roads on Majorca radiate from the capital, Palma. They are all in good condition, but often – particularly in the hilly regions – narrow and enclosed between walls. Minor roads are sometimes only wide enough for a single vehicle but they are well provided with passing places. The roads in the Sierra del Norte tend to be winding, with numerous sharp bends.

Minorca

The main roads, particularly the road which runs the length of the island from Mahón to Ciudadela and the side roads leading to the coastal resorts, are well constructed and maintained. The smaller secondary roads, however, are usually very narrow and enclosed by drystone walls, and on these roads, when two cars meet, one of them may have to reverse to the nearest passing place. Many small side roads come to a dead end, with no room to turn.

Shopping and souvenirs

The principal craft products of Majorca and Minorca are leather goods, glass, and, on a smaller scale, pottery, and these are very popular holiday souvenirs. The large leather and shoe factories are in and around Inca; visitors are conducted around the factories, which have showrooms and sales points. It is worth while comparing prices carefully; the shoes are often little cheaper than those, mostly imported from Spain, which are sold in chain-stores at home. When buying leather garments visitors are well advised to take their time and check carefully on quality; there are bargains to be had, but in Spain as elsewhere quality goods have their price.

There are many glass factories on Majorca where visitors can watch the glass-blowers. With astonishing dexterity they fashion a variety of animal figures from the molten glass and offer them for sale at a modest price. It is true that the glassware displayed in the large showrooms at the glass factories is predominantly mass-produced and of questionable taste, but by looking carefully it is often possible to find individual items of quality. Unfortunately visitors travelling by air are limited in what they can take with them, and glass and pottery are liable to suffer from the rough handling of passengers' baggage.

Typical Majorcan products are the archaic pottery figures known as *siurels*, made of white clay painted red and green, with a small whistle at the foot.

An internationally known speciality of the Majorcan town of Manacor is the production of artificial pearls. Manacor pearls can scarcely be distinguished from the genuine article; they come in all sizes and arrangements, and, though not cheap, they are extremely attractive.

Spain produces good and reasonably priced spirits, notably brandy. Distilled from wine, this resembles French cognac but has a fruitier taste and a more generous bouquet. Among the best brands are Lepanto and Duque de Alba; cheaper brands are Veterano Osborne and Carlos I. *Hierbas* ("herbs") is a palatable liqueur which may be sweet (*dulce*) or dry (*seca*). There is also the aniseed liqueur found all over Spain. A Minorcan speciality which goes back to the days of British rule is a locally produced gin. *Palo* is a liqueur made from carobs.

Visitors will also be tempted by the wide range of candied fruits on offer, and perhaps also by the flaky pastries called *ensaimadas* (see Food and Drink, Local specialities).

Telephone (Teléfono)

International calls can be made from coin-operated public telephones. These take 25, 50 and 100 peseta coins (varying from machine to machine; check before telephoning and have plenty of change ready). 5 peseta coins can only be used for calls within Spain.

Telephone

Telephone calls from a hotel will probably be considerably more expensive.

To the United Kingdom 0744
To the United States or Canada 071

International dialling codes from Spain

Time

During the winter Spain observes Central European Time, one hour ahead of Greenwich Mean Time and six hours ahead of Eastern Standard Time, From the beginning of April to the end of September the country observes Summer Time which is two hours ahead of Greenwich Mean Time and seven hours ahead of Eastern Standard Time.

Tipping

In Spain, as in most other countries, a service charge (*servicio*) is included in the bill in hotels and restaurants, but it is customary to give a small tip (*propina*) to a waiter (*camarero*), a chambermaid (*camerara* or *muchacha*), a porter or a page-boy (bell-hop; *mozo*), etc, particularly when they have performed some special service. It is also usual to tip a porter (visitors do not normally carry their own luggage). Custodians of monuments and other tourist sights, and the attendants who show people to their seats in theatres, cinemas and bullrings also expect a tip. It is therefore advisable always to carry plenty of small change.

Travel documents

Visitors from the United Kingdom, the Commonwealth and the United States must have a valid passport. No visa is required by nationals of the United Kingdom, Australia, Canada and New Zealand for a stay of up to three months, or by United States nationals for a stay of up to six months, provided in each case

Personal papers

that they are not taking up any paid employment. An extension of stay can be granted by the police authorities.

Motoring documents

A national driving licence is acceptable in Spain, but must be accompanied by an official translation stamped by a Spanish consulate. It may be easier and cheaper to carry an international driving permit (which in any case is required for business trips).

The car registration document must be taken and the car must bear an oval nationality plate.

An international insurance certificate (green card) is required, and also a bail bond (issued by an insurance company with the green card), since in the event of an accident the car may be impounded pending payment of bail (see Motoring).

Health insurance

British citizens, like nationals of other EU countries are entitled to obtain medical care under the Spanish health services on the same basis as Spanish people. This means that they can obtain medical and hospital treatment but will be required to pay charges for prescribed medicines and for dental treatment. Before leaving home every visitor should ask the local office of the DSS for a booklet called "Medical Costs Abroad" (SA 30) which contains an application for form E111. This is the document which must be presented to a Spanish doctor or hospital when treatment is sought.

It is nevertheless advisable, even for EU nationals, to take out some form of temporary health insurance which provides complete cover, as there is always a possibility of bureaucratic delay.

Nationals of non EU countries should certainly have adequate insurance cover.

N.B.

It is advisable to make photocopies of travel documents and to take them with you. This makes it easier to obtain replacements if the originals should be lost.

Vacation apartments

All over Majorca and Minorca there are flats (*apartamentos turisticos*) and villas which can be rented (often as part of a package deal) for a week or longer period, allowing visitors to make their own arrangements for catering. Like hotels they are officially classed into categories, indicated by one, two or three key symbols (three being the best).

The Spanish Ministry of Transport, Tourism and Communications publishes annually a list of hotels and apartments which can be obtained from tourist information offices (see Information).

Walking

There is beautiful walking country on the islands, particularly in the hills of Majorca (Sierra del Norte and Serranías del Levante). The Consell Insular de Mallorca has produced a booklet (available also in English), describing twenty walks on Majorca; this can be obtained from Tourist information offices (see Information).

Water sports

The coasts of Majorca and Minorca offer opportunities for every conceivable form of water sport.
The principal beaches are supervised and bathing conditions are indicated by coloured pennants (green = bathing permitted without restriction; yellow = bathing dangerous; red = bathing prohibited).

The most popular bathing beaches on Majorca are on the south-west coast, particularly in Palma Bay (though these beaches are often crowded) and in Pollensa and Alcudia Bays on the north-east coast.

On Minorca there are sandy beaches of some length only on the south coast, particularly at Son Bou and Sant Jaume Mediterrani. The other coasts are predominantly rocky, with only occasional small sandy coves.

The rocky stretches of coast are ideal for snorkelling and scuba diving. Diving excursions are often organised from the larger holiday centres and harbours (enquire locally for details).

If you bring your own aqualung it may be necessary to fit an adaptor to enable cylinders hired locally to be used.

Wind-surfing is now a very popular holiday activity, and equipment can be hired at all beaches suitable for this purpose. Regard should be paid to any signs indicating that wind-surfing is prohibited.

See entry   Boating harbours and
                                             anchorages

When to go

The very temperate climate of the Balearics is pleasant at any time of year. Winter holidays, which brought many people to the islands before the great tourist boom developed, are again becoming popular, and for those who want a quiet and restful holiday a winter visit, in a well-heated hotel, can be thoroughly recommended.

In January and February the almond blossom on Majorca is an unforgettable sight. Easter is also a good time for a visit, since the real spring is beginning and bringing with it a fresh growth of lush green. The very mild weather of the Balearic spring can, however, be capricious and only the hardy will bathe in the sea at this season.

The height of summer is less to be recommended on account of the crowds of visitors, the considerable heat and accompanying heat-haze (*calina*), and, particularly on Majorca, the dust. Of course, there are many who can not go at any other time, and summer is undoubtedly the best time for swimming in the sea and acquiring a sun-tan.

Weather table	Temperature in °C (°F)				Sunshine (hours per day)	Rainy days	Relative humidity of air (%)
	Air			Sea			
Months	Max.	Mean	Min.				
January	20·4 (68·7)	10·1 (50·2)	0 (32)	13·3 (55·9)	5·1	8·3	76
February	18·8 (65·8)	10·3 (50·5)	−3 (26·6)	13·2 (55·8)	6·1	7·1	75
March	22·6 (72·7)	11·5 (52·7)	−2 (28·4)	13·5 (56·3)	6·4	7·5	74
April	25·5 (77·9)	13·9 (57·2)	1·7 (35·1)	14·5 (58·1)	7·2	6·5	72
May	29·4 (84·9)	17·2 (63·0)	6·2 (43·2)	16·8 (62·2)	9·3	4·8	71
June	34·2 (93·6)	20·6 (69·1)	10·2 (50·4)	20·2 (68·4)	10·2	3·1	67
July	35·6 (96·1)	24·3 (75·7)	14·4 (57·9)	22·5 (72·5)	11·1	1·0	65
August	36·0 (96·8)	24·7 (76·5)	14·2 (57·6)	24·6 (76·3)	10·6	2·5	67
September	33·0 (91·4)	23·1 (73·6)	11·0 (51·8)	23·2 (73·8)	7·7	5·7	69
October	27·1 (80·8)	18·1 (64·6)	6·0 (42·8)	20·7 (69·3)	6·3	9·7	73
November	24·0 (75·2)	14·5 (58·1)	3·6 (38·5)	17·6 (63·7)	5·3	9·0	76
December	20·4 (68·7)	11·8 (53·2)	1·4 (34·5)	15·0 (59·0)	4·2	10·7	78
Year	27·3 (81·1)	16·7 (62·1)	5·6 (42·1)	17·9 (64·2)	7·5	76	72

Since Minorca has no coastal hills the heat is tempered by a continually blowing breeze.

Autumn is generally regarded as the ideal time for a visit to the Balearics. Then the main tourist rush is over, and the warm settled weather makes bathing possible in coves sheltered from the north wind until the end of October. On the northern coasts, particularly on Majorca, however, there are violent storms and the cool *tramontana* from September onwards. (See climatic table above.)

Youth hostels

Young visitors can obtain accommodation at reasonable prices in youth hostels (*albergues juveniles* or *albergues para la juventud*), which are usually open from July to September for members of national youth hostels associations affiliated to the International Youth Hostel Association. The stay in any one hostel is limited to three nights. At the height of the holiday season advance booking is advisable.

Majorca has youth hostels in Alcudia and Ca'n Pastilla (near Palma); there are none on Minorca.

Index

221

Index

Notes